The Boy Who Shot the Sheriff

HERBERT NICCOLS--MURDERER OF SHERIFF JOHN WORMELL
AT ASOTIN WASHINGTON. AUGUST 7 th 1932 1931

THE BOY WHO SHOT THE SHERIFF

The Redemption of Herbert Niccolls Jr.

Nancy Bartley

UNIVERSITY OF WASHINGTON PRESS

Seattle and London

© 2013 by the University of Washington Press
Printed and bound in the United States of America
Designed by Dustin Kilgore
Composed in Chaparral Pro typeface designed by Carol Twombly
17 16 15 14 13   5 4 3 2 1

University of Washington Press
PO Box 50096, Seattle, WA 98145, USA
www.washington.edu/uwpress

Library of Congress Cataloging-in-Publication Data
Bartley, Nancy.
The boy who shot the sheriff : the redemption of Herbert Niccolls
Jr. / Nancy Bartley.
p. cm.
Includes bibliographical references and index.
ISBN 978-0-295-99245-7 (pbk : alk. paper)
1. Niccolls, Herbert. 2. Juvenile homicide—Washington (State)
3. Murder—Washington (State) 4. Juvenile delinquency—
Washington (State) 5. Juvenile justice, Administration of—
Washington (State) I. Title.
Hv9067.H6B37 2013   364.152'3092—dc23   2012035614

For James

From a single crime know the nation.

—VIRGIL (70–19 BC)

Contents

Preface

THE LONG, low beams of late afternoon sun poured through the windows as trapped flies tapped at the glass. A strip of flypaper hung above the stairs to the basement where the black coffin rested on sawhorses. The keeper of the mortuary-turned-museum handed me the keys and told me to drop them off at the house next door when I was finished. Then I was alone.

It was a Sunday, a quiet day in Asotin, Washington, a small town on the banks of the Snake River. No one was asking to tour the museum, to walk down the winding stairs into the dark basement and peek into the coffin. I suspected few came here, except local history buffs committed to preserving the stories that have been passed down for generations. The most familiar of those concerned a boy, a gun, and a murder.

Amid the period dresses, farming implements, branding irons, and embalming tools were photographs—one of Sheriff John Wormell, a serious man with a handlebar mustache, and another of a boy in ragtag overalls staring at the camera with a puzzled look. The boy was thin and had no shoes. He was the reason I was in this dry and dusty town with my twelve-year-old son riding his mountain bike in the soft dirt just outside the museum window.

My fascination with the story began one day when I was at the Indeterminate Sentencing Review Board near Olympia, Washington, reading a file on seventeen-year-old Walter DuBuc. DuBuc attended school through the fifth grade, came from a large family where food was often scarce, and holds the record for being the youngest person in the state to be put to death for murder. In 1932 he was executed in the state's only double execution, his accomplice taking the adjacent place on the gallows. With the exception of a few letters from family members begging the governor for mercy, there was no public outcry. No one questioned why a seventeen-year-old, whose involvement in the crime was minimal, should pay for the death with his life.

While sifting through files filled with stories of violence, loss, grief, and injustice, I found one concerning a twelve-year-old boy who had been sentenced to prison for life. The case had shocked the nation both for the crime and the punishment. Herbert Niccolls Jr. was regarded as an example of what citizens in 1931 feared—the increasingly violent youth. Correspondingly, the public became increasingly intolerant.

More than thirty years earlier, Illinois had established a juvenile court to deal with such children, and other states had taken similar measures, including Washington, where DuBuc and Niccolls committed their crimes. The Washington juvenile court system was created in 1905 based on the *parens patriae*, or government as parent, concept. Like most of the nation's juvenile courts, it began during the Progressive Era, those years of social change early in the twentieth and late nineteenth centuries when laws concerning child labor, mandatory education, and other laws were introduced. The state opened a juvenile reformatory in 1892 but it, like many states' early juvenile courts and reformatories, did not take young murderers.

Niccolls's story seemed incomprehensible as I read the yellowed pages of the files, a departure from common sense and reason. A child with a baby face and unruly dark hair posed in typical prison mug shots, full-face and in profile. I would find more about him in the state archives—prison documents, press clippings, and letters written by Washington state governors and scores of citizens. He would become a cause célèbre and in the process have every detail of his personal life, from his hygiene to his mental health, open to public discussion.

Niccolls committed his crime during the Great Depression, the bloodiest years in the nation's penitentiaries, when more people were put to death than at any other time in history.

Prisons were filled not only with notorious gangsters but also with those who broke the law simply to provide food and shelter for themselves or their families. Some were too ill or developmentally disabled to defend themselves. In states where sentencing review boards determined when an inmate was released, prisoners could be held for years on charges that today might warrant a one- or two-year sentence. The justice process itself often was corrupt and unconstitutional, from the police investigation to the prosecution and defense. It would be decades before reforms would be made.

That day in Asotin, as I watched my own son ride his bike, I wondered if there ever is a time when a child is beyond redemption. It's a question that is not easily answered. All crime leaves trails of suffering.

Despite the current public belief that violent juvenile crime is a recent phenomenon—a sentiment common whenever high-profile crimes occur—juvenile crime is not new nor are the defendants younger. A survey of headlines from earlier eras shows how long juvenile crime has been a problem. In 1850, a British fourteen-year-old shot two bullies who had been tormenting him. In 1874, a fourteen-year-old Boston boy killed two and assaulted seven others before he was imprisoned in solitary confinement for nearly the rest of his life. In 1929, a six-year-old Paintsville, Kentucky, boy shot and killed his playmate over the ownership of a piece of scrap iron they had found and were going to sell. This child was convicted of manslaughter but released to his parents on $500 bail. In 2000, a Michigan six-year-old shot his first-grade classmate after she complained that he had spat on her desk. But unlike the Kentucky case, the Michigan boy was not tried. Prosecutors said that what he needed more was "to be loved."

A 2003 case from Ephrata, Washington, closely parallels that of Herbert Niccolls Jr. In both, the defendants were twelve years old and considered by judges to be beyond redemption. The crimes drew national attention because the defendants were so young.

The immaturity and impulsiveness of youth, the effects of poverty, violence, and child abuse, and the lack of stable and loving families when children must raise themselves are formulas for juvenile crime at any time. From century to century, generations have always feared nonconformist youth and the demoralization of the young. What changes is our reaction, our laws, and the sentences as the public-opinion pendulum swings from rehabilitative to punitive solutions and back.

While it is too soon to know what choices the Ephrata youthful murderers make in their adult lives—one is serving a fourteen-year-sentence and the other twenty-six—for Herbert Niccolls on that night in Asotin, one life was forfeited but another was found.

The Boy Who Shot the Sheriff

Chapter 1

Asotin, Washington, August 5, 1931

MOONLIGHT spilled over the banks of Asotin Creek, where frogs chorused in deep pools. It was after midnight when he awoke cold and damp, unsure of his surroundings. This was not his grandmother's house—his grandmother with the big stick and the Bible. He had escaped. He was free and curled up in a hole along the bank. But unlike the small animal that had once made its home there, he shivered with cold. He was dressed in a thin shirt and worn overalls. His feet were bare. And he was hungry. He was always hungry.

He felt the gun thud against his chest inside the bib of his overalls as he crawled up the bank. The frogs stopped singing. He walked to the lumberyard and on toward the dairy, creeping about the sleeping town in the hope of finding something to eat. A car was parked alongside the road and he sat on the running board, wondering what to do next. Then in the distance he saw the gleam of a headlight. He darted into the shadows and hid behind a shed until the car passed and the chug of the engine faded.

Earlier in the evening he had hidden beneath the Asotin County Memorial Bridge as a family with eight children picnicked nearby, the fragrance of their food filling the air. He had hoped to stay with Murphy Watkins but Murphy's grandfather ordered him off the place. He left for a while and then returned. He didn't know where else to go. When the old man caught him a second time, the sheriff came. That's when he retreated to the only place he knew would be safe: the hole in the earth.

Now it was dark and he was alone. The creek murmured as he crossed the bridge and walked toward town. He had never been alone in town at that hour of the night. Storefronts, the solitary courthouse, the square jail with its barred windows, all cast shadows.

•

Except for Anatone, twenty miles south, Asotin is the last pinprick of civilization on the southeasterly corner of the Washington State map. It is a small town where the Asotin Creek races east from the Blue Mountains to the Snake River. In the 1890s, it was a hub of commerce situated on the route to the gold mines farther south along the Snake. Before that, it was the winter hunting ground for the Nez Perce. But in 1931, it was a town of ranchers and wheat farmers whose lives had been hard for decades. The Depression had brought nothing new.

As the boy walked, he could feel the gun swing in the holster he had made from the leather top of an old boot by threading a belt through the loops and hanging it from his neck. He had taken the gun from Colonel Fulton's cellar while he and Fulton's son Jimmy were playing. Jimmy was only ten and told him all about the guns the colonel had collected during the Philippine Insurrection. But Jimmy was no doubt asleep in bed and Junior—as Herbert Niccolls was known then—was alone in town after midnight.

With the gun Junior felt powerful, like Pretty Boy Floyd who robbed banks. He had heard about the robberies on the radio as the hour of prayer slipped away to the news, and then he'd read about them in the *Asotin Sentinel*. As he walked from the park down the quiet streets he knew that if his grandmother caught him she would lock him in his room to pray for forgiveness, without food or water. Each time the punishment was longer. But this time, he wasn't going back. He had made that decision when night fell and he wasn't home. She must have been furious to send the sheriff after him. This time there would be no stopping her as she meted out the punishment of the Lord. He hadn't thought any further than the momentary desire to run down the hill and play on a sunny day. Now in the dark, he was approaching the lynching spot, the jail at the corner of Filmore. How many men had died there? His grandmother said that's where he'd end up—a criminal. He'd always be haunted by her wrath and accusations.

In the shadows of the buildings, the stream's song was muffled. At Peter Klaus's People's Supply store he saw cigarettes through the window. Cigarettes and whatever else he could find inside the store would comfort him on this cold summer night. The pavement was cold against his bare feet. He hadn't owned shoes since he first went to the state reform school two years earlier.

He walked to the side of the building and peered into the store through the window next to the door. He turned the doorknob but it was firmly locked. He slammed his frail shoulder into the door but it wouldn't budge. Slowly, he walked back around the building. Across the street at the Asotin Hotel a light the color of cherries gleamed over the desk.

Junior walked around to the side of the store, took out the .32-caliber Iver Johnson and smashed it against the door. The glass tinkled like ice. He reached through the gaping window and unlocked the door.

The store was cool and fragrant with tobacco and the tang of fat pickles swimming in the shadows of the vinegar barrel. Moonlight streamed in through the broken panes and he could see the rack of tobacco, candy bars, and gum. First he opened the cash register, pulling down the heavy lever and watching as the numbers popped up and the drawer flew open with a zing. He scooped out $2.82 and put it in his pocket. Then he snapped open a paper bag as he had seen the Klauses do so many times before—even the day before when he had bought shells and charged them to his grandmother's account. Into the bag went Lucky Strikes and Adams gum. His plan was to return to the stream, feast on gum and candy and smoke. When morning came, he would meet Murphy and they'd go fishing or shoot jacksnipes up by Hen Lee's old place. Maybe he would hide out there, living off fish and stealing watermelons from the farm up the road and fruit from the orchards.

He knew he would have to lie low until his grandmother stopped looking for him. She would pray for his black soul, pray that he not be cast into the fiery depth of hell for his sins. He had done a lot in his twelve years. He had stolen everything from cars to candy.

Perhaps that's why his mother got rid of him and all the other boys. Like most children, he blamed himself for being forced to live with his grandmother. He wondered if his mother ever thought of him.

Hazel Niccolls's face had become blurred with time and tears. Someday he would return home to her with plenty of money and be able to buy her things so she wouldn't have to work so hard, so she wouldn't have to give all her children away just so they could be fed. That's what his mother had said the day the social worker came, which was not long after the police had arrived and arrested his father.

He wondered why they hadn't come for his father earlier. He could remember that day hiding in the barn while his father looked for him, carrying a shotgun. Over and over his father shouted his name. "Who dared bring that dog home?" Bert Niccolls had screamed. "Who dared bring that barking dog here?" It was forbidden. His brother had tied the puppy up by the porch and it whimpered loudly. Over and over his father yelled for him, "Junior! Junior!" And finally he found him in the barn, pointed the shotgun at him, and asked him if he had brought the puppy home.

"No, not me, Papa," he said. He could see his brother Wesley's horrified face in the yard beyond, pleading with him wordlessly not to implicate him. "Not me." Lying came easy when it was the only way to survive.

His father had lowered the shotgun and walked slowly from the barn. Junior's brother was trying to untie the dog but his trembling fingers wouldn't move fast enough. Junior heard his father laugh, heard Wesley cry out as the dog began to frantically bark. Bert Niccolls raised the shotgun to his shoulder and aimed at the puppy's small brown head. Then he pulled the trigger.

•

As Junior was filling the bag in the dark, he suddenly became aware of three shadows by the front door. There was a murmur of deep voices. He dropped the sack and scurried softly to the back of the store, slipping behind a vinegar barrel and a pile of boxes next to a rolltop desk. Then the front doorknob rattled and the door swung open, the little bell jingling.

"Come on out."

It was John Wormell, the sheriff of Asotin County. Inside the store there was nothing but silence.

"Come on out, now."

Again there was no answer. The sheriff repeated the words once more and cocked the hammer on his revolver. He nodded to Charlie Carlisle, deputy and county clerk, and Peter Klaus, the grocer. Then he and Klaus stepped inside.

Peeping over the rim of the barrel, the boy could see the sheriff silhouetted in the moonlight and the glint of light on the gun. The man moved closer.

"Come out before someone gets hurt."

The sheriff's voice was calm. After serving four terms as sheriff and about as many as deputy sheriff, he knew that patience paid off.

Suddenly the store's lights came on and the boy ducked, blinking in the harsh light and fumbling to remove the pearl-handled revolver from the holster. Listening closely, he could hear two maybe three sets of footsteps.

Deputy Sheriff Wayne Bezona stood inside the side door near the broken glass as the sheriff and the grocer walked slowly up the aisles. Klaus saw the bag the boy had dropped and stopped to retrieve the items as the sheriff crossed the room, listening for the softest flutter of sound. He had walked almost the entire length of the store with his gun in his hand and was standing close to the vinegar barrel when he heard a familiar click and a roar.

Both Klaus and Bezona heard the blast from the gun, saw the sheriff spin and pitch forward as if still walking, and they ducked for cover. But who had shot him and from where? There was no smoke from a gun.

Bezona ran out into the street to the hotel, where a man had stumbled outside after hearing the shot.

Bezona told him that the sheriff had been shot and yelled for the doctor, and then ran back inside the store with Carlisle. In the silent room, he could hear his heart and the ragged edge of his breath. Across the store, his eyes met those of the others. Where was the shooter?

He took a step forward, kicking a cardboard box out of his way and shouted for the shooter to surrender. He heard the sound—a scurry, a faint rustle of paper. He trained his revolver in the area of the desk. Where was he? There was no place big enough to hide a man. He took another step forward and kicked another box out of the way, keeping his gun trained on the site. No one behind the molasses barrel; no one behind the vinegar barrel. Where had he gone? Had he slipped down the cellar steps a few feet away? He hoped not, as it would be even more dangerous to hunt for him among the crates in the dim light of the bare electric bulb.

Then Bezona saw a small corner of faded denim near the back of the rolltop desk. But no one could possibly hide in the few inches that separated the desk and the wall, unless the person was very small. Again, he ordered him out. Bezona could hear the shouts and tire screeches outside in the street as others came to help. He tried not to look at Johnny lying so still on the floor. Seventy-three years old! John Wormell should have retired long ago. Bezona had tried to tell him that.

"Come out or I'll kill you!" His voice boomed through the store but there was no reply.

Minutes passed and then, as Bezona trained his gun in the area of the desk, the boy threw a revolver over the top. Bezona kicked it to the other side of the store, keeping his own gun trained on the desk and waiting to see what madman would emerge from the shadows to own the deed.

Bezona ordered him to raise his hands and come out. It seemed like forever before two small hands appeared from behind the desk, then the frail arms. In the end, a boy less than five-feet tall stood up and looked nervously around, his face white, his body trembling. Bezona rushed forward and grabbed him.

The deputy's face was red and close to the boy's, as he gripped the boy's shoulders.

"What did you do this for?"

The answer to the question would be published in newspapers everywhere: "I was told to," the boy cried. He had re-cocked the gun and was ready to shoot Bezona, when surrendering seemed to be the better idea. The body of the sheriff lay face down on the floor, a bullet hole just above the right ear. Everywhere there were spatters of blood like drops of dark rain.

•

Rain. That's what the Niccolls children would remember about that day long ago when they came home from school and pushed open the gate to find a woman lying in the yard with a bullet hole in her back, a farmer shouting, the sheriff's siren wailing, their mother screaming. Their father's face was bloated and red as he chased her. She carried a baby boy in her arms as she fled into the fields.

The neighbors stood stunned in their sun-bleached front yards, except for the dead woman's family who had gathered around the still form. She was a gentle soul, a Quaker. Why kill such a kind woman? She gave her life to protect another, they said.

"Why did you do it?" A police officer had asked his father as the sheriff handcuffed him and led him to the squad car.

•

"Why did you do it?" Bezona asked the boy again. The doctor had arrived and was kneeling beside the sheriff. Men and women in their nightclothes, having been roused from sleep at the hotel across the street, gathered to peer in the windows. Even in the pre-dawn hours, the boy knew they were angry and speaking of lynching and punishment and what a good man poor Johnny Wormell had been. Poor Johnny slain by Mary Addington's juvenile delinquent grandson. Johnny, who had never had a chance to protect himself. Too bad Johnny hadn't gotten in a shot. What a blight Mrs. Addington had brought on the town when she let the boy stay. Tears began flowing down the boy's cheeks.

"I was told to. Bill Robinson put me up to it," he said.

"Robinson!"

The boy said that Robinson had waited at the side door while he went in and got tobacco and money. He planned to give the boy $2 and a ticket to Canada for his trouble. Bezona took the boy to the sheriff's office in the courthouse, telling Carlisle to summon Halsey, the coroner, and Merchant, the undertaker. Bill Hostetler, the part-time night deputy who worked as the state brand inspector by day, also arrived on the scene and stared in disbelief at the prone body of the sheriff.

The ticking of the regulator on the office wall echoed through the quiet building. It was almost 1 a.m. and the boy was very tired. Bezona again asked him to tell him how the shooting occurred. The boy had only been in town since May and he'd been nothing but trouble to his grandmother. Once again the boy repeated the story. Bezona sat behind the desk. The boy was sprawled across two polished oak chairs and seemed to be slowly melting into them as he sunk into the realm of sleep.

He was small for a twelve-year-old—sixty pounds, four feet, eight inches. Too much food creates a rebellious spirit, his grandmother believed, and she locked her pantry. With each infraction of her rules, she gave him less. It was God's will, she said, taking her seat in the rocker by the oil stove. She would purse her lips and read the Bible in the halo of lamplight. He would wait until she fell asleep and try to take her key.

•

The dark streets bustled with the chug of automobiles, a flurry of whispered urgency. Bezona rose from his desk and nodded to Hostetler, instructing him to stay with the boy, who was sleeping stretched across the oak chairs. In the meantime, Dr. John McElvain stood at the entrance of the store, looking weary. Elmer Halsey had just arrived. The three men entered the store where the sheriff's body lay.

Nothing could be done. The sheriff had been killed instantly, McElvain said. The bullet went right into the brain.

Elmer Halsey had seen crime in the many years he had spent in Asotin—a rape back in 1896, a murder in 1903, bank robbers, horse thieves, cattle rustlers. Sheriff Johnny Wormell always neatly wrapped up the cases. He'd served his town well. A fine man he was. A devoted community servant, a state representative, and a charter member of the Anatone Odd Fellows. Halsey knew someone would have to tell Annie Wormell. It would be a hard job.

Halsey was not only the prosecutor, he was also the elected coroner. Filling in as sheriff if the current sheriff was unable to serve was just part of the job. Halsey, well into his seventies, was grim about the prospects. He never thought he'd be writing up the death certificate for Johnny. But Bezona knew he would have to be the one to break the news to Annie. He walked slowly from the store, vowing that Robinson would pay for putting the boy up to this. Even though it was still several hours before dawn, word of the shooting had spread. Men milled about the courthouse, talking in low tones. Bezona asked Carlisle to round up some men to go out to the Robinson place and arrest Bill. But Carlisle looked puzzled.

"Old Bill Robinson?"

"Put the boy up to it."

Bezona told him to take several other men with him, cautioning them to be careful because if Robinson was capable of this, he was capable of anything.

•

The new Ford V-8 with the red lights hummed north along the road to where Bill Robinson lived with his daughter, Della Watkins, her husband, Jim, and their seven children. Young Murphy Watkins was jarred from sleep by the barking dog, the roar of the car engine, and the winking of its red lights. He rose on one elbow and looked across the screened porch where his mother and sisters also slept. His mother quickly rose, wrapping a bathrobe around her. The dark shapes of the lawmen came to the screen door and their fists pounded on the frame.

"Open up, Robinson!"

They had come to arrest him and Della ran to the door to block their path. They pushed her aside. She asked what they wanted with her father but they shoved passed her to open the door to the bedroom where Robinson was still sleeping. They demanded he get up and get dressed because he was being arrested.

"What? You want to arrest me?" the old man said, sitting up in bed, startled.

"For the murder of John Wormell."

"Murder? The sheriff?"

Murphy's little sister, Jean, ran past the men and threw herself at her grandfather, crying. She clung to the lawmen, pleading for her grandfather's release as they led him from the house, "Please don't take him! He didn't do anything bad. Don't take him away."

Murphy and Jean followed the men into the yard, watched the deputies handcuff their grandfather, saw him duck his head to get into the backseat of the patrol car. The dry grass hissed against the lawmen's boots. Car doors slammed. The engine again came to life and the lights streaked red against the backdrop of night. Jean and Murphy stood in the yard; the soft dust—so hot against their feet during the day—was now cool. Jean whimpered softly and ran to cling to her mother. The car traveled down the ribbon of road, its red lights winking until at last there was nothing but darkness and a scattering of stars.

Della told her children to return to bed, that the arrest had been a misunderstanding and it would be straightened out in the morning. But when she tucked them in, Murphy noticed that she was fully dressed. Shortly afterward he heard the screen door creek open and softly close and the engine of his grandfather's truck come to life.

In the distance a coyote yipped but there was no return chorus, only darkness. Murphy would say years later that his world changed that night. No longer would his world revolve around games of marbles and kick-the-can and mumbly peg or paste and blackboards or the white-starched shirts for Sunday school. All that had existed—the humming, contented, familiar melody of his childhood—had vanished. His world was now uncertain, a place where anything could—and had—happened. It was a dark, silent emptiness.

Chapter 2

JOHN WORMELL had been dead less than eight hours, his body still lying at the Merchant Funeral Parlor when farmers, merchants, and reporters from Lewiston, Spokane, Reno, and Boise began to fill the courthouse. They gathered in amazement around the door and gazed at the boy, curled across two chairs, sound asleep. He looked more like eight than twelve, with his delicate face, long eyelashes, and very thin frame.

"Is he the one?"

It was the question all the reporters, including J. F. Anderson from the *Lewiston Morning Tribune*, wanted to know. Anderson had seen murderers in his day. They were cold, steely eyed, and ruthless, not pretty children with curling lashes.

Hearing voices, the boy finally stirred, opened his eyes and blinked, unsure of where he was. A reporter smiled and the boy smiled back, and then stretched and rose. Then it all came back to him.

Anderson said good morning and asked the boy if he could tell him what had happened the night before. The boy looked around at the faces. Anderson had a kind face, ready to listen to every word. So the boy began telling the crowd about how he wanted to go to Canada to be an adventurer. He also said that he wanted to be away from his grandmother because she whipped him. When the reporters asked what for, he replied, "For doing things I'm not supposed to." Then he told them how Bill Robinson had said he'd give him $2 and a ticket to Canada if he robbed the store.

The recitation came matter-of-fact. He told the reporters that he and Robinson had the whole robbery planned for days and that he was at Robinson's house the night before making the final arrangements. He said they had walked into town the back way so nobody would see them, following the creek and then cutting through a field until they were almost to the bridge. There were two women and eight children all having dinner at the park. That's when Bill laid low. The boy said they hid out at Hen Lee's old shack until it was time.

Anyone in those parts of the territory knew Hen Lee, the old Chinese man who had been a cook at the hotel. He always cooked for friends. Murphy Watkins had told Junior that Hen Lee would give children who fished near his place plates of fried chicken and chocolate-chip cookies. Junior wanted more than anything to meet him. Gentle Hen Lee. Generous Hen Lee. Hen Lee, the God of Fried Chicken. Then Murphy had spoiled it all and told him Hen Lee was dead.

Anderson asked where the boy got the gun. He said that Robinson bought it secondhand in Lewiston and took him out to the fields to teach him how to shoot.

At his desk behind the wall of reporters, Bezona listened intently. The story fit the one the boy had told the night before almost word for word. He had taken the boy through town, made the boy show him exactly where he and Robinson had stopped. He was unwavering as he told it, looking you straight in the eye. The only problem was that when they had arrested Bill Robinson, he had clearly been asleep in bed. With Bezona's tolerance for reporters over, he rose to usher them outside.

Anderson then turned to the boy and asked if he was sorry.

"If I didn't get him, he would have gotten me!" Junior said. "Bill said if anyone came in before we were done to shoot to kill."

Before Anderson left, he took the boy outside. Already it was a searing hot day under a pale layer of clouds. The sky was white and blank like the paper the boy had rolled his ink-blackened fingertips onto last night. The boy stood erect, his arms at his side, gazing into a camera lens. Suddenly, he wasn't a cherub-faced child, but a young man in tattered overalls that were worn thin as tissue in places, and his gaze, some would believe, was cool and calculating. At that moment, he seemed not only capable of one murder but also a second. With a snap of the shutter it was over and Bezona took the boy by the arm and led him to jail, a small square building with barred windows, a dirt floor, and an iron ring in the center used for shackling prisoners.

Robinson, gray and disheveled, looking like the boy had never seen him, sat on a bunk and blinked as a bar of light from the open door fell across him. The single room radiated heat and intensified the stench of human waste rising from a bucket set against the wall. A fly tapped against the window and then buzzed around the room, settling on the bucket.

Robinson stared at the boy who had turned his back so he didn't have to meet the old man's eyes. Robinson had always been a mean old man as far as the boy was concerned. He had ordered him from the house when he had no place else to go. That would make anybody sore.

The boy paced the dirt floor, tracing the writings on the wall with his fingers. "Life is a game of chance. Death holds the winning cards, spades." And "take advice young man and leave alcohol alone, for this is my benefit of it, being shut up here for being drunk and gun in my pocket." Then over by the window, the boy found another: "If it had not been for you, I wouldn't be here." The boy read it and glanced at Robinson to see if he had noticed it. But the old man fanned his face with his hand and stared up at the small barred windows that only let in minimal light.

Outside the jail Junior could hear voices. They were loud and angry. He recognized Bezona's voice and that of Judge Kuykendall, a man who always tipped his hat whenever he saw a lady.

He heard the clank of the iron bar and the door opened again. A woman from the hotel stepped in, carrying a tray of food. Bezona, carrying another one, opened the cell and she handed the trays in. They had walked past the angry crowd, many with tears in their eyes when they spoke of John Wormell, their protector, friend, and neighbor for nearly half a century. His loss was the loss of a life lived for the community—everything his killer had never known.

•

Della Watkins wished that her husband would return from harvesting up in Anatone to aid her in this crisis. As she explained to the deputy, she had been sleeping on the porch and would have known if her father had gone out. The boy was just angry because he had been forced to leave. His grandmother had been looking for him and sent the law to scare him home. The family didn't want to interfere. Although he is such a little boy, she said, her dark eyes welling with tears. She recalled how Murphy had told her of the beatings the boy got with a club if he was late. He is just a child, she reminded the deputy.

Bezona studied her carefully and told her that he was investigating the case and if Robinson's version of the story checked out, he would be released soon.

Grasshoppers whirred in the dry grass outside the jail. It was shortly after nine a.m. and crowd had gathered. Their voices rose in a chant.

"Hang them! Hang them!"

Each word fell like the thunder of fists. Robinson pleaded with the boy to tell the truth. Did he want responsibility for hanging an innocent man on his conscience?

But the boy was more interested in the untouched food on Robinson's plate. He had never seen such wonderful food—thick, fluffy pancakes swimming in maple syrup, eggs with golden eyes. He had dreamed of food like this. But for Robinson, the thunder of the mob was impossible to ignore.

The town had a history of lynching. John Wormell once stopped a lynching in 1893, in his very first year as elected sheriff. A man had set fire to the hotel, wrongly believing his wife was inside. An innocent man died in the fire. To keep a mob from lynching the arsonist, Wormell moved him back and forth across the state line. When the mob found him in Lewiston, Idaho, Wormell moved him to Dayton, Washington, and then to Uniontown, Washington. Finally, the man was tried, convicted, and executed at a public hanging in Pomeroy.

In 1897, a young woman from Enterprise, Oregon, was on her way home on horseback after visiting friends across the border in Lapwai, Idaho, when a few miles from Asotin, she was overtaken and "outraged." She made it in to town to tell her story. Her assailant was arrested but a band of men overpowered the deputy sheriff. Her attacker was hanged in the jail yard.

In 1903, Mabel Richards, the twelve-year-old daughter of Sheriff Robert Richards, was murdered on her way to Sunday school near her ranch home in Anatone. A man described as a "moron" in the local press, was arrested later and then confessed. Hours later, dozens of men, faces hidden behind handkerchiefs galloped down the hill, removed the man from the jail, and debated whether to torture and burn him or simply hang him. As thousands from nearby towns turned out, the mob covered his head with a black hood and hanged him with an electric guy wire from a telephone pole. The crowd broke into a loud cheer when the deed was done. The *Asotin Sentinel* wrote that Mabel's murder had been avenged without the aid of a trial.

When the mob swarmed outside the jail in 1931, Junior seemed unaware. It was easy to escape reality by turning inward, drifting like a piece of dandelion down in a shaft of sunlight.

"Hang them. Both of them!" The crowd shouted.

The boy did not want to hang. He could hear Bezona's voice, urging everyone to go home and let justice be done. As he sat on his bunk a rock was hurtled through the glass of the barred windows, hit the opposite wall and fell to the ground. Then came another and another, and the voices rose like the sound of a storm.

Suddenly, the bar lifted and the door swung wide. Bezona and Hostetler stepped in. They ordered Robinson and the boy into the police car, telling them that they were being taken to the Garfield County Jail in Pomeroy for protection.

As the boy moved from the jail into the car, he glanced at the crowd. It included his neighbors, people his grandmother did business with. He settled into the backseat. A row of bars divided the front from the back. Robinson looked gray and unwell as he hunched into the corner of the car. Out the back window of the car the boy could see several other police cars—the police chief from Pomeroy and a deputy sheriff from Garfield County—following behind. Slowly, the town faded as the road curved west along the Snake River, higher and higher, leaving the rolling brown hills and the Snake River far below. Then they descended slowly down the winding Alpowa Grade into the valley. The Blue Mountains were ringed in distant clouds. The boy had never been this way before.

Lewis and Clark took this route on their expedition. Wayne Bezona knew this because he was a self-educated man who envied his five children's opportunities for education. He felt no sympathy when they complained about walking the five miles from the ranch to school in Anatone. As far as he was concerned, it should make them value the lessons.

He had never had many opportunities for schooling back in Missouri. But he had learned about the Golden Rule and the law. There were times when he got whipped but it never made him cry, he often told his children. It had made a man out of him.

He glanced into the back seat. The boy was pretty and spoiled, without a conscience or pangs of guilt for the Wormell family, for Annie and the kids.

The Wormell children—a daughter and three sons—were grown and Annie was left alone in her little white house that was flanked with her daisies and pink peonies. He remembered seeing her in her broad straw hat and checked pinafore tending the garden in the midday sun. She had never lost her New England ways—she was proper, always ladylike. She was a blue blood and could trace her ancestry all the way back to the Boston Tea Party. She had been born to preside over the pink teas of ladies auxiliaries and she did it so well. But she was no fragile flower. Stubborn as hell, that's what Johnny said. She had been an excellent ranch wife and did not complain. Johnny loved her. And she loved him.

Just a few hours earlier, Bezona had been the one to tell her it was over. It wasn't that he hadn't done things like this before as a deputy and during his term as a sheriff. But this was Annie. And John was the deceased. Even though some thirty years separated their ages, he and John had been close friends. For years, he had been Johnny's deputy. Then Johnny encouraged him to run for sheriff and Johnny had been his deputy. Bob Richards had his stint as sheriff for a while, until the death of his daughter. Then a few years ago, it was the Wormell-Bezona team again. Over the years, they'd been almost like father and son—except better.

When Bezona had pulled up outside Annie's dark house and slowly got out of the car it was about three a.m. Annie met him on the porch, concerned because John had not returned home. Bezona paused and suddenly was overwhelmed with grief. It was his job to comfort her but she was calm and strong. He fought down the swelling in his throat, the urge to blurt it all out, the words of sympathy he had to say. Then he would accept her wrath, her blame. He would always regret not going in the front door of the store with John and wondered if Annie would blame him and question why he hadn't been at John's side. As the thoughts ran through his head, Annie sat in the cool, dark evening with stars all around and ribbons of moonlight streaming in the river. He didn't want to burden her with his grief.

Annie's once delicate face with its high cheekbones was lined now but her blue eyes were still bright. Like John, she was advanced in years. John had been looking forward to retiring. His son, Earl, was taking care of the ranch, and he and Annie had planned to spend their leisure time in town, watching the birds soar and the boats and barges chug down the Snake laden with wheat.

Annie's dreams would have come true had it not been for the boy in the back seat—a boy who seemed unconcerned with what he had done. The law would change that.

Chapter 3

THE GARFIELD COUNTY COURTHOUSE was impressive with its venerable white brick, stately cupola, long windows, and golden statue of justice with the scales in her hand on the rooftop. On the front lawn was a bronze statue of Sam Cosgrove, a Pomeroy native who had been governor for three months.

The boy, who had grown up so poor he had to hide food from his siblings so he'd have something to eat, would have been impressed at the opulence. Few, if any, twelve-year-olds ended up in the county jail in those days. Although the Depression brought new concerns about what was coming to be known as juvenile delinquency, and Washington, like many other states, already had new juvenile court systems in the more populous counties, sleepy Asotin had no need for a juvenile court before the boy came to town. Not that he would have been eligible anyway. According to the law, juveniles went to the reformatory for all crimes except murder. The public attitude was that juveniles who committed adult-size offenses should get adult-size punishment—even hanging.

Bezona was relieved to turn the boy and Bill Robinson over to Sheriff James Patterson at the Garfield County Jail. Bezona had been up all night and knew he couldn't hold back a lynch mob if things got worse. Then he asked for one of Patterson's deputies to work the case. Patterson said he would put Deputy Sheriff William Gilliam on it.

In a time when the average age for a criminal was thirty-two, the "barefoot boy murderer" was a curiosity. Deputies and citizens alike gathered around the patrol car. The deputies walked the boy through the side door and down the hall to a row of cells. The sheriff's key ring jingled in the rusty lock and a cell door swung open. Robinson would be placed down the row, in the adult area, at least until all the questions were answered.

The boy took a seat on the bunk. It was a small cell with a toilet and a wash basin. Daylight came in through a barred window high above. There were other prisoners farther down the row where Robinson was sent. He could hear murmurs of conversation. But no one was in the juvenile section. He sat quietly on his bunk and wished he had his cornet. He would play "Red Wing" or "Home on the Range."

How excited he had been to take lessons when he lived with the Mitchells in Shoshone, in southern Idaho. Mrs. Mitchell had been good to him, kissing him on the forehead when he went off to bed, laughing at his jokes, feeding him great platefuls of chicken potpie teeming with golden gravy and fresh vegetables and his favorite dessert—apple pie. He was in charge of the vegetable patch. He was supposed to work in the fields with Mr. Mitchell. That was the plan. Many ranch families took in foster children because they needed ranch hands. But the Mitchells were kind. They had offered more.

Mrs. Mitchell was the principal and a teacher at the Shoshone School, and she had taught him all about history and geography, math and literature. It was easy and she always put gold stars by his name on the chart at the front of the class, told him how smart he was. She also gave him a pocket-size New Testament that he read through several times, memorizing verses. "With God everything is possible." Mark 10:27.

Despite the Mitchell's kindness, he stole from them, too, and ruined the relationship. The girls and Mrs. Mitchell all cried when he left. His grandmother told him that the devil made him do it, and that she was well acquainted with the devil. From the Mitchells' ranch, he had been sent back to the children's home in Boise. The superintendent had had an earnest talk with him, and the boy promised to make good in the future. But on August 2, 1929, he had tried to persuade another boy to help him rob the safe in the office of the home. When the other boy refused, Junior Niccolls had stolen a Ford parked across the street. He could barely see over the steering wheel when he drove the car down the street. Faster and faster he went into the countryside, and when the road curved he lost control and wrecked the car. He got out, dusted himself off, and returned to the home that night on a stolen tricycle. A judge sentenced him to the State Industrial School in St. Anthony, Idaho. But shortly after he was delivered there, his grandmother interceded with two of the fiercest attorneys in town. She told the judge that she would be able to control him, and he was released to her care. The two of them then moved up north to Orofino so she could be near his father, who was in the insane asylum there.

Saying she was trying to make a good boy of him, she whipped him and starved him. But it seemed like the more she did, the more he shot from the house in wild abandon, like one of Murphy's marbles. He broke into the post office with another boy and stole a package, thinking it would be full of candy. When he found that it contained bandages for the hospital, he festooned them around a tree. He stole candy, cigarettes, and anything else he wanted whenever he could and lied so much that the line between fact and fiction blurred. Yet he never forgot to say, "please" and "thank you," "yes, ma'am" and "yes, sir. " He was a little gentleman, the women in town who didn't know him well said.

Impressed by the boy's intelligence and good manners, the superintendent of the Orofino School District was convinced he could help him and took him into his home. But while he was there he still got into trouble, stealing an automobile from the woman for whom his grandmother worked as a housekeeper.

This time when he got into the car, put the key in the ignition, and drove off, it was a profound moment. For the first time, he felt free like he had never felt before, driving eastbound toward the Rocky Mountains where the clouds' shadows moved across the fields and the world was full of possibilities. With each press on the gas pedal the car went faster. He was flying. But moments later, the police were behind him and forced him off the road. He leaped from the car, grabbed a rusty old revolver, and threatened them with it.

His grandmother came and collected him from jail. She beat him and locked him in his room. Later, he repented before God and his grandmother. The next Sunday, he slipped into the church pew next to her and snuggled close. Moments later curling smoke had drifted into the sanctuary, and suddenly men and women were screaming and scrambling from the burning building. On his way out, he stole the collection plate. Finally, there was nothing even his grandmother could do and once again he was sent to the State Industrial School. It wasn't bad there as far as he was concerned. He had shoes. There was food. On Friday nights there were movies—the first ones he'd ever seen.

Then after fifteen months, he returned to his grandmother who was launching a new campaign to free his father from the insane asylum. She had moved to Asotin, hoping to persuade the authorities that if they released his father to her care in her Washington home, he would no longer be Idaho's problem. She had bought a small house with a plot of alfalfa and enough space for a few rows of corn. It was located a short ways from downtown on the road to Anatone.

•

When Herbert Niccolls had arrived in Asotin in May 1931, he arrived without history. At first, mothers who knew him held him up as a model child—intelligent, well-mannered, and charming. For the first time, he was free of his family's legacy of poverty and violence. He was not insane Bert Niccolls's boy and not yet Mary Addington's delinquent grandson. He descended on the town with the courtly politeness his mother had taught him, a willing spirit with a pleasing smile that veiled a desperate heart. No one knew him, except for his one attachment in the entire world—a gray kitten.

He was watering the patch of alfalfa one day and the kitten trotted up to him meowing insistently. He lifted her up and she curled against his neck, purring. From then on, he had saved some of his own meals for her, and whenever he went to work in the garden, she was there. When he awoke, with the soft light of dawn coming through the window, he would find her perched on the sill, surveying the morning.

Who would feed her now that he was in jail? He sat on the bunk watching the shadows change as day passed.

•

When it came to violent crime, Garfield County Sheriff James Patterson, like others in his town, was appalled when he read the headlines or heard the messages from the pulpit about broken families and teenagers gone wild. The state created the juvenile reformatory at Centralia in 1891 and started the juvenile court system in 1905 but nothing stopped the influx of juvenile delinquents. Nathan Leopold and Richard Loeb, the young men from Chicago who killed for nothing more than to see a child die, helped bring the Progressive Era of social change to an end in '24. Those two, who had come from wealthy families, had had no motive to kill a fourteen-year-old. It wasn't for money, shelter, food, revenge, or even sex.

Who hadn't heard kids on the courthouse lawn, playing cops and robbers, except in this case both sides wanted to be the robbers. During the days of unemployment, farms being taken over by the banks, the stock market collapse, it seemed that only the robbers were getting ahead. The officers, too, sometimes crossed the line, going from law enforcers to law breakers, addicted to power, lured by money. One by one, Patterson hung the wanted posters with their faces up in the post office.

Patterson shuddered to think of the difficulty of enforcing the law in bigger cities. He shook his head as he locked his office for the night, happy to be going home to a home-cooked meal and a pretty wife to serve it.

Of course, how the newspapers covered the news made all the difference. When an eighteen-year-old daughter of a prominent Boston bacteriologist joined a ring of robbers, her photo played across the three columns of the front page of the local paper. The story carried a headline that was impossible to ignore even in communities on the West Coast. The fear-mongering media message was clear—times were changing and, rather than regard the case as an anomaly, it seemed to portend what the future held.

•

The Union Pacific line thundered through town at midnight, bisecting the rolling hills of wheat, shaking houses on their foundations and making the pendulum of the courthouse clock quiver. The boy was curled up, sleeping soundly as an infant.

At dawn, trucks full of grain trundled in from the country. The morning trains chugged into town, brakes screeching, engines hissing, steam gushing as they pulled up to the grain elevators, ready to ship Palouse Prairie gold to points east. And while the workers arrived at the courthouse and the jail, and the janitor began the daily mop up, pail clanging as he whistled, still the boy slept on.

Finally, balancing a breakfast tray in one hand, Deputy William Gilliam took his nightstick and rattled it against the bars. The boy leaped up and seeing the tray, smiled. Nothing pleased the boy more than food.

At ten o'clock, Patterson unlocked the cell and summoned Junior to the office. Bezona had asked him to talk to the boy about the shooting to see if his story had changed.

As the boy told his tale, Gilliam and A. G. Farley, who would donate his legal services to the boy, crowded in the doorway. Patterson asked again what Robinson told him.

"Shoot to kill," the boy replied. Robinson had bought the gun at a secondhand store in Lewiston the week before, the boy said. Robinson gave the gun to him, instructing him how to use it if they were caught. For many hours, he lay out in the cold shivering, until it was time to do the job. And then he heard someone at the door to the store. He said, "I hid behind the vinegar barrel. When I saw him coming, I pulled out my pistol and fired. I aimed at his body."

After the others had left, Gilliam took a checkerboard off the sheriff's desk and brought Junior into the office for a game. By afternoon Junior had an impressive number of wins and Gilliam told him he was the best checkers player he had ever encountered. Later, Junior jumped from his bunk and went to the cell door when he heard footsteps. Wayne Bezona stopped at the door to the cell and summoned Gilliam to unlock the door and usher the boy down the aisle into the sheriff's office. Once again he was asked to repeat the story. But, Bezona told him, no more lies. The boy recited the story without changing any of the details, insisting that Robinson had bought him the gun at a secondhand store across the river in Lewiston, Idaho.

"Colonel Fulton says it's his. You stole it from his basement two days before the sheriff was shot," Bezona said. The boy vigorously denied stealing the gun but Bezona was relentless, questioning him, making him recite again how he came to get it and the route he took to the bridge that night. There was only one set of footprints, he told him. And they were just a boy's size.

The boy began to invent stories about how the second set had been erased, but Bezona pressed on. If Robinson was outside the door of the general store, did he help break in? Despite the boy's insistence that he had not acted alone, Bezona stared intently at him and told him that only his fingerprints were on the glass.

If he didn't tell the truth now, Bezona told him, he'd recommend hanging. That's how they handled murderers in the state. As far as Bezona was concerned, the boy wasn't too young to start being a man and, if necessary, accept man-sized punishment. Finally, the tears started and the true story came out. "I was just sore because he wouldn't let me stay the night," the boy said. Gilliam guided the boy back to the cell.

Bezona asked for Robinson's freedom so he could take him home to his family. "Della has been at the courthouse waiting," he said.

Gilliam came back to Junior's cell a few hours later and handed him a harmonica because the boy had told him how much he loved music. He had told him how he also hoped to be reunited with his beloved cornet and again create music, the dancing notes like arithmetic games except better. Then the wailing strains of gospel hymns and cowboy tunes echoed through the jail as another day turned into night.

•

The body of John Wormell lay beneath the grove of willows. Baskets of roses and standards of gladiolus and carnations, daisies and chrysanthemums lay in Asotin Park where—lacking any other facility large enough to handle the crowd—the funeral was to be held. Women with hats and men in dark suits filled the shaded grove. Law enforcement officers came from Idaho and counties throughout Washington State. Fellow Democrats came, as well as merchants, lodge brothers, family. Annie, dressed in black, was accompanied by her daughter and three sons. In all, 1,500 people from three states gathered to mourn.

The Asotin Male Quartet sang "Sometime We'll Understand" and "Sweet Bye and Bye," and Reverend J. B. York gave the funeral address.

In a *Lewiston Morning Tribune* account of the funeral, York stepped up to the pulpit and gazed out across the mass of tearful faces. "We're here," he began "because of an inherent thirst for cigarettes . . . and the lack of proper home environment. They are directly responsible for the untimely death of Asotin County's most highly respected citizen and a crime, which shocked the world.

"If parents would stay home with their children," he admonished, "instead of spending their evenings pleasure seeking, there would be no such crimes committed by the youth of the country." He said that the sheriff had come to his death because a youth's desire for cigarettes had led him to rob the store where the murder was committed.

"The life of John Wormell was too well known by everyone for me to attempt to explain his virtues," he said. And then the quartet began to sing as Bezona, Carlisle, County Commissioner Frank Campbell, and three members of the Anatone Odd Fellows carried the casket through the trees.

As Sheriff Patterson and his wife were leaving the park, reporters—men in rakish fedoras, carrying notebooks and pencils—gathered around him.

"Tell us about the boy . . . "

"Is he talking about the crime?"

"Is he sorry?"

"He talks freely about it," Patterson said. "He doesn't understand the seriousness of his act. In fact, he seems quite indifferent."

In a small cemetery near the Wormell homestead final rites were said in keeping with the traditions of the Masonic Order. Annie and her family watched as the casket was lowered into the ground to take its place next to other Wormells who had come to the region in 1880, even before Washington was a state.

When she had met Johny, she was Annie Ramsdell. That was more than forty years earlier. She had been drawn to him because of their common New England roots. She bore his children, worked long days on the ranch, sweating over steaming kettles at canning time, cooking vast quantities of food for harvest crews, nursing one baby while helping another with his penmanship lesson, wiping noses, tying shoes, feeding chickens, and nursing sick calves. But how restless she had been at the ranch, so far from town. Yet, there had been the golden hills of wheat and the band of green in the horizon as the tree line faded into the Blue Mountains beyond.

As was typical in the valley, there were picnics and barn dances with fiddlers coming from nearby ranches to play. The men would clear out the loft and everyone danced. There were waltzes and Virginia reels. Annie and John were a handsome couple—both dark-haired with blue eyes.

But while John moved with quiet deliberation, Annie was high-spirited. After she and John built a house in town, she threw all her new dishes into the river in a temper. When she was like that, Johnny knew it was best to keep out of her way. Whatever family drama had brewed through the seasons, all became calm sooner or later. The year of the great blizzard she lay beside him, listening to the softness of his breath as the cares of the day melted into sleep.

Now that she was elderly, she was alone. A boy with a gun had altered the path of her life. Annie was content to leave the boy's fate and his punishment in the hands of God. She often told her Sunday school students that forgiving and loving your neighbor were steps to heaven. She had instilled in her children, too, the importance of charity and had always made food baskets for the poor and championed any child in need. How could she strike out against the boy who would forever live with the memory of what he had done? She bore the boy no ill will and refused to speak about it. Hating would not bring Johnny back; it would only dishonor his name.

For the first time in her life, Anna Margaret Ramsdell Wormell felt old, as if a part of her had died with John. And, seven years later, suffering from poor health, she would join him, being buried at his side in the nearby Anatone Cemetery where every spring wild flowers and the gnarled branches of lilacs burst into bloom.

Chapter 4

A METEOR passed over the Lewiston-Clarkston Valley on August 7, 1931, apparently burying itself in the Blue Mountains near the B. H. Brown home, the harvest crew reported. "It appeared to be traveling about 200 miles-an-hour as it flashed low across the mountains and dipped into the foothills."

Wayne Bezona set his copy of the *Lewiston Morning Tribune* on the table, his breakfast half-eaten. John Wormell had been laid to rest the day before and the town seemed to have simply picked up and carried on. The *Tribune* reported that Louis Folch, whose foot was crushed when it was caught in the cogwheels of a combine, was improving. The forest fire that broke out in the Blue Mountains southwest of Anatone was almost extinguished; teas and anniversaries were still occurring; and men and women were traveling to other communities to see friends and relatives. There was also a notation about the Board of Commissioners meeting to pick a new sheriff to fill out John's term. Six had applied for the job. He would make the seventh, if he officially applied.

Halsey had asked him to consider taking the job. But suddenly the burden of enforcing the law without Johnny seemed hard. People were angry at anyone in government, and they blamed government for all their problems—banks foreclosing mortgages and taking farms and homes, unemployment, poverty. Prohibition didn't help either. If anyone thought he was going to turn a blind eye to all the bootlegging going on in the hills, they would be very disappointed. He was going to uphold the law, regardless of whether he agreed with it. The law was sacred. Sacred as a father's word. That's what he told his children. And that's what he told the voters back in 1923 when, after being urged to campaign by some of his fellow Anatone ranchers, he stood on a street corner in Clarkston talking about the need for a tough law man who wouldn't be soft on criminals. He wasn't. There weren't many who dared to challenge him, at six-foot-two and 230 pounds. And he prided himself on being the toughest lawman around. Even with his children. If he thought they were so much as catching fish out of season, he would make them show him their hands and sniff them for the telltale aroma. He loved his children, but being soft wouldn't make them good, law-abiding citizens.

"Obey the laws of God, the laws of your father, and the laws of the country," he told them. His children were turning out fine, all of them.

Grace, his wife (or Queenie because she was the Queen Bee of the family), cleared the kitchen counter and table and placed the dishes in the sink, leaving him to brood. A hint of early fall was in the air, a barely perceptible chill, with the crispness of apples. Summer was leaving; fall would be upon them soon. The boy remained in jail and Johnny's death was yet to be avenged.

As the days passed the letters that flooded the county courthouse increased, as did the calls from reporters around the world. Could it be true that a twelve-year-old boy had slain a respected law enforcement officer, a boy who now faced execution or life in prison? Which were they more upset at, the fact that he had committed the murder or the fact that he was going to have to pay for it? Bezona knew the answer and it angered him.

Day by day more strangers appeared in the town looking for the "bare-foot-boy murderer," hoping to catch a glimpse of him. Bezona bristled at Junior's growing celebrity.

Patterson had needed to send a doctor in to treat the boy's trench mouth when his mouth started to bleed. As the doctor said, he probably had never been taught to brush his teeth. His mouth was full of open sores.

Bezona was anxious to have the charges filed and the trial over. But Halsey was determined to plod along at his own pace. When the pressure was on, Halsey would only smile, lean back in his chair, and fold his hands. He'd file the charges in the near future, he told Bezona. Reporters had asked him the same question. It made little difference because the boy wouldn't be arraigned until Judge Kuykendall, the circuit court judge, convened court in the next few months. Halsey then assigned Bezona the task of putting together a solid case. Halsey said he wanted all of the information possible so he could let the jurors know that Herbert Niccolls is a menace to society. If they failed to do that, they would be crucified in the press for prosecuting a mere child. And that concerned Halsey greatly. The case was going to be a difficult one. Halsey had no doubts about the boy's guilt, but he had never in his fifty years as a lawyer tried a case that was open to so much public scrutiny and he had never prosecuted someone so young.

Halsey decided that what he needed most was psychological information about the boy, so he sent him to Eastern State Hospital, where spinal fluid and blood had been drawn in an attempt to find any physical clues to back the state's belief in the boy's innate criminal nature. Junior was later returned to jail and Asotin County's health officer, Dr. McElvain, interviewed him for the prosecution's report.

No records suggest that any of the boy's three attorneys were with him during the invasive medical procedures or the interviews with the prosecutor or McElvain, who would later testify that the boy was a psychopath. Criminal defense, as it is known today, was still in its early stages for adults. Appropriate legal defense for juveniles was even less likely, especially in geographically remote areas.

In the town of Clarkston about ten miles north of Asotin, John C. Applewhite, attorney at law, had an office with a window facing the street. Like Halsey, he was not a young man. Though he had practiced law in California and Oregon before coming to Washington, he'd been in Asotin County so long that most people assumed he had been born and raised there. He served several terms as the county prosecutor and had his own practice, which gave his wife standing in the women's clubs, and their home was always open to guests. So when the boy's grandmother said they were unable to afford an attorney, Judge Kuykendall appointed Applewhite, along with Clarkston city attorney Edward Doyle, to represent young Niccolls.

Defending the boy—no matter how necessary under the law—was not a popular role to play in the small town of 200, where the public would just as soon lynch him as give him due process. For attorneys out of town, however, it was a different matter. A. G. Farley of Pomeroy had volunteered his services. Farley was a tall, strikingly handsome man—a contrast to Doyle's humble demeanor or Applewhite's warm fatherly image.

•

Applewhite pulled a pocket watch out of his coat. His wife had given him the watch when he passed the state bar exam in 1903. He had been forty-two years old at the time. He held it in his hand, watching the second hand tick across the ornate face of the watch, recalling all the high hopes that had come with the gift.

He had not been to Pomeroy to see the boy, though Farley had. Farley had conferred with Doyle about strategies for the defense. The most plausible plea was not guilty due to insanity or mental irresponsibility. The fact was that the state legislature had not anticipated being faced with a twelve-year-old killer. There were conflicting laws. One prohibited any child who had committed a violent offense from being sent to the state reform school and another prohibited juveniles from being sent to the penitentiary. The state law did not rule out executing someone young or sending them to a hospital for the insane.

The attorneys met in Applewhite's office on a hot August afternoon.

A fan hummed and rotated the breeze across the room and unsettled a stack of documents that Applewhite half-heartedly fought to control. There was only one choice, he acknowledged: plead not guilty due to mental irresponsibility. Who could testify to that? The prosecution had Peter Klaus, the eyewitness and a church-goer. They also had the county clerk, the county doctor, so many solid citizens who were ready to testify against the boy. Finding someone to address the boy's mental state was their only hope. When Junior spoke of the crime, he spoke without emotion, even when he was told he could hang. It was as if he was detached from reality, Farley noted. His experience working with underprivileged children told him that young Master Niccolls was indeed walking the thin line of sanity.

But who really knew the boy? A school teacher? A minister? His grandmother? Doyle fretted, full of nervous energy. Unlike the other two lawyers who studied on their own, and then took the bar exam without formal legal education, Doyle was a graduate of the University of Washington Law School and had a teaching degree from Lewiston Normal School. Born in Boulder, Colorado, he taught school in order to put himself through law school and had since become a success. In addition to his law practice, he was on the board of Farmer's Bank in Uniontown, where he also had a part-time practice. He was on almost every civic board imaginable, was active in the Knights of Columbus, had a wife and five children. What more could a man of fifty-one years want?

If only Herbert had been younger. Under the state statute, children younger than eight were considered incapable of committing a crime. From eight to eleven was gray area. But the law presumed a child of twelve knew right from wrong as well as any adult. Had Herbert been ten, like he said he was when he was first arrested, the case would have been much easier.

Doyle, as a father, felt especially bad about the case. Unlike his own children, raised in the solid structure of the Catholic Church and in the embrace of a loving family and community, Herbert had no one. His family had failed him. His church had failed him. His school had failed him, and his community had failed him. Although instructed not to sell merchandise to him, the People's Supply store had sold him the shells—not just once but twice. Colonel Fulton left the guns around, even though his own son and others played in the basement. The boy had no one to turn to even when he was hungry or in need of shelter. Doyle fully planned on raising the issue of the community's responsibility to him during his argument. It was a defense that Clarence Darrow had used in defending young killers Leopold and Loeb just a few years earlier.

Junior's attorneys knew that the only hope in the trial was to send him to the state mental hospital. Not only had he confessed, but his written confession had been published in the *Lewiston Morning Tribune*, which made it unlikely for them to find jurors who didn't know details of the crime or the defendant.

•

A white-haired man with a full mustache stood at the door of the cell on a late August morning. A deputy stood next to him. They called the boy's name—Herbert Franklin Niccolls Jr.

The boy stumbled off the bunk. The old man nodded to the deputy.

Deputy Gilliam led him into the office, read him the documents charging him with first-degree murder in connection with the death of Sheriff John Wormell, on August 5, 1931, in Asotin County.

Never had the deputy served a subpoena on one so young. The boy was little more than a baby. Halsey took no joy in the sad task of seeing him held accountable.

Gilliam told the boy that if he was to be convicted he would be sentenced either to life in prison or death by hanging at the state penitentiary at Walla Walla. Then he asked the boy if he had anything to say. He did not and signed as he was told to in his best grade-school penmanship.

Chapter 5

THE TROUSERS were long and the bow tie a sporty bright red. Deputy Gilliam tied it for him and helped him into a jacket. The boy beamed when Gilliam told him he looked quite the dandy in the new suit. He couldn't believe his luck. A wealthy Pomeroy wheat farmer, J. B. Tucker, had come in with a tailor the other day. They measured him and fashioned him a fine, gray-striped suit and a bow tie like none he'd ever worn before. He was speechless as he stood before the man, unable to even thank him. Now on the day of the trial, he was all dressed up, looking like a cherub-faced nine-year-old. His dark curling lashes and dimples made him look like he "stepped right out of one of Booth Tarkington's Penrod stories," a *Seattle Post-Intelligencer* reporter wrote in his account of the trial.

The boy hadn't been back to Asotin since his arraignment on September 3, when he had pleaded not guilty due to mental irresponsibility. While the courtroom had been packed at that time, hours before jury selection began, it overflowed with so many people that they spilled onto the lawn outside.

Enterprising members of the nearby First Methodist-Episcopal Church began frying chicken in the morning, preparing to sell lunches to the spectators when the court broke for recess at noon.

From the window in his chambers, Judge Elgin Kuykendall watched as the Asotin police car pulled up before the courthouse. Immediately, the crowd surrounded it until a deputy forced them back. Bezona, the newly appointed sheriff, emerged from the car, scowled at the crowd and then opened the rear door. Bright-eyed and smiling, the boy stepped out. Cameras clicked and voices called to him. Obligingly, he turned his head to each and beamed, until Bezona, holding him by the elbow, guided him through the crowd into the courthouse.

As he passed through the heavy doors into the room, spectators in the gallery buzzed and turned, craning their necks to get a better look. He smiled and waved to them and a ripple of laughter filled the room. But then came a shriek, and Herbert saw his grandmother flapping her way toward him, her arms outstretched. His smile quavered, and then he broke into tears.

She paused, clasped her hands to her bosom, gazed down upon him, and sobbed. Then his grandmother reminded him—and all who watched—that it was never too late to repent. Cameras clicked like crickets and Applewhite and Doyle drew the boy to the table at the front of the courtroom.

In his chambers, Judge Kuykendall read the trial briefs on *State v. Niccolls*. Never in the many years since he had passed the bar had he seen someone so young facing such serious charges. It was inconceivable. The laws of the state were not set up to handle such cases. The state reform school dealt with thieves—not murderers. The whole affair was troublesome.

During his years as a state senator, he and his colleagues never once considered that a murderer might be a child. Kuykendall couldn't help being angry. The case had even made the European press. The trial hadn't even begun and he'd received hundreds of letters from around the country calling him, the prosecutor and the deputies the most uncivilized names. "May every possible bad fortune descend upon you and all your family. May every evil over take you. May you suffer the eternal condemnation . . . of the damned," one anonymous scribe wrote. "Crackpot," Kuykendall muttered as he filed the letter away.

The boy was responsible for the predicament facing them all. The eyes of the world were trained on little Asotin. Herbert Niccolls had emerged as a symbol of the new generation of troubled, violent youth that brought with them a new era of social-minded, sentimental do-gooders who had no sense of justice.

As far as Kuykendall was concerned, the world was an open slate of opportunity. All one had to do was obey the law and work hard. Kuykendall was raised a doctor's son and grew up on the Yakama Indian Reservation where his father worked. He had been expected to go into medicine, too, but he bucked tradition. He became a teacher and the Pomeroy superintendent of schools. Then he took an interest in law and hired on as a clerk at Sam Cosgrove's office in Pomeroy. Sam taught him all he knew about law. Going to fancy law schools was unnecessary, if you studied and worked hard. Be respectful to your elders and you can get somewhere in this world, Sam had said, and he had. Sam was a most influential mentor who went on to be governor. He would have made a fine one, too, had he not become so ill that he cut his term short. Some said, as his own career climbed, that he had become a living tribute to Sam. Kuykendall was pleased when the town saw fit to erect a bronze statue of Sam right in front of the Garfield County Courthouse. He always paid silent respect to Sam when he passed by.

As the circuit court judge for three counties, Kuykendall was often overworked. He would be glad to dispose of the Niccolls matter and get on with the more routine matters he usually encountered—divorces and larceny. None prompted the passion this case did. It had gone on too long, since it was already October. On that morning he had awoken in his home in Pomeroy to find ice flowers scrawled across the windowpane. As he drove up the Alpowa Grade and then dipped into Snake River country and Asotin, the sun rose higher, washing the wheat fields the palest rose. In Asotin, he parked in front of the courthouse and glanced down the block at the general store. There were pumpkins in the window and a sheaf of cornstalks. His grandchildren would soon be getting their costumes ready for trick-or-treating. He almost felt silly when he thought of them.

The case would be over soon. He had appointed Ed Doyle to handle it with John Applewhite's help. Farley had asked to be appointed, too. Kuykendall suspected that Farley was merely interested in receiving the publicity that came with the job. Doyle was a sharp attorney who would do right by the boy and didn't need Farley's help. But at Farley's request, Kuykendall had appointed him anyway. It wouldn't be much longer and the Niccolls case would be history. Whatever the result, he welcomed an end to the ordeal.

•

Silver-haired and in a black robe, Kuykendall was an imposing figure as he took his place at the bench. Already the courtroom was warm with the press of bodies, and the odor of soil and sweat filled the room. Thirty-five prospective jurors had been called. It would take all day before the jury was impaneled. The room buzzed with the undercurrent of whispered conversations. Kuykendall rapped his gavel sharply and the room grew silent.

State v. Niccolls had begun. Was Mr. Niccolls present? The boy raised his hand, which caused the crowd to chuckle. Kuykendall rapped his gavel again.

Bearing placards with numbers, the men and three women on the panel of jurors sat in the benches at the front of the courtroom. Kuykendall nodded to them respectfully, thanked them for their attendance, and praised them for their citizenship.

The jury would decide whether the boy was guilty of first-degree murder, and if they voted to convict him, would decide whether he should be sentenced to death. If the jury did not specify what the punishment should be, the boy would be sentenced to life in prison, according to the laws of the state of Washington.

A veteran of Asotin County Superior Court, Halsey began the voir dire, questioning the jurors with ease about their private lives and convictions. For capital punishment or against? If they were against it, he would put a check mark by their names to eliminate them. Although he would not ask for the death penalty, the question, "Shall the death penalty be inflicted?" was on the jury's verdict form. It would be solely up to the jury to decide. He wanted nothing to stand in the way of justice being done.

When Herbert's attorneys began to interview the jurors, they discovered that many of the thirty-five called had read stories or had personal knowledge of the crime and most had already formed opinions on the subject. Others declared sentiments that would prevent them from seeking the death penalty. By the time the jury was reduced to the final twelve, the state had exhausted six of its peremptory challenges and the defense eight. The three women in the panel were dismissed, because Halsey believed women were too emotional to be able to render a guilty verdict. The final jury consisted of a lumber-mill executive, a barber, a teacher, four farmers, two laborers, a cherry grower, a real estate man, and a bus driver.

Throughout the proceedings the boy fidgeted in his seat, turned to the crowd and smiled. A curious thing had happened, Halsey noted. Unlike the angry mob of several months ago, many of the men and women in the courtroom had become sympathetic, having heard stories from the boy's attorneys and jailers of what a well-mannered young man he was and how bright he was. Instead of the dirty boy in tattered overalls, Junior in his smart new suit looked like the model child who could easily take his place in any schoolroom or Sunday school class. Halsey, too, had heard stories about how the boy loved to play checkers and could best any of the deputies. He also knew that the boy loved music and Boy Scout books and had spent hours in his cell reading them. Once the testimonies began, Halsey would destroy that image.

In the meantime, the boy squirmed, examined the sleeve of his coat, his buttons, and shoes, and grinned.

Then it was time for lunch.

State brand inspector, night cop, and self-described "cow-town clown," Hostetler had been called to join Deputy Sheriff Bob Campbell in keeping an eye on the defendant. They were seated around a desk in the sheriff's office during the lunch recess when there was a soft knock at the door. Campbell opened it and D. Harold McGrath stepped inside. McGrath spoke softly to the deputy. The deputy nodded.

McGrath, assigned by the International News service to cover the trial, asked if the boy would mind if he stayed with him. The boy rose to his feet, shook hands and said it would be fine. Then the boy asked for a deck of cards, wanting to show his captive audience some card tricks. Stunned by the boy's innocent candor, McGrath put his notebook away and simply observed, noting later in the story he would eventually file, how the boy beamed with pleasure when he surprised the men with his tricks. Then the boy took out a harmonica and began to play. The tune floated through the open window of the courtroom, out into the fall sunshine where the crowd had gathered on the lawn. The notes danced with the calling of birds and the occasional shush of a passing car.

"From this valley, they say you are leaving.
We will miss your bright eyes and sweet smile."

By three p.m. the jury was impaneled and the boy had returned to the courtroom. Kuykendall gave the jury the instructions: "Don't discuss the trial with anyone except other jurors, not even family members. Ignore any publicity about the case—and there had been plenty—and don't read the newspapers. Reach a verdict based solely upon the evidence set before you. Any questions?"

Of the witnesses who were subpoenaed, many gave their impressions of the boy's state of mind—even though Dr. Semple from Eastern State Hospital was the only one qualified to testify concerning Herbert's mental health. J. B. Tucker, a wealthy Pomeroy wheat rancher, had merely provided the suit. Edward Bucholz, the city clerk and member of the Chamber of Commerce and Methodist Church, was called, as were the boy's jailers in Pomeroy—Patterson, Campbell, and Gilliam.

Halsey opened the case with an eloquent address: "I am an old man, and this lad's life lies ahead of him. There are cases when I demand the Mosaic law of an eye for an eye, a life for a life, but I will not ask that in this case. The question is not whether the boy was of unsound mind, but whether, when the crime was committed, he knew right from wrong. He shot Mr. Wormell, and the pistol used, found with the hammer pulled back, indicates he was ready to shoot again."

Then Halsey detailed how the boy had stolen all his life, had stolen the gun and practiced shooting, premeditated breaking into the store and having to kill if necessary.

"We of society are equally guilty with this child in the death of Wormell," Doyle said in his opening. "We now have two alternatives for we do not want to kill this boy. Our alternatives are penitentiary or institution. The boy is deficient now and always has been deficient mentally. He did not commit this crime from foresight. He is intelligent but he had no plans for robbery or murder. He has no inhibitions."

Farley then detailed the boy's sordid early life with an insane father and a mother so poor there wasn't enough food or clothing for her seven children. "A child is not responsible for his parents," Farley said. "Of course, the boy was lying now and then. There was a vacant place in [Herbert's] life and he filled it with imagination."

Doyle added, "I'm not trying to win this case. I'm only trying to do the best I can for society."

Halsey called his first witness, Charlie Carlisle, who, among other things, operated the telephone exchange. Carlisle explained how he heard a noise in the store and called the sheriff. And then Bezona took the stand, relating how he went to the store with the sheriff, Carlisle, and Peter Klaus. He related, too, how Johnny insisted on being the one to go in first. He noted how he heard the shot but couldn't see where it had come from.

"Why was that?" Halsey asked.

"Smokeless cartridges," Bezona said.

Then he related that when he spotted the boy he told him, "Come on out or I'll kill you!" And then he told the court how the boy had confessed.

Halsey asked about the condition of the gun when it was found. Four chambers were loaded, one discharged, and the hammer was resting on a loaded cartridge. It showed, Bezona added, that after the boy had shot the sheriff, he re-cocked the weapon and was ready to fire again, before he threw it over the desk.

Halsey asked Bezona what the boy had told him about the gun. The newspapers carried Bezona's answer: "He said he had only got one shot in because the gun jammed. I asked him if he had planned to shoot me and he said he didn't see me but he probably would have had he had the chance."

•

As the boy's attorneys bickered over points of law and court procedure, Junior was more concerned about seeing Murphy Watkins and hoped he would have one more chance. He hadn't seen Murphy and his sisters since the day of the shooting. He never really planned to run away. With every beating his grandmother gave him, he had vowed to do better. But when he saw the opportunity for escape, a world of possibilities opened to him.

Several days before the murder, he had gone to the general store just after Peter Klaus had gone for dinner and left his fourteen-year-old son in charge. Junior told the youth that his grandmother had sent him to buy some .32 caliber smokeless shells for his father's revolver. He charged them to his grandmother's account. That afternoon, he went out on the river with Murphy and, with the gun stolen from Colonel Fulton's trunk, shot at jacksnipes. The following day he returned to the store again while the youth was working and asked for more. The youth said that there were no more, so Junior persuaded him to take $1.50 out of the till and go to another store to buy some and give them to him. When he returned home, Junior asked his grandmother to read the Bible to him, as was their custom. She read six chapters from the Book of Job and then she and the boy knelt in prayer. He then asked her to continue reading. She said she would if he would first go outside and turn off the water that was irrigating a few rows of corn.

He had stepped from the darkened house that afternoon and all of summer bloomed before him. The rows of corn danced, the poplars shook their cascade of leaves, and children down the road laughed. He drifted toward them. He knew he was not supposed to leave the yard, as he had been in trouble for stealing. But the darkness of the house propelled him into the light and he began to run. He ran into town and down the streets, coming to Murphy's house where he whistled sharply. Murphy appeared at the door and motioned him into the yard.

The Watkins family was poor. The seven children in their ragtag clothes hung out of the windows and doors and had worn what little lawn there was down to bald patches around the small white house near the river. Della was always somewhere in the middle of them, cooking beans on the stove, dabbing antiseptic on a scraped knee, or kissing a forehead. Junior had never seen a house so welcoming.

"Hey, Junior. Wanna shoot some marbles?"

Murphy walked to the edge of the yard. Murphy was deadly at marbles and had huge sugar sacks full of the aggies he had won off other boys. Junior had no marbles of his own but Murphy always spotted him a few dozen. Murphy knew he'd always win them back. No one ever beat Murphy Watkins at marbles.

Dinnertime came and Junior crowded around the table with the rest of the brood. Della smiled as she spooned red beans and fried potatoes onto his plate. Murphy's grandfather entered the room just then and muttered that there were already so many mouths to feed, they didn't need one more. Della paid no attention.

Murphy asked his grandfather if Junior could stay the night. With seven children, some sleeping out in the backyard because there wasn't space in the house, they had no room for an eighth. Junior must leave and right now, Robinson had said.

"But he can't go home," Jean pleaded. She and Murphy knew how often the boy was beaten. They had witnessed it themselves. If he was late from school, the old woman greeted him with a club that she'd swing against his backside and his legs until he collapsed, crying. When she was really angry, she'd refuse to let him eat. Jean, Murphy, and their sister Bonnie frequently would go to the house and engage Mrs. Addington in conversation ("Yes, Mrs. Addington, we know Jesus died for our sins.") while Junior crept in the back door to take fruit from the pantry. It would be all he had to eat all day.

Robinson grumbled that a good beating might be what the boy needs.

The boy wandered along the creek to the bridge and ducked beneath it, where he found a hole in the bank. He curled up in it and slept for a time but when he awoke, the lavender dusk of the fading daylight was settling in and with it a chilly breeze.

He walked back to Murphy's and they played hide-and-go-seek. He was standing in the kitchen when the old man discovered he had returned and ordered him out again. But before he could leave, a heavy fist slammed against the door and everyone jumped. Robinson opened the screen door, and Junior heard the sheriff say he was looking for him, that his grandmother said they should pick him up and put him in jail.

Junior leaped from the table, grabbed the gun off the icebox, and fled out the back door, letting the screen door slam behind him. He ran through the mulberry bushes toward the river. His night as a fugitive had begun.

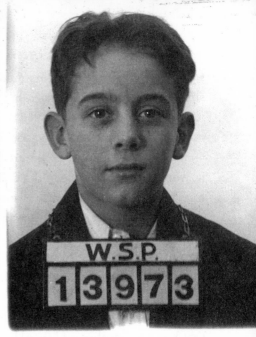

Fig. 1 Herbert Niccolls Jr., age twelve, was photographed in the typical prison mug shot and given his prison number at the Washington State Penitentiary. Courtesy of the Washington State Archives.

HERBERT NICCOLS--MURDERER OF SHERIFF JOHN WORMELL
AT ASOTIN WASHINGTON. AUGUST 7 th 1931 /93/

Fig. 2 J. F. Anderson, a reporter for the nearby *Lewiston Morning Tribune*, took Herbert Niccolls outside the courthouse for a photograph, which would appear in newspapers from coast to coast and in Canada. Courtesy of the Asotin County Museum.

Fig. 3 Sheriff John Wormell had not only served multiple terms as the lead law enforcement officer of Asotin County but had been a state legislator and one of the region's pioneers. Courtesy of the Asotin County Museum.

Fig. 4 The entire cast of players in the trial were requested to pose for a photograph outside the courthouse, adding a surreal element to the trial. From front left: Deputy Sheriff Wayne Bezona, Herbert Niccolls Jr., Mary Addington, Asotin County Clerk L. A. Closuit, and Deputy County Clerk J. Swain. Back, from left: defense attorney John Applewhite, prosecutor Elmer Halsey, defense attorneys Ed Doyle and A. G. Farley, and Judge Kuykendall. Courtesy of the Asotin County Museum.

Fig. 5 Governor Roland Hartley clashed with those who wanted to parole Herbert Niccolls to Boys Town. Courtesy of the Washington State Archives.

Fig. 6 Father E. J. Flanagan took his campaign to free Herbert Niccolls to the radio in frequent broadcasts. Courtesy of Boys Town.

Fig. 7 Mrs. Armene Lamson was greeted with roses by a Boys Town resident when she arrived at the Omaha, Nebraska, train station on her campaign to bring Herbert Niccolls to Boys Town. Courtesy of Boys Town.

Fig. 8 While Herbert Niccolls was in prison, there were frequent executions, including the execution of seventeen-year-old Walter DuBuc, who had a fifth-grade education. Courtesy of the Washington State Archives.

Fig. 9 As an adult, Herbert Niccolls lived in a Hollywood apartment filled with books. Courtesy of Jonathan Niccolls.

Fig. 10 James Ashe was a literary agent who, while serving time for bilking a society matron out of money she paid him to get her book published, became Herbert Niccolls's mentor. Courtesy of the Washington State Archives.

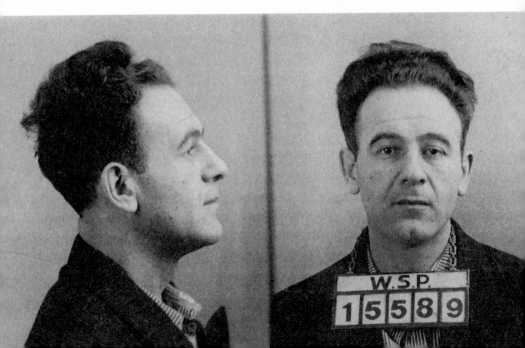

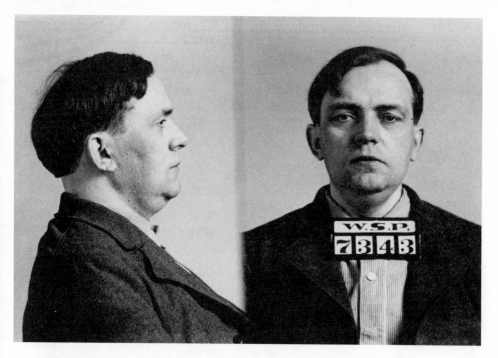

Fig. 11 Inside the penitentiary, Peter Miller was known for starting the prison library and a fund to help inmates when they got out. Courtesy of the Washington State Archives.

Chapter 6

THE SECOND DAY of the trial came, and the boy once again wore his sporty new suit. This time Hostetler tied Herbert's bow tie. Hostetler had spent the night with him inside the small jail. Bezona had thought that not only might the boy need the added security but he might also be afraid of being alone in the jail at night. Hostetler said he'd make sure that the boy got dinner and had a walk for a little exercise.

•

Dressed in his worn overalls, Junior walked down a country road along the river at a brisk pace. Suddenly, he shouted that he was challenging Hostetler to a foot race. He darted down the road, leaving eddies of dust as each bare foot struck the soft dirt.

Hostetler was at first startled but then set out after him, keeping up with an easy stride. The boy carefully gauged the deputy's pace and then stopped with a sigh. Hostetler knew it wouldn't do to have the boy get away from him. And while he was a man in fine condition, he would have lost the race if it had gone on much longer.

That night he listened to the boy talk of airplanes and automobiles, cowboys and catching bees, and how he'd very much like to see a circus. The boy then noted that if one were stout enough, he could break out of jail just by undoing those hinges. Beside him in his bunk, unbeknownst to Hostetler at the time, was a rock wrapped in a piece of cloth that the boy had torn from a sheet. If he had had the chance he might have been able to strike his jailer and run to freedom, an opportunity that apparently did not arise. The boy's young voice faded as he drifted in and out of sleep. Outside the crickets sang as he spoke of his mother, an image blue with tears.

Hostetler lay on the bunk in the small jail. He had children of his own and couldn't imagine giving them away because he could no longer afford to feed them. But then again, he supposed it was different for a woman who was alone with no income, no man to protect her. What was she to do? So many children. So many mouths to feed. Then he too drifted to sleep as all around the small barren jail the night sounds unfolded.

•

The boy again burst into smiles when he saw the crowd. He had never felt so important. Not only were Hostetler and Campbell at his side, but so was McGrath, the reporter. They escorted him into the courthouse where he met his attorneys. A woman in the crowd leaned over the rail and handed him a bag of gingersnaps. The boy's eyes brightened with delight.

The prosecution called the Klaus boy to the stand, and he explained how he had sold smokeless cartridges to the boy. Then Halsey called Colonel Fulton who identified the gun used in the murder as the one the boy had stolen from his basement.

"He's a murdering little thief. He should be hanged," Fulton shouted.

After about an hour, Herbert was pale and tugged on Doyle's shirtsleeve. When Kuykendall called a recess, Herbert ran into the lavatory and vomited. It seemed his entire insides would come out, all the blackness that colored his soul and made him do the things he did was pouring forth. His grandmother often told him that sin makes your heart black, so he figured his heart and everything else inside must be the color of coal. Then about thirty minutes later, he left the courtroom to vomit again.

"Too many pancakes," the court clerk told the gathering.

When he returned to the courtroom, Hostetler asked if he was feeling better. He said he was and glanced around the courtroom again, smiling whenever he caught someone's eye.

Bill Robinson testified next about the events that occurred at his home on the evening of the murder, and how the boy had lied and got him into trouble.

"He has no conscience," Robinson said. "None whatsoever."

Sheriff Patterson said that the boy was pleasant and had the intellect of a sixteen-year-old.

"Would you say he was sane?" Halsey asked.

"Absolutely," the sheriff said.

J. B. Tucker, who had bought the suit for the boy, said Herbert Niccolls was mentally deficient and had a below-average mental capacity.

The prosecution concluded with testimony from Eastern State Hospital's first psychiatrist and superintendent, Dr. John M. Semple, who came out of retirement to testify. Semple was a product of the Progressive Era, but unlike some of the more liberal-minded progressives who looked to the environmental causes behind a crime, Semple was a conservative who believed that eugenics—or one's heredity—determined one's failure or success. For Semple, who read the reports concerning the Niccolls family, the answer was easy.

"He's a congenital psychopath with bad heredity," Semple said. "He may become a menace to society."

At about noon, the boy was whiter than ever and returned to the courtroom lavatory to vomit again. Doyle suggested a continuance, and Kuykendall asked how ill he was. Would it serve justice better if the proceedings were continued the next day?

Halsey objected, reaching under the table where the boy had been seated and pulling out an empty bag of gingersnaps. He turned the bag upside down.

"No wonder he's sick," Halsey said. "He ate them all."

The crowd began to laugh. Kuykendall rapped his gavel and announced a recess until one p.m. Locked in the sheriff's office for the hour, the boy took out his harmonica and began to play.

When the court reconvened the defense attorneys knew that they had to hone their efforts to make the jury believe Herbert Junior was mentally incompetent. The wild card in the defense was Mrs. Mary Addington, the boy's grandmother. During pretrial interviews she had told them about the boy's home life and the boy's father, but how credible would she be with her periodic wanderings into religious dogma? Would she be dismissed as a religious zealot who could see sin in a soapbox and insanity whenever it was convenient? They would have to take their chances.

Formidable in a black dress, Mrs. Addington peered over the lenses of her rimless glasses. She raised her right hand, swore she would tell the truth, and then was seated.

Could she describe young Herbert's home life before he came to live with her?

Junior and his eight brothers and sisters lived next door to his grandmother's ranch in Star, Idaho. His mother, Hazel Niccolls, was neglectful, and most of the time the children were unwashed and unfed. When they did have food, their mother would throw the plate on the bed or the floor and the children would eat like animals. The children always went without shoes, sometimes tying burlap bags around their feet in the wintertime when they had to walk to school. Hazel never displayed any maternal warmth toward any of her children. She deserted them several times and when she was home, she let them run wild. From one Sunday to another they did not go to church and spent most of their days outdoors, even when the weather was very cold.

"Who knows how they kept from freezing to death? And food—whenever they could they'd hide bread and things in the turkey house for future use," she said.

She described Bert Niccolls as a Christian, called by God to preach to sinners but saddled with a nagging wife who, when he came back from a mission trip to California, greeted him most uncivilly. The arguing and lack of Christian love in the house eventually forced him to move back to his mother's home, taking his twin daughters with him, she said.

But one day when fury overtook him, he took his rifle and went to the house where Hazel and the boys lived, intending to kill her, but he shot her friend Mrs. Frazier instead. And now he was living at Orofino State Hospital for the Insane. Mrs. Addington delivered her story calmly, slinging blame, whenever possible, on her daughter-in-law, who was too afraid of her to come to the trial.

After Mrs. Frazier was murdered, Hazel abandoned her four oldest children, Mrs. Addington said. One boy was put up for adoption, the oldest two went to work for a rancher in Ketchum, and Junior was sent to a foster home in Shoshone, Idaho.

Mrs. Addington detailed how Junior rapidly got into trouble, stealing his teacher's pocketbook. He stole money and then a car. He was sent to the state reformatory and after fifteen months was paroled to his grandmother. She told the jurors that she had tried to bring him up to be a good Christian.

On the day of the murder, Junior had requested that she read chapters from the Book of Job, where Hebrew spies entered the city with "40,000 prepared for war" and marched around Jericho, blowing trumpets and attacking until they "utterly destroyed everything in the city, both man and woman, young and old . . . with the edge of a sword." Then they looted and burned the town. "It was the will of God," she said."

Doyle asked if she thought Herbert Junior—who has killed, like his father killed—was insane as well. "No," she said. "He's possessed by a demon."

Junior's aunt, Mary White, then took the stand. "He doesn't know right from wrong," she said.

"But is he insane?"

"I don't rightly know."

Then Mrs. Hilda Cooper, the boy's sixth-grade teacher, stepped forward. She smiled at the boy as she passed him and whispered how handsome he looked. She told the jury that he was very bright, working at or above his grade level. Then she added that she found him to be so trustworthy she let him play with her own young children. "He has the nicest manners," she added.

Doyle called Dr. W. J. Sherfey, the Garfield County health officer, to the stand.

"Is Herbert Niccolls of sound mind?"

"The boy has no conscience, shows no remorse and sees no harm in committing crimes," Sherfey said. This lack of emotion or remorse indicates insanity, Sherfey asserted.

•

When the court broke for recess, the attorneys conferred. It was not going well. There was only one thing left to do—put the boy on the stand and hope that his candid recitation of facts, or perhaps his childish charm, might sway the jury.

Junior walked smartly to the stand and smiled at the crowd, the jurors, and the reporters. When the judge asked, he spelled his name for the record.

"H-e-r-b-e-r-t F-r-a-n-k-l-i-n N-i-c-c-o-l-l-s, J-u-n-i-o-r."

Doyle noted that Junior was a good speller.

"I'm better at math. I think math is just dandy," he said.

The crowd began to laugh, and Kuykendall rapped the gavel and scowled. Doyle asked what other things he liked to do.

"I like books and magazines about Boy Scouts," he said. "They're good for boys to read."

Doyle asked him to explain what had happened the night the sheriff was shot. Without emotion, the boy recited the events that led to Wormell's death.

"I saw some tobacco in the window and wanted it. So I broke the pane and went in," he said. "I was filling a sack with tobacco and gum when I heard the door rattle. . . . I did not want to shoot him."

Then the attorney asked him about his home life. The boy explained how his parents fought and about the day he came home to find Mrs. Frazier dead, lying like a broken toy on the hard earth. And then he couldn't think of anything else to say.

In cross-examination, Halsey asked him if he was in trouble much at his grandmother's house. The boy answered affirmatively and said that he was often spanked. When Halsey asked why, he replied, "For holding a duck under water." The crowd again laughed and the reporters added more quotes to the stories they would file that afternoon.

Judge Kuykendall recessed the court until the following morning when the attorneys would give their closing remarks. As the defense attorneys were packing up their briefs, a reporter asked them, if the boy did not make the insanity plea, would he be found guilty? He would be convicted, the boy's attorneys all agreed. That was why they had stipulated the facts in the trial and were merely hoping to persuade the jury that he was guilty due to mental irresponsibility. As far as the attorneys were concerned, anything they could do for the boy amounted to little more than show.

•

Back in the jail, Junior hung up his suit and set his new shoes neatly against the wall. He slipped beneath the cover of his bunk and drifted as far away as the stars, until the nightmares came. He was haunted by them—he'd wake up hearing the sound of a gun and think he saw the sheriff falling, or sometimes he saw Mrs. Frazier. He wanted the dreams to go away.

From his bunk he could see the house across the street, the golden squares of light and the family inside. Finally the lights went out.

The dark brought memories. He and Francis were punching each other. Suddenly, everyone was yelling. Papa was hitting Mama, smacking her again and again until her face was bloody. The children had all stood frozen as his fists split flesh, and they wondered if he would ever stop. He had not been sad to see his father leave.

He was six years old when his father went to a revival meeting in Boise and became convinced that he was destined to be a great evangelist. The next morning, Bert Niccolls packed up and left for a Bible college in Sacramento, California, leaving his wife and children without any money or means of support. While he was in California, he contracted syphilis. It went to his brain and on June 14, 1924, he was committed to the asylum for the insane at Imola, California. In November, Mary Addington convinced the authorities there to release him into her care. She then returned him to his family.

They walked silently around him after he came home, avoiding him, because risking his attention was risking a beating. Then something strange happened. Since their father had given up smoking, when Wesley found a cigarette butt in the barn, he picked it up and was on his way to tell Mama. Then he heard the calf bawling. He rounded the corner to see the fifteen-month-old heifer tied in the stall, with his father, his pants dropped to his knees, mounting her.

Hazel Niccolls pleaded with her children, "You must not tell anyone. Ever."

Later on, as Hazel Niccolls was close to delivering her ninth baby, she walked into the barn and caught him with the same heifer. The children could hear her yelling that she would never live with him again. Then she stormed inside where her mother-in-law, Mary Addington, was visiting. Through her sobs, she told her everything she had seen.

"Forget about it," Mrs. Addington said. "And tell no one."

But Hazel packed her bag that night and went to the Salvation Army Home. Four days later she delivered her last child, Paul. When she returned home, Bert had moved in with his mother, taking the twin girls with him. Her mother-in-law had the heifer in question slaughtered. Mrs. Addington told her daughter-in-law that she had consulted a veterinarian who claimed that her statements about the heifer were false.

One day the twins ran to their mother's home to warn her that their grandmother had let Bert have a gun, that he said he was coming to kill her.

When Bert Niccolls took the gun that day on his slow walk through town, he first stopped to threaten the veterinarian who refused to vouch for the heifer's virginity. Then he proceeded to his wife's home, occasionally firing shots at random.

Hazel Niccolls and Mrs. Frazier, her sister-in-law who lived nearby, were sitting in the living room sewing baby clothes for the new infant, when Mrs. Frazier looked out the window and saw Bert coming up the walk, carrying a pistol. The women fled out the door. He caught up with Mrs. Frazier first.

She had always bothered him. She came to the house to help but as far as he was concerned she simply interfered with his authority.

"Prepare to meet your Jesus!" he shouted.

He lifted the rifle to his shoulder. Her hands were clasped before her as she pleaded for their lives. Strands of her usually tidy hair sprung loose. He saw her mouth moving and heard nothing. As she turned to run after Hazel, he pulled the trigger.

The shot reverberated across the wheat fields where a farmer was plowing. He looked up to see a woman, infant in arms, running toward him and behind her a man with a gun. He shouted to his farm hands, and they ran toward him.

It took six of them to take Bert down and hog-tie him until the sheriff could arrive. After the struggle was over and Bert lay facedown in the prairie soil, the farmer stood with his heart pounding. Instead of the whir of grasshoppers and the soft plodding of the horse's hooves and creek of leather as the mare pulled the plow, all around him was silence.

Inside the house the children were softly sobbing as Mrs. Frazier's body lay in the front yard of the small, white house with the peeling paint.

The murder was too much for Hazel. For the previous few years, she had worked two or three jobs, taking in laundry and working as a cook and a housekeeper. But still she could barely keep her children fed. The large Quaker community in town had been very helpful and kind. But it had hurt her pride to ask them for help.

Now there were nine children and no hope that there would ever be an income again. Not that Bert had ever been much good at holding a steady job, but he did hunt and fish, which meant food on the table. But now the shame, humiliation, and sorrow were too much. Bert had always disciplined the boys, but they still were a wild lot. They'd be better off in places where they might have a man around. That way at least they wouldn't starve.

In June 1927, a social worker from the Children's Home-Finding and

Aid Society came to the house. Hazel's four oldest boys had their meager possessions packed and watched solemnly as the social worker gingerly picked her way through the broken toys and up the sagging steps.

It would be a new life, full of new opportunities, the woman said. They followed her out to the car. Eldon was thirteen; Wesley, eleven; Junior, just days away from turning eight; and James Francis, only five. Their little sisters cried as they left the house, their tears creating dirty streaks on their small thin faces.

As the car pulled away from the house on that warm afternoon, Junior looked back. His mother stood in the doorway. It would be the last time he'd see her for many years. As the car rounded the corner, the social worker told them that they were just going to love Boise.

Chapter 7

CLOSING ARGUMENTS in the trial heightened the public frenzy. Gone would be the tedious bickering between attorneys over legal points, and each side would simply sum up the testimony. Then the case would be in the hands of the jury. Would John Wormell's death be avenged? Would a twelve-year-old be sentenced to life in prison? Sentenced to death? Put in a hospital for the mentally ill?

Reporters from all the major wire services and newspapers took rooms at the Asotin Hotel and stood in line before the phone booth to call in stories to editors across the country. Their articles ran on both the East and West coasts, in the Great Lakes states, in New York and New England. The case became a symbol for the nation's growing concern and intolerance for juvenile delinquency, which had seemed to run rampant alongside every other kind of lawlessness since Prohibition went into effect in 1920.

The case even bumped Los Angeles "trunk slayer" Winnie Ruth Judd off the front pages. She had been a frequent feature after she murdered two friends, hid their body parts in a steamer trunk, and shipped the trunk from Phoenix, Arizona, to Los Angeles. She had been caught when she tried to claim the malodorous trunk at the railroad depot. The medical experts quoted in the press explained that her wide-set eyes were clues to her insanity. How could a woman of such a naturally delicate constitution carry off such a heinous deed? How could a cherub-faced twelve-year-old kill a respected officer of the law? The social order of the nation was spinning. What could one count on? Not government. Not the banks. From the pulpit, preachers spoke of Armageddon.

In the meantime, near the Asotin Superior Court, the Methodists had sold so many chicken dinners that they had exhausted the town's supply of chicken and had to bring them in from Lewiston.

•

Junior turned his usual beam on the crowd when he took his seat. Never had so many people paid so much attention to him. He especially loved the reporters who took his picture and followed him and his attorneys around, scribbling down anything they had to say. Then they wrote their stories, and people all over the country read about him. He was famous. Almost like Pretty Boy Floyd. But his favorite among the reporters was Harold McGrath, because he was also a Scout master and talked to him about the Boy Scouts.

While the Progressive Movement changed the image of children from being miniature adults to those needing special protection, the concept escaped prosecutor Halsey. He detailed every past offense, called the boy a cold-blooded murderer, and hammered down on facts surrounding the boy's heredity: Bert Niccolls and Junior's paternal great-grandmother were both in insane asylums. Junior simply has "bad heredity," Halsey said. As he pontificated, occasionally twirling his thick mustache when he paused to think, the boy fell asleep and remained so throughout the morning.

Halsey told the jury about how Junior went from the Children's Home to live with a fine family in Shoshone, Idaho. He told them about the violin and cornet lessons they gave him and how they doted on him. How did he repay the family? He stole from them—jewelry and money—

and he habitually lied. Finally, these kind people returned him to the Children's Home. Then he stole a car, broke into a safe, and even stole a tricycle.

Junior was to be sent to the Industrial School at St. Anthony, Idaho, but his grandmother intervened. Then he was placed in her care and taken to Orofino.

"Did Herbert reform under the loving care of his grandmother?" Halsey asked.

He did not. He burglarized the post office. He stole another automobile. He stole from homes and stores. His grandmother attempted to give him a solid religious education but he stole from the collection plate and set fire to the church. He was again sent to the reform school. When he was paroled, he came to Asotin. During his few months in town, he burglarized the Asotin County Cooperative Store and stole a bicycle and then a gun.

Halsey paused for dramatic effect. "He shot Mr. Wormell, and the pistol used was found with the hammer back, indicating he was ready to shoot again." Then Halsey asked the jury to do the right thing, in honor of the memory of John Wormell.

In his closing, Doyle played to the jury's sympathy when he said, "With an insane father, with a mother fear-stricken because of poverty, without food enough to satisfy a growing boy's appetite, Herbert's twelve years of experience gave him a distorted view of life."

By noon, the arguments were over. After a break for lunch, Kuykendall reconvened the court at 1:35 p.m. and turned the case over to the jury.

Hostetler and Campbell led Junior from the courtroom downstairs to the sheriff's office where he would remain until the verdict came in. Through the window he could see boys playing kick-the-can, and he wanted to run after them. He watched as they rounded the corner, the can clattering on the pavement.

The door to the office closed with a click and Campbell, Hostetler, and McGrath gathered around the desk. Someone broke out a deck of cards.

Campbell, who ran a dance band in his off-duty hours, suggested that the boy play a tune. "Wayne told me not to. It might disturb them," he said, pointing to the ceiling where a floor above the jury was deliberating.

Campbell asked if the boy was hungry. When he vigorously nodded, the deputy suggested that he, McGrath, and Hostetler take the boy to lunch. It might be the last time the lad would eat anything but prison food. Damn shame. Seems like a nice kid, too.

At an Asotin cafe, they gathered in a booth and let the boy order whatever he wanted. He ordered a hamburger and apple pie a la mode. The pie was fragrant with cinnamon, and the ice cream melted into pools on the plate. The boy ate with vigor.

"Better have some of this, Bob, for dessert," Junior told the deputy. A sympathetic woman seated nearby recognized the boy from photographs in the newspaper and gave him fifty cents.

"Thank you," he replied. "I have twenty-five cents here. That makes seventy-five. Maybe when I get to Walla Walla I can go down to Montgomery Ward's and get me a cheap watch." The men telegraphed silent messages to each other over the boy's head.

•

Meanwhile at Applewhite's office down the street, the attorneys were reviewing the case. It was a tough one. Halsey had so much to work with. After all, the boy had a record. He had stolen everything from candy to cars. Halsey even mentioned the time he stole a tricycle. Doyle had brought up the community's contribution to the crime. Would that argument sway the jury to leniency? Doyle hoped so. Maybe they shouldn't have let the boy take the stand. He was bright, charming, childishly naive, and well-mannered, answering questions with "yes, sir" or "no, sir." He spoke with chilling candor about the murder—and Doyle hammered on that fact during his closing, but had the boy come across as mentally irresponsible or insane? They feared not.

In the late afternoon, a deputy strolled into the office to tell the attorneys that the jury was in. They had deliberated for three hours and three minutes. A short deliberation time was never good for the defense. It nearly always meant the worst.

As usual, Junior appeared more interested in the group of reporters clustered around him, than the findings of the jury of his peers. The courtroom hummed with speculation until Kuykendall rapped his gavel and the jurors filed in. Kuykendall asked the boy to stand. "Do you have anything you wish to say?"

"Nothing," he said.

Had the jury reached a verdict? Williams, the foreman, answered that they had and handed Kuykendall a paper. The jury found the defendant, Herbert Franklin Niccolls Jr., guilty of first-degree murder. The crowd buzzed. What would happen to the boy who had played in the courtroom for most of the trial? Would he be sent to prison for life or hanged by his tiny neck? The answer would come the following day.

Before that happened, however, a photographer asked them all for a group photo. Applewhite stood next to Halsey, who was next to Doyle, who was next to Farley, who was next to Kuykendall. In the front row, Bezona was on the far left, the court clerk and his deputy were on the right, and Mary Addington was in the center with a smiling Herbert Niccolls, looking like a tiny actor in his bow tie and suit. The assembled players in the drama stood before the courthouse, smiling slightly as if for nothing more than the curtain call for a community play.

Chapter 8

WHAT HERBERT NICCOLLS JR. had that most other juvenile offenders of any era did not was a powerful advocate with a national platform, who unequivocally believed in the boy's potential for good despite the crime he'd committed. Although Father E. J. Flanagan never met Niccolls, he was convinced that "there is no such thing as a bad boy," and that included young murderers.

Flanagan was at Mercy Hospital in Denver, October 29, 1931, when he read the newspaper account about Niccolls being accused of murder and facing life in prison. He considered the notion barbaric. Although he had been urged to rest, he could not be idle any longer.

Not only did the boys at his farm need him, so did Herbert Niccolls. Flanagan summoned a nurse to take a telegram.

To Mr. J. C. Applewhite and Mr. E. J. Doyle: Have read convicting of 12-year-old murderer and his probable commitment to penitentiary for life. Judging from background, I feel this boy has never had a chance.

Would you ask the court that this boy be given such a chance now? I will take him to my home and be responsible for him.

Have cared for three thousand neglected and homeless boys during past fourteen years. My home is at Omaha, Nebraska, known as Father Flanagan's Boys Home. Answer me here, Mercy Hospital.

Flanagan had read all about the boy's life, from the thefts to the murder. For days it had been on the front page of the *Denver Post*, but only today he had read with shock of the boy's conviction. Now, he would have to pray and wait.

•

It was nearly over and Bezona, for one, was very glad. Maybe then the town could get back to normal. Not that it would ever be the same without Johnny. Annie and the other Wormells had not attended the trial or spoken on the issue. And as for the crowd gathered in the courthouse, he regarded them as curiosity seekers. Anyone who knew Johnny felt no sympathy for the boy. John Wormell had been a wise and good leader, beloved by many.

As the boy entered the courthouse, Hostetler pushed his way through the crowd, carrying a gray kitten. The boy cried out in delight, and Hostetler set the kitten on the floor. When the boy called to it, it promptly leaped onto his shoulder. The boy nuzzled it and stroked it, and the kitten curled around his neck. Who would take care of it when he was gone?

"Stand up, Herbert," Judge Kuykendall said, and the boy slowly rose. "Do you have anything to say for yourself?"

"No, sir," he said.

The judge then read the sentence: life in prison. The jury had swiftly made the decision, calling only once for a ballot.

It really mattered little to the boy. He was, as always, detached from the reality of his future. McGrath and the NEA Service reporter Sherman Mitchell were among the reporters in the crowd shouting questions.

"He's a boy who wanted much but had little," a court attaché told Mitchell. "From infancy he was under-nourished. He craves food and tobacco. He doesn't hesitate to steal if he can't get something by honest means. He lies when it's convenient. His case is typical of a shattered home, diseased mind, and poverty."

"Junior!" a reporter called. "What do you think of the sentence?"

"I'm glad they didn't send me to an insane asylum, for even smart men go nuts in a madhouse," he told the reporter.

Then through the open door of the court, he saw Murphy and Jean and he ran outside and hugged them.

"We wanted to say good-bye," Murphy said. Junior apologized for getting Murphy's grandfather in trouble. Murphy muttered his reply and handed him a present: his best aggie shooter. It was blue like a souvenir from picnic-day skies. During the 105-mile journey to the prison in the city of Walla Walla, the boy kept it in his pocket—a fragment of his childhood.

•

In his hospital bed, Flanagan watched the clock. On the West Coast it would be one hour earlier but surely by now the telegraph had been received. He heard footsteps and then his nurse stepped into the room, a telegram in her hand. Her face was solemn as she handed it to him.

It was too late, the attorneys wrote. His offer had been received one hour after the boy had been sentenced. He was already on his way to prison. Again the nurse sat at his side with her steno book and pen. Flanagan would write to the governor.

He was about to begin the bitterest campaign of his life.

•

"Barefoot-boy murderer gets life," the news vendors called from the street corners in the largest cities across the country. Within an hour after the verdict, the Associated Press wire had transmitted the news from coast to coast.

A *Seattle Post-Intelligencer* reporter wandered past the office of Kenneth Mackintosh, a former state supreme court justice recently appointed by President Herbert Hoover to the National Commission on Law Observance and Enforcement and a nominee for the Ninth Circuit Court of Appeals.

"What does the Honorable Judge Mackintosh think about sentencing a child to life in prison?" the reporter asked.

"The boy had previously shown a criminal tendency and should have been removed from contact with society before he committed this murder," Mackintosh said. "He undoubtedly always will be a criminal—a constant menace to society. It is reasonable to expect that at some future time he will again be at liberty. . . . Life under our present system means only a few years in the penitentiary. He should have been hanged."

Mackintosh was a member of Herbert Hoover's Wickersham Crime Commission, the group of lawyers and jurists who were putting together the first comprehensive national study of crime, enumerating its causes and the importance of probation and parole in U.S. history. Only three months earlier, the commission had found that juveniles in trouble had the right to be dealt with as wards of society, not as its outcasts. Mackintosh was also up for presidential appointment for a vacancy on the U.S. Ninth District Court. The boy's sentence was shocking but Mackintosh's comments took the case to another level. Newspapers from the largest to the smallest, and even to those that had not yet joined the fray, wrote editorials of condemnation.

"That the boy should be hanged is almost unthinkable," wrote the *Appleton Post Crescent*, which was located in Wisconsin.

> This pre-adolescent youth was not more guilty than his parents and the kind of home training he had or the possible influence of boy companions, or the community environment which brought him to such a pass. . . . The responsibility of the community does not end with his conviction. It has just begun. Much could be written about the increase of youthful crime since the war. The growth of organized banditry due to changed social conditions, the flagrant display of crime motion pictures and the casting of murderous gun-toters and infamous crooks in the roles of gallant outlaws, have all had their influence in lessening the value of human life in the minds of impressionable and susceptible youths.
>
> The crime of the Washington boy may well serve as an incentive to his community to give introspective study of its own negligence and guilt.

Flanagan was so enraged by Mackintosh's comment that he issued a statement of his own to the newspapers of the country: "It is a statement without mercy or gentleness." Who is he "to pronounce judgment . . . upon a mere child, a victim of society? What a travesty of justice to commit a 12-year-old boy to life imprisonment and to speak of hanging him, when all of the crime commissions, special enforcement societies and government prosecutors congratulate themselves upon sending such an arch criminal as Al Capone to jail for eleven years!"

Katherine Lenroot, acting chief of the National Children's Bureau, weighed in as well on Herbert's sentence and the death sentence of an Illinois seventeen-year-old.

"No 17-year-old boy should be sentenced to death, nor should any 12-year-old be sent to prison for life." She said the Niccolls case was contrary to juvenile court standards that were worked out under the auspices of the Children's Bureau, "not by sentimentalists but by persons of experience and judgment." Murder cases involving children under sixteen are usually either accidental killings "or involve some kind of mental abnormality," she said. Her opinions apparently were given little weight in Washington, where in a few months a seventeen-year-old with a fifth-grade education would be hanged. Meanwhile, plans were being made for Herbert's incarceration at the penitentiary.

Flanagan tried to intervene in Herbert's case and sought help from Kuykendall. It's too late, the judge had told him. Flanagan then tried Warden Clarence Long and got the same answer. When Sheriff Wayne Bezona called Long with the verdict, Long was not pleased. The Walls, as the penitentiary was called, was no place for a child—even if the child was a murderer. He would be exposed to some of the most vicious men around. If he were a murderer now, he'd be worse off if he mixed with the likes of those at the prison. Besides it was illegal, the law forbade young offenders from being housed with older criminals. No one seemed to have thought much about that. Can't you just build him some kind of separate quarters? Kuykendall asked. The judge wanted him to bend the law. Long said he'd come up with something.

In the meantime, the boy would have to be isolated in a cell away from the others. Long put C. F. Rose, the librarian, in charge of him during the day. They would work something out to see that the boy got some sort of schooling. But Long didn't like the idea at all. Prison was no place for a child. His physical needs for food and shelter would be met, but what of his social needs to interact with others? Given his age, there seemed to be no other choice, but if they allowed the boy contact with the others, the criminal tendencies he already had would only be fine-tuned. Perhaps the boy could be transferred somewhere else later.

Junior stood outside the courthouse with a wooden box of tattered clothing, a book, a blue marble, and a harmonica in his arms, all topped with his beloved cornet. The wind blew in from the north, carrying with it a slight chill and the scent of sage and fallen apples. Bezona glanced down at the boy. He had grandchildren that were this boy's age.

Bezona was now beyond the rage he had felt that night in Klaus's store. Instead a deep vein of sadness ran through him as he turned the boy over to Campbell for the drive to Walla Walla. Campbell opened the door of the police car for him. Carrying the wooden box, the boy got in front, his head barely visible over the top of the seat. Then Campbell slipped into the driver's seat and McGrath took the other side.

As the town faded into wheat lands, the boy was quiet for the first few miles. Then McGrath turned to him and asked about the book resting on top of the box on the back seat. The boy's face lit up as McGrath reached for the book and opened it. On the inside cover it read, "E. E. Halsey to his friend, Herbert F. Niccolls." McGrath was stunned. Few prosecutors send defendants parting gifts, and Halsey had been anything but gentle with the boy. But Halsey did tell one reporter he felt as sad about the boy's lot "as if it were my own son."

"Have you read it?" McGrath asked.

"No," the boy replied, taking it from him and lovingly stroking its cover. "I want to save it until I get there. I'll have more time."

"What kind of books do you like?" McGrath asked.

"Books about animals and birds," he answered. "I like picture shows, too. Funny ones. But I only saw them when I was at St. Anthony's."

"Have you ever read the Bible?" McGrath asked. The boy produced a thumb-worn, small New Testament from his pocket.

"I have read this a lot. I read it all through once," he said.

Then the boy took out his harmonica and played as the wind from the open windows blew his hair and the car sped along the two-lane highway, like a silver ribbon through the harvest-shorn hills.

The boy played various tunes but when he began "Home Sweet Home," the men felt lumps in their throats, McGrath would later write. But the boy showed no emotion.

"'Red Wing' is my favorite," the boy told them, in between songs.

"Do you know 'Irish Eyes'?" Campbell asked.

"No, I don't believe I do," he said. "You see, I don't know the latest tunes. I have been in jail the past three months." To the child, McGrath noted, it had seemed like years.

"Play something on your cornet," Campbell asked.

The boy eagerly produced the cornet from the backseat and carefully readied it, cleaning the mouthpiece and explaining what he was doing with each step. Then he played a few notes and rested a moment. A gust of wind blew into the car, rustling paperwork on the backseat like autumn leaves. Then the boy lifted the cornet and played "Taps."

When the white-brick Garfield County Courthouse came into view, the boy asked if he could stop and say good-bye to Deputy Gilliam. But Campbell told him it wasn't possible. After all, he was taking the boy to prison, not on a field trip.

Through the farmlands between Pomeroy and Dayton the boy again grew quiet, looking at a countryside he had never seen before. Occasionally, he'd break the silence, saying, "Pretty near hit that pig, Bob," or "There's some woolies," when he saw a flock of sheep. He also asked how it was possible to get water up to the tops of the hills to irrigate the crops; his experience with farms had been entirely with irrigated regions near rivers, McGrath later noted. At Dayton, they stopped for a rest.

"How much farther is it?" the boy asked.

"About thirty miles," Campbell answered. "Won't be long now."

McGrath, craving something to drink, saw a soda fountain across the street, and then patted his pants pocket and realized he had left his wallet behind.

"I have my seventy-five cents, Mr. McGrath," the boy said. "You can have that."

Campbell said that they should be heading down the road. The prison officials would be waiting. He was anxious to put the whole affair behind him and not think about the boy again. He couldn't help but feel that the whole situation was a horrible tragedy from the loss of the sheriff's life to what might as well be the loss of the boy's. What kind of future did he have behind the Walls?

Campbell pulled the car back onto the highway. The sun was dipping lower in the horizon. The wind picked up and the clouds scudded across the sky, their shadows crawling over the hills. The warmth of the sun had faded and with it came the chilly reminder of the presence of fall. The wind blew through the car, carrying memories of school days, holidays, and harvests and the gentle passing of another season, another year. Campbell glanced at the boy whose eyes were darting across the horizon and wondered what he must be feeling now.

A car pulled up behind the unmarked police car and passed it.

"Step on her, Bob," the boy said. "See how fast you can go. You can pass him. You're only doing forty-five now. Go ahead, pass him."

Campbell smiled.

"How are you feeling about going to prison?" McGrath asked.

"I have tried to picture what it's like," the boy said. "Maybe it will be like the industrial school. It isn't in a one-horse town, is it?"

"No," McGrath said. "How do you feel about staying there the rest of your life?"

"I won't know until I get there," the boy said.

Then he turned in his seat and removed his Boy Scout handbook from the box in back and thumbed through the pages. "I already know part of the Boy Scout oath," he said, beginning to recite it. McGrath, who was a scoutmaster, filled in the missing words.

As the first signs of the town came into view and the car hummed along the highway, the boy raised his right hand in the Boy Scout sign.

"Upon my honor, I promise to do my best to do my duty to God and my country."

And then the town unfolded before him—an oasis of gold and green on a hot, dry prairie. There were maple-lined streets with quaint bungalows and stately old houses. There were gardens and yards where children raked leaves and then leaped into the piles. There were blue tendrils of smoke rising from small garden fires and fat pumpkins sitting on porches and black cats and cornstalks for Halloween.

There were boys on bicycles and mothers calling from screen doors. The bloom of dinners cooking mingled with the pungent decay of leaves.

"This is a pretty town, isn't it?" the boy asked. Campbell nodded. The stately Whitman College came into view and then the small shops—a meat market, a bookstore, a shoe-repair shop, car sales lots full of sleek, shiny Buicks parked side-by-side like chrome-teeth beasts waiting to spring to life at the turn of a key.

"It would be nice to live here," the boy said.

The men were silent as the last of the shops flashed by and the car turned onto a small road leading to the north of town. They rounded a corner, and then the imposing brick walls of the Washington State Penitentiary came into view. The building sat on a hill, surrounded by prison-owned farmland, cared for by convict labor. Campbell slowed the car and pulled into the path leading to the administration building.

At the sound of car wheels crunching gravel, the door opened and Assistant Warden Hans Damm stepped out. Campbell got out of the car and shook hands with the man briefly. The boy slipped out behind him and stood small in the shadow of the imposing building, with its four gun towers that were guarded by men with machine guns. The catwalk at the top of the wall was where guards patrolled.

Campbell handed the boy his box. "My cornet, too, please," the boy said. "And the mouthpiece."

The boy turned toward the building. Dressed in his proper gray suit and vest, his face lined and eyes keen, Warden Long emerged from the building and stood at the top of the stairs. Slowly, the boy mounted the steps with Damm at his side. He looked up at the warden, flashed an engaging smile that dimpled his left cheek and said, "Please to meet you, sir."

Then he stepped beyond the walls.

Chapter 9

BEYOND THE WINDOW PANE in Governor Roland Hartley's office maples shimmered in their November gold and a flock of ducks flew across the gray sky in a perfect V. It was three o'clock and already the edges of night had slipped across the capitol campus in Olympia.

A few blocks away in the redbrick mansion, the governor's wife would be fussing over dinner, moving in and out of the kitchen, not leaving the staff alone to cook, smoothing the tablecloth as if the King of England himself were coming to dinner and not just Henry Broderick and friends. Hartley was in no mood for company, no mood to be charming. It had never been his strong suit anyway.

When the people had elected him governor of the state of Washington, he promised to be a governor who was hard on excess, who would run the state with a tight rein. He was a no-nonsense leader, not afraid to be unpopular. And he believed if it weren't for him the bleeding hearts would have given the state away by now.

When it came to those hanky-wringing crybabies, there were none worse than the growing pack who were concerned with the Niccolls boy. That a man of Father Flanagan's standing would throw himself among them and lead them in defiance of the governor of Washington incensed Hartley. As with all bleeding hearts, Flanagan, Hartley believed, was terribly misinformed. His offer to take charge of young Niccolls was ludicrous.

Hartley was convinced that Niccolls was a killer, not some namby-pamby mama's boy down on his luck that the priest could take under his wing. Hartley had other things to worry about. The Niccolls matter and Flanagan's persistence annoyed him.

Hartley's secretary, Amy Albright, popped her well-coifed head in the doorway and handed him a letter from Mrs. Armene Lamson, adding that Mrs. Lamson had called twice asking to meet with him. Although the Lamsons were Republicans and earlier had been Hartley supporters, Hartley was annoyed that the esteemed doctor's wife didn't know her place.

As the heavy door to his office was swinging shut, the young woman in her trim black suit popped her head in once more to ask about the press.

Hartley thought they were nothing but varmints, news-mongering varmints. And he didn't hesitate in saying so. There were calls from, Miss Albright paused to read a list, the *Seattle Times*, the *Seattle Star*, the *Tacoma News Tribune*, the *Walla Walla Daily Bulletin* . . .

He wanted them all to go to hell. But he ordered his secretary to tell them he had no comment—on anything.

The door to the office closed swiftly and Hartley eased himself back in his leather chair. It seemed easy back in 1924 when he won the election on the promise to be a champion of the taxpayer and to reduce the size and cost of government. Shortly after he was elected, he made the unprecedented move to adjourn the legislature until fall so he could assess the needs of the state.

"The people are not asking for more laws," he told the legislators in a joint session. "Their insistent demand is for as little legislation as possible . . . fewer taxes and more economies. Such a plan cannot be evolved hastily and haphazardly."

By the time he reconvened the legislature in November, he had laid the groundwork for getting rid of the liberal Henry Suzzallo, president of the University of Washington, and squeezing out the others who did not share his vision. He did battle with the Lands Commission plan to sell off timberland cheaply and set straight the education lobbies. He took exception to the location of the proposed Legislature Building—he believed that if it weren't for him it would have sunk in no time—and he ordered the site to be buttressed with monster slabs of concrete. He also questioned the money spent on the new building's furnishings— embossed leather chairs, fancy hat racks, and golden "spitunias," as he liked to call them. He put the chair and a gilded spittoon in the back of a truck and drove throughout the state inviting taxpayers to step right up and have a sit and a spit.

The press dogged him. Whatever he did and said, they recorded it. Somehow the things he did and said took on different light and seemed ridiculous when they were stamped in hot-lead type on the crisp sheets that filled the newsstands. He bitterly recalled how they howled like jackals over the recall effort in 1926 but didn't say much when it failed. Despite the reporters, he was reelected to a second term in 1928. He showed them, and he would show them again. He fully intended to be the first governor to be elected to a third term. What would the state have done without him?

He was sixty-seven, and with the Depression upon him, governing was becoming harder than ever. The people were demanding more. They looked to the state for a cure for everything instead of looking to them- selves. The bad economy came at a time when the state's revenues, which relied greatly on property taxes, had already been diminished because people were unable to pay their taxes.

"The American people today suffer from too much government," he told the legislature. "We are striking at the very vitals of the Republic by robbing the individual of his independence, his self-reliance, his will to work and his zeal to achieve, thereby reducing him to the status of a ward of the government."

Hartley believed that much of the Depression was just an illusion, created by the press. He had been a bootstrapper and he had succeeded. He had been born in New Brunswick, Canada, in 1864 and had graduated from Minneapolis Academy. He then became secretary to the mayor of Brainerd, Minnesota, got a start in the lumber business, and then was appointed as secretary to Minnesota Governor David Clough. While in Minnesota he fell in love with the governor's lovely daughter, Nina, and they moved out West in 1902. He landed a job as a timber executive with a company with lucrative returns, and the couple moved into a four-story mansion in Everett, north of Seattle. He became mayor of Everett and later a state legislator. Sometimes he thought of simply retiring to the Everett home, putting public life behind him, but, no, it was part of him. It was in his blood. More important, however, there was no one else around to pull in the reins of government spending, no one with common sense. He couldn't trust his fellow Republicans to do the job.

Now the press was badgering him about Niccolls. The reporters hadn't even stopped howling over DuBuc. The seventeen-year-old deserved to be executed. The boy took part in the cold-blooded murder of an eighty-seven-year-old man.

Hartley had shown leniency earlier in his term toward two young men who had killed a Seattle policeman. When one of their mothers came to him with tears in her eyes and pleaded quietly without the knowledge of the press, he had complied. It seemed so long ago.

He took a sack from his desk drawer, opened the door to the balcony and stepped out into the chilly afternoon. There was a spatter of rain, a gust of wind that carried with it the scent of cedar. Gulls wheeled across the gray flannel sky. He removed the crusts of bread and tossed them onto the lawn. The birds descended, beating the air with their silver wings, swooping low to retrieve a piece and then sailing back upward into the clouds. They cried to one another and circled, but none landed on the railing as Tee had.

The press wrote about her, too. It made him look silly. "Hartley's forces in the Legislature may desert him and his enemies may say all manner of evil things about him falsely, but nothing can shake the undivided devotion of Tee, the seagull. Tee . . . his best friend," or so the *Seattle Star* wrote.

He began feeding Tee shortly after he took office in 1925. When his office was moved into the new wing of the capitol building, Tee soon figured out he was on the north side of the building. For most of the day, the bird would sit on top of the flagpole at the Temple of Justice and all he'd have to do is wave his arms and she'd swoop down for a meal. But he hadn't seen the gull for several years. He still looked for her, still hoped. He didn't like to think she'd moved on. He crumpled the bag, surveying the sky.

•

From his apartment upstairs, he could hear the voices of the guests arriving at the mansion, the cooing of his wife in return, and the soft sweet voice of his daughter. And through the trilling of feminine voices came Broderick's hearty boom. Hartley adjusted his tie and trotted down the stairs to meet him. As the maids scurried to take coats and umbrellas, the guests milled about the foyer, ruffling feathers and preening before the gilt mirror like ducks walking in the morning beside a lake.

It seemed the controversies of the governor's office followed him even to his own dinner table, and the guests had the audacity to question his policies on youth and crime. Henry Broderick, of course, was in his camp but there were days when he found the Seattle real estate tycoon irritating. The way he "collected" celebrities, for example, fancying himself a patron of the arts because he had met the burlesque queen Gypsy Rose Lee. But H.B., as Broderick preferred to be called, was a powerful ally and had certainly been a benefit in his campaign. They shared the same no-nonsense approach to crime and criminals. That's why he had let him sit in as a prison control board observer for the last three years.

Without pausing in his attack upon the roast beef, Broderick asked what Hartley thought of the Niccolls kid. The *Times* had said that the priest from Nebraska wanted to take him. Hartley acknowledged that Flanagan had written and said he "intended to give it careful consideration." After all of his years in politics, he had a stock supply of phrases to get him out of the line of fire; giving something "careful consideration" was one of them. But it seemed these days he was using it more and more, especially where youth and crime was concerned.

In Hartley's den, the fire burned brightly. The men slipped into the leather chairs and Broderick lit up a cigar and launched into stories about Gypsy and her fans. Then he added, with a chuckle, that the governor certainly wasn't afraid to be unpopular.

·

It was a moonless night and a soft rain pattered against the leaves of the trees as Hartley walked across the campus toward the capitol building with its mighty dome. It was a grand old building, a replica of the nation's Capitol and to Hartley, the center of his world. It had been for a very long time. He had worked hard to get to the place. He ran for governor in 1916 and 1920 but failed to win the Republican primaries. However, the election of 1924 was a different story. No one had ever called him a quitter and here he was—a living example of tenacity.

The capitol building had never stopped amazing him. He remembered the first time he had seen it after coming to Olympia to meet with lobbyists representing timber interests. That was so long ago. He stood in the rotunda, at the edge of the golden state seal, all roped off in heavy purple cord, then walked through the dim corridors to his office. A current of cool air rushed past him, rustling the draperies in dark corners. He paused at the door to his office. In the silence it seemed the passions of the day—the shouting, pleading, cajoling, imploring, sanctimonious lobbying for causes and crusades, the brisk clip of pages—lingered in the shadows. He could almost smell the fresh ink of the new laws, waiting to unfurl like a banner, carrying with them the many possibilities for change. But in this quiet hour, he could study what would be best for the people, study the issues wisely as a father. If only his detractors would understand that he would lead the state as a father leads his children.

He removed a ring of keys from his pocket. They jingled as he found the right one and inserted it into the lock. The heavy door swung open. He switched on a light and walked over to Miss Albright's desk. He had been through so many secretaries since 1925 he could hardly remember their names. He took a stack of mail addressed to him and retreated to his office, where he set it on the desk, removed his wet overcoat and hat, and turned on a desk lamp. The circle of light fell across the spidery handwriting on the envelopes. He removed an ivory-handled letter opener from his desk and ripped open the first envelope and laid it aside.

He opened the file cabinet drawer marked "clemency" and retrieved several files. There were stacks of letters, some with the square handwriting of children, others with the elegant handwriting of pleading wives and mothers, and still others, the formal typed letters from attorneys and businessmen. So much of his day, it seemed, dealt with requests for clemency. As the number of crimes and convictions rose, so did the clemency pleas. But he believed that sitting in on the parole board meetings gave him insight into the criminal mind. As chief executive of the state, he had the sole power to pardon or parole inmates or commute sentences from death to life. With each plea for clemency, he carefully read the files. But only rarely did he reverse a court's decision.

It was hard when the letters came. Every day it was someone new. Since he took office, ten men had been executed for their crimes. Three more waited in the wings. With each execution there were waves of protests from the grieving relatives who believed in the inmate's innocence until his last breath.

Hartley believed infirmity or youth shouldn't absolve anyone from the death penalty or life in prison. Before him were two files, each detailing a murder committed only two weeks apart, one on the Chamber's Creek Prairie south of Olympia and the other in a small farming town on the Snake River. Both of the high-profile crimes had been committed by young people, and they attracted sympathizers who begged Hartley for clemency.

Walter DuBuc's crime had been especially horrible. His ne'er-do-well cousin Ethel had introduced the boy to her latest live-in boyfriend, Harold Carpenter. The three traveled from their home in Yakima to Olympia where they camped out. They had heard that Peter Jacobson, an elderly rancher, kept a fortune stashed in his house and made plans to rob him. They drove to the house and DuBuc knocked on the door. When the old man answered, the boy told him his daughter was sick and if he would come, he would take him to her.

"He was standing in the doorway where I could hit him, but I couldn't do it," DuBuc wrote in his confession. "Then he went in the house to get his clothes on. I was in the doorway a little inside the house . . . then before I knew it, I hit him with my fist. I hit him about three times and he fell and I saw Carpenter come there and hit him with his . . . rifle barrel on the head. I got scared and run [sic] to the car and started it. While I was turning around, Carpenter jumped on the running board and told Ethel to tell me to meet him on the road close to the bridge, said to load all the camp stuff on the car and pick him up. . . . So I picked him up and turned around and started for Yakima. Carpenter told me he only got $2.60 from the man and he got a watch and knife and some groceries. I asked him about the rifle and he said that he broke it all up on the man's head."

The trial had concluded a month earlier. The woman was sentenced to life in prison and the thirty-one-year-old Carpenter and DuBuc were to hang.

Now DuBuc, like Niccolls, was at the Washington State Penitentiary. DuBuc was about to become the youngest person in the state to be executed for a crime. DuBuc had pleading relatives and the press. But Niccolls had Father Flanagan. If Flanagan heard about DuBuc he'd be trying to spring him, too, Hartley knew.

Hartley studied Flanagan's letter, dated November 4, 1931, only days after the boy had been sentenced. "I have been deeply moved by the conviction and imprisonment of . . . the 12-year-old boy murderer, who is now serving a life sentence in a penitentiary of your state. It is pathetic that a child so young must meet the fate of the worst of adult criminals."

Flanagan argued that his Boys Home could be a service to the state by taking the boy off the prison officials' hands. "Were it not that we have had considerable experience in the caring of real problem boys during the past fourteen years, I would not attempt to ask for such a parole. My experience has taught me that through the influence of our Home where kindness, love and an understanding interest in these boys' problems play such an important part, I am certain our Home can bring to this forlorn and dejected boy, hope and future success."

Flanagan asked Hartley for the same consideration that he had given other similar requests made in behalf of adult prisoners in the past. But more than anything, Hartley hated anyone who tried to usurp his authority as the chief executive of the state. This priest had deliberately done that by going to the press first. Now they were all clamoring at him. It made a monkey out of him and he wondered if he paroled the boy to Flanagan what message it would send to other criminals? That he was soft on crime? That all they had to do is cry to the newspapers?

He rose from his desk and retrieved his hat and coat. For the moment he would take no action, and that, too, would be a message. The lights blinked out and the heavy door swung shut behind him. The lock fell into place with a dull thud that was soft and final.

Chapter 10

THE SOUND of happy children always made Father Flanagan smile. But as much as he loved them and delighted in seeing them clatter down the hall like colts galloping, it also pained him with worry. The farm's finances were grim but somehow the farm must survive. Lack of money would never cause him to turn a child away.

Flanagan had left the hospital against the doctors' orders and the sisters fretted and fussed at the door. But he had been in bed too long, been away from his boys too long. There was urgent work to be done.

He quickly went through the pile of mail—letters for some of the boys, bills, several letters with contributions, but no letter from Governor Roland Hartley of Washington State.

Across the playfield, sun glinted off a boy's head as he caught a football, then cocked his arm and hurled it. The ball soared into the bright blue sky.

Every child was dear to him, given to him by God, he believed. They were blessings, and he could see Herbert at the farm, see the boy on the playfield, running breathlessly, the bloom of winter upon him as he burst through the door into the warm room. There was no such thing as a bad boy, Flanagan believed. No matter what the child had done, each was a product of his environment. Why that was such a novel idea Flanagan couldn't understand. The best way to curtail crime was to prevent boys from being brought up in poverty and environments where crime can breed. A youth who makes a mistake may be compared to a plant growing in depleted soil and deprived of health-giving sunshine, he wrote in one of his many public speeches. A boy in such circumstances hasn't got a chance. Most boys with criminal records start by stealing food or money for the bare necessities. If no one intervenes, it becomes a way of life.

Flanagan had come to that conclusion long ago when he was at St. Patrick's Church in Omaha in 1915. So many homeless, jobless, hungry men had flocked to the city when they couldn't get jobs on farms because of the wheat crop failure. Each day more and more got off the train and wandered through the city, looking for work, food, shelter, and hope. The parish, of course, offered a meal or two but it was impossible to keep up with the demand. There were just so many. With the help of the St. Vincent de Paul Society, he had opened the Working Man's Hotel in 1916 and filled all forty cots the first night.

They were a rough lot those men, many being gamblers, drunkards, or dope addicts, but they were all God's children. And the stories were often the same—childhoods of poverty, neglect, and homelessness. That was the challenge, Flanagan knew. In order to save the man, one must save the child.

Omaha's streets were full of homeless, delinquent boys—orphans and runaways or children turned out because their families were too poor to feed them. With Archbishop Jeremiah Harty's blessing and $90 borrowed from a friend, Flanagan rented a rickety house at 25th and Dodge streets in downtown Omaha. He took in two boys who had been referred to him from the juvenile court and three boys right off the street. In days, the number grew to twenty-five children. The archbishop had arranged for two nuns and a novice from the School Sisters of Notre

Dame to help with the household tasks, but there wasn't any money or food to provide for his home. Each night he prayed for a miracle.

On the snowy Christmas Eve of 1917, the sisters came to him. There was nothing, absolutely nothing, for any of them to eat. As the wind moaned around the eaves of the old house, he heard the clip-clop of horses' hooves, the creak and jingle of a harness, and the groan of a wagon. He had thrown open the door to see a man, pulling a barrel off the wagon and toting it up the walk.

The man mumbled something about thinking that maybe he could use it. He set the barrel on the porch, tipped his hat, and retreated into the storm. It was Christmas dinner. It was manna from heaven. It was divine. It was sauerkraut. A humble holiday fare and Flanagan sank to his knees that night in gratitude.

How his home had grown since those days that seemed like yesterday. By the spring of 1918, 100 boys lived at his home and friends donated clothing and shoes. Food again was plentiful and he was able to rent a horse and wagon to transport his band to school and church. In April, a fundraising dinner had been attended by 4,000 and brought in $5,300. Soon thereafter he was able to rent the Omaha German-American Home with its playground, bowling alley, and pool tables. And still the number of boys grew until once again they were pushing at the seams of the home.

It hadn't, of course, always been easy for the boys. They stood out in public school because their clothes were worn. Many had never attended school regularly before and they easily fell behind. And worst of all, his boys faced ostracism. But he insisted that all were children of God and he would not refuse a child because of his race, creed, or color. He told his critics that he saw danger for all in an ideology that discriminated against anyone racially, politically, or economically.

So it had seemed like a good idea to start a school in the home, and better still to move to a farm out of the city. While there he could weave a protective cocoon around the boys that would allow them to grow and heal away from the rest of the world. That was the way to turn lost boys into confident young men—give them guidance, protection, structure, and love.

He, of course, had already had his eye on the ideal site, the 160-acre Overlook Farm west of the city. He told the owners about the boys and about how, with a farm that size, he could increase the number of boys he cared for to 500. In the end, he convinced them to trade the farm to him in exchange for a forty-acre farm that he had bought earlier.

"Your greatest business asset is your faith," they had told him. And faith had carried him through.

It was one of those times when his faith had been tested. He had always been a dreamer—ever since he was a boy in Ireland, dreaming of being a priest. He knew what he wanted this city of little men to be, a Boys Town. Although prominent Omaha businessmen had raised more than $200,000 for the construction of the main five-story building at the farm, there were still monthly mortgage payments and the increased costs of running the farm as the number of boys increased. With the stock market crash in 1929, the amount of donations had declined as well.

He had campaigned nationally, knowing that when he spoke money poured in. And he still ran the home with a small staff that included his mother, brother, and other family members. But in August 1931 he had become short of breath and dizzy and had slumped across his desk. The doctor scolded him. The doctor warned him. And he knew that the boys' futures depended on his health. He agreed to go to the sanitorium in Denver, writing letters, taking phone calls, and enduring the sisters' fussing over him, insisting that he was working far too hard for his health. But what could he do? The lives of so many boys depended upon him.

From his hospital bed he wrote a letter to his supporters that he had hoped he would never have to write.

"The Boys Home, for which I have worked so hard and for so many years, must be closed unless the necessary money is raised immediately. . . . If the home closes it will break my heart. That won't matter much. But it will break the hearts of these two hundred boys and deprive [them of] a chance in life" and a "chance for the hundreds of boys to come."

They needed $87,500. It would take a miracle in those times of unemployment and poverty. Flanagan was determined that it would be done somehow. The lives of boys like Herbert Niccolls counted on it.

Numerous letters had been sent to the farm in response to the newspaper articles announcing his willingness to take in the boy. And he opened a folder full of letters and read them again. They were good people. All of them. If they would only spur the governor into action. After receiving the letters from the Garfield County sheriff and the boy's attorneys, Doyle and Farley, he was more convinced than ever that the boy must be saved.

Patterson had written,

The history of this lad goes back to the age of six years. He has a record of stealing from that time on. . . . He was released to his grandmother, who is a widow woman, and unfit to care for a youngster of his type. He testified she whipped him with a club the day he committed the murder of the sheriff at Asotin. He left home and was trying to get to Canada, and decided to rob the store. . . . His father is now serving time in the insane asylum at Orofino, Idaho, for murder. The lad is an underprivileged boy from the start, his home environment has a great deal to do with his act.

I have had him as a prisoner here for about 90 days and find him a model prisoner, an exceptionally bright boy, perfect manners and command of the English language and a very pleasing personality.

And, according to Ed Doyle,

The judge had no discretion in the matter and life imprisonment, under our laws . . . is the only thing that could be done except, of course, to have him found not guilty for insanity which would not have been any real help to the boy.

This little fellow was sent away by his mother to the Children's Home. . . . He has been knocked about as the saying is, from pillar to post. He has been deprived of proper clothing, home life, the companionship of his brothers and sisters and everything that goes to build up the moral side of a child's life.

The boy, although [transferred] from one institution to the other, has a wonderful school record. He has a marked talent for music, his language is refined and he is very cultured and polite. It seems to me something could be done with the boy. I am relating these circumstances because I know of your great interest and success in handling boys.

An attorney named Farley also had written: "The little fellow sat between Mr. Doyle and myself, and I have to admit he is one of the most likable and attractive little fellows that I have ever met. I have been connected with the Home Finding Societies for over 30 years and can point with pride to several homes where one or the other . . . neglected child with my help was saved. . . . I believe that this little fellow will make good if given the chance which he has never had. You could not sit through this trial and listen to all the pitiable trials of this child without wondering—is this possible?"

Flanagan knew, of course, that it was all too possible. He had encountered children living in conditions not fit for animals, children abandoned because the parents could not afford to feed them, children beaten, children who had to beg, children who labored day and night in cities and on farms without a chance for education, children who committed crimes, children who had shot their mothers and fathers or their playmates.

The letters about the case began to fill his mailbox. They came from Minnesota, Washington, Wisconsin, Illinois, and Missouri, just to start. Wherever a newspaper ran the story about his fight to free the boy, letters about the case followed.

"The Divine Master forgives over and over again, surely the Governor of the State of Washington will understand that we human beings should at least try to follow in His steps . . . had we more Father Flanagans in our country, our jails and prisons would soon crumble and decay," wrote Elva Timms from Kansas City.

There were many letters that supported Flanagan's stand and his work with boys. Occasionally, they came with contributions, one dollar here and there, and sometimes more. Keeping his ministry before the public not only brought in contributions, it made the public aware that beneath the tarnished exterior of crime and poverty these boys, regardless of their deeds, were children.

A letter from a Mrs. O. F. "Armene" Lamson, child psychologist and author from Seattle, and a newspaper story she had written, especially attracted his attention. Mrs. Lamson was overjoyed that he was interested in Herbert Niccolls and wanted to know all about Overlook Farm and his boys' school. "I've been approached from many sources in our state for an opinion about the offer you make," she wrote.

Mrs. Lamson was a product of the Progressive Era; she had started the free Parental Clinic in Seattle, a place where low-income families could find medical help. "You have . . . my interest as well as my good wishes and admiration for the very great work you are doing," she wrote.

He wrote back to her immediately, describing the home and its advantages. "We aim first to build up our lads physically, to give them healthy bodies and minds. It is much easier afterwards to break through their seemingly hard crusts to the tender injured souls beneath."

If there was a formula for redeeming a boy who was thinking of turning to crime because he had no home, no work, or no friends, that was it. "Easy money and the rackets would get nowhere if he knew he had a home and friends. Every child at Overlook Farm is made to feel that this is his home, and that he must live up to the fine things expected of him, and whenever possible, he must achieve something worthwhile for his alma mater, whether it be on the football field, classroom or in the performance of his daily duties about the home. Surely there can be no more glorious work than saving boys and making men."

At Overlook Farm, Flanagan was continuing to strategize ways to get Herbert paroled. More than anything, he wanted him to have the same chance as the home's other boys. He was grateful to have a potential ally in Mrs. Lamson. Herbert's attorneys had been little help.

In a second letter, Doyle urged him to let the boy remain in prison for a month or so and then "if approached in the proper spirit," he believed Hartley would relent. Flanagan shuddered at the thought of a child that age among the worst of men. The governor had not replied yet.

Tucked in the file of correspondence was another letter he had somehow overlooked. He opened a thin white envelope and read a letter from a Ruth E. Johnson in Spokane, Washington. It was typical of many letters about the case in that those who had never met the boy had taken a personal interest in his fate. Much of the public response was no doubt a result of the detailed newspaper and radio coverage that both violated the boy's privacy and fueled the campaign to release him.

As Johnson wrote, "The lack of understanding that this boy's case has received from teachers, psychologists and judges, who should know the effects of environment, is astounding. They seem, in this case, to have given heredity entire emphasis."

Flanagan had read the stories and many others like it about other boys. In Herbert's case, nothing had been left out. Even though he was only twelve, not a single family fact was kept confidential. The boy was condemned because his father was in an insane asylum and because the family did not have the funds to buy the services of able lawyers and the testimony of psychiatrists. Clarence Darrow's defense for Leopold and Loeb was that those young men were victims of an educational system that took no account of character training or emotional development. The experts upheld that defense. But no one thought that Herbert Niccolls might likewise be a victim of faulty training, or at least no one but this Mrs. Johnson. The boy's crime was not even premeditated.

"I am ashamed of the way my state has handled this case. I have been sorry that I have not the influence or the funds to do something for the boy," she wrote. "If you would be permitted to take the boy you might do wonders with him. His statements show that he is bright. He would probably be willing to prove that he can be a real man and adapt himself to life as well as the other boys can."

•

Nathan Leopold and Richard Loeb filled the headlines of the mid 1920s. Flanagan had pondered their fate. Two brilliant young men—Nathan Leopold had graduated from the University of Chicago at eighteen, and Richard Loeb from the University of Michigan at seventeen. They were capable of doing so much good in the world. But they kidnapped a fourteen-year-old and plotted the "perfect murder" for the "intellectual thrill" of killing. One struck the boy on the head with a chisel and stuffed a gag in his mouth. The boy died almost instantly. Then they left his body in a culvert, but Leopold's glasses were found there, too, and the trail eventually led to them. Leopold's wealthy family hired Darrow to defend the young men. And although he couldn't keep them out of prison, he did keep them from the gallows. Where had the two young lives gone so wrong? The public reeled in shock at the seemingly new generation of criminal—one that they believed was more ruthless than ever before.

As heinous as the deed was, Flanagan firmly believed that young lives could be changed, but the older the child was before intervention, the less the chance of success.

Ruth Johnson's letter was like many others, yet with it came inspiration. If Governor Hartley was content to allow the boy to linger in prison, he would intensify the fight. He was after all an Irish parish priest at heart—a scrapper, a David in a land of Goliaths. It was one thing to have people write to him, and another to have them approach the governor directly.

He put sheets of typing paper into the trusty black typewriter and began to type.

"Within the gray walls of the penitentiary at Walla Walla . . . Washington is a youth placed in solitary confinement. He was convicted and sentenced on the charge of murder."

Within days of receiving the letter, fifty radio stations in the central and eastern states, all twenty-three radio stations in Washington State, and stations in Texas, Arizona, and Canada all agreed to broadcast his speech over the air. On the clear cold evening of November 12, the voice of the Irish priest sailed into the living rooms of thousands of homes like a heaven-sent meteor. His voice burst into the public consciousness between the symphonies and the prizefights, and men and women and children paused around their Motorolas and Bendix to listen.

"Dear Radio Friends: A few weeks ago a jury of twelve . . . sat in judgment against a youth accused of murder. Unlike most criminals, this murderer was but a boy 12 years of age, and while the jury was deliberating concerning the fate of this boy murderer, the boy himself did not pay any attention to the case, but played around the courtroom with toys and a harmonica some kind friend gave him. A little later one could see him cuddled up in a chair fast asleep. He was not interested in his fate."

"The boy's conscience did not seem to hurt him. He was just a child, interested in the things of a child, doing things a child would do, and did not realize that his fate rested in the hands of the twelve jurymen deliberating in the adjoining chamber," Flanagan told his listeners.

Flanagan continued to paint a portrait of a boy with no father or even a tearful mother in the court to support and comfort him. The boy was "forlorn and abandoned" at a critical moment, without relatives or friends to speak a kindly and encouraging word to him.

There was no Clarence Darrow to plead the case "of this lonely, homeless, and hungry little urchin."

Flanagan placed the blame on society "for its disgraceful treatment of this poor boy." In the public mind, the boy was just a murderer and he must be put away. Society must protect itself against a twelve-year-old "hungry, homeless child," he wrote.

When the jury reached its verdict and order was restored in the court, the boy entered the court, with only his attorneys there to support him, Flanagan told his radio audience re-creating the scene on the air. "This is indeed, an important moment in the life of every criminal whose fate has just been decided upon, a moment when every nerve is tense, and . . . eyes are focused on those grave faces of the men who have decided his case. . . . But not so with our little child murderer."

Herbert Niccolls will be placed in solitary confinement for the rest of his life, he told the listeners. He was led from the court with his toys and harmonica, unmindful of his fate, "because he did not realize the seriousness of the sentence. . . . Life has not meant much to him. . . . In consideration of this boy's pitiful condition and the injustice dealt him by a cruel society, Father Flanagan's Boys Home of Omaha, Nebraska, has petitioned Governor Hartley of the State of Washington to parole this boy to our institution for boys and turn him over to me to receive that care and training that has been denied him during the 12 years that have comprised his short life."

Flanagan had set the stage for the ultimate public fight. Delivered in his melodic brogue, he invoked the audience's sentimental feelings for their own young, calling on their gratitude to God. Flanagan thus dealt Hartley a swift blow that the governor would hold against him forever, the antipathy intensifying each time Hartley heard "Dear Radio Friends."

As Flanagan signed off that evening, he reminded listeners that God was protecting their boys "from such a fate as little Herbert Niccolls and in gratitude to Him you want to see little Herbert get a chance that has been denied him. . . . It will cost you nothing but an airmail stamp. . . . Kindly write a letter today to the Honorable Governor Hartley, Olympia, Washington, and ask him to parole this little boy . . . to Father Flanagan of Father Flanagan's Boys Home, Omaha, Nebraska. Send that airmail letter today."

The speech could not have been worse for Hartley. Within a few days, the letters began coming to him by the bagful. Pleading, threatening, cajoling, the more they wrote the harder Hartley resisted. Although it seemed like it would be easy to simply turn the boy over to the priest and be done with it, to Hartley it was a matter of principle. The governor, as he told his constituents earlier, would not be hoodwinked by anyone who wanted to circumvent his authority.

•

At the state's maximum security penitentiary, Herbert Niccolls was alone in his cell at the far end of Cellblock 1 when he wasn't in the library studying. It was at night when the terrifying sounds surrounded him. He heard the voices of grown men, sometimes a cry and dull thudding—and he pulled the black wool blanket over his ears to block out the sound when they called to him.

The Boys Town mail came and went. Father Flanagan rifled through the pile, hoping for a letter from Hartley. There was nothing. In the past, he had a vision of the governor dictating a letter, setting in motion the chance for new life for the boy. But now the vision had gone and the silence from the state capitol was like a dark curtain that had fallen—impenetrable and final. It filled him with panic. More than anything, he could not tolerate the suffering of children. And he imagined Herbert in a small dark cell—alone and frightened. He imagined, too, how easy it would be for him to be preyed upon. He was such a little child. Surely, no man could allow a child to suffer such a fate.

He would go to Seattle to plead with the governor himself. In the meantime, he would write another radio speech. Just then the phone rang and he lifted the receiver to hear the friendly voice of Morris Jacobs in Omaha. Jacobs, a crackerjack public relations man, said he had an idea that might help the boy in the Washington prison. He offered to contact his newspaper and radio sources in the state on Flanagan's behalf, adding that "more publicity would be sure to shake things loose."

The Bozell & Jacobs public relations firm had helped the farm in the past, but Flanagan needed them more than ever now, and accepted. Once again, he began to write.

On November 15, his gentle voice floated into the living rooms of America. Farmers hurried in from feeding stock, women abandoned pots and pans, dinners ceased, homework stopped, grandmothers put down crochet, and grandfathers, paused, pipes in hand. It was Father Flanagan, talking about "that boy again!"

> Dear Radio Friends: I want to thank all the friends of our poor, abandoned child murderer in their efforts to save him from life imprisonment. These many letters sent to the Governor, appealing to him to pardon or parole the child, will do much good. I have had no answer from Governor Hartley as yet to my letter to him requesting this pardon.
>
> We must rest our case of mercy in behalf of this unfortunate child until the governor and his parole board sees fit to act. But we must not remain idle. We can do something that will prove most beneficial, and that is [placing] our case . . . in the hand of a higher and superior court. We can beseech heaven with our prayers . . . God looks into your hearts and mine, and He is looking into the poor forlorn child's heart today as he sits in his dreary cell, helpless and alone. Here was a young murderer. Regardless of

the fact that he had to seek food by stealing, he was a dangerous criminal, they say, and he must be put away. Society must be protected. And thus it goes with the judgment of men.

Then Flanagan took on Mackintosh for his statement that "startles the world of sane men." He wrote, "It was his deliberate judgment that this 12-year-old boy should be put to death. I care not what a man has been or is, or what position of influence he may have attained . . . such a man issuing a statement such as Ex-Judge Mackintosh gave utterance to, is deserving of the contempt of all men. This so-called great and influential man has made men bow their heads in shame.

"Mr. Mackintosh, I know, would never condemn his own son to death if fate had dealt as harshly with him as with little Herbert Niccolls. I know Mr. Mackintosh would fight to the bitter end to save his boy from the death penalty or solitary life imprisonment were he the victim instead of Herbert Niccolls."

As far as Flanagan was concerned, society was to blame for Herbert Niccolls's fate.

"I want to say right here to the citizens of the State of Washington, from the governor right down to the lowliest person privileged to be a citizen of that great and beautiful state," Flanagan said. "The eyes of the world are watching you to see what steps you will take to give this boy a chance."

Chapter 11

ON HERBERT JUNIOR'S first day in prison, Hans Damm took him aside for a stern talk. Damm later reported that the boy broke into tears and said he was sorry for killing the sheriff, that he didn't intend for it to happen and from then on he promised to do the right thing.

When asked what made him finally tell the truth about Robinson, the boy answered, "Prayer." Damm asked him about the checkerboard he had brought with him to prison and told him he couldn't play alone.

"Maybe you could play with me?" the boy asked.

•

Having plenty of food, guaranteed shelter, and freedom from beatings, the boy quickly adapted to prison routine. Mr. Rose, the librarian, Damm, the warden, and those who taught him were his companions. Occasionally, he'd get one of them to play checkers or dominos with him. The crime had made him a celebrity and people he didn't know sent him things. He had more gifts than he had had in his entire life. But the only gift the staff let him keep was a picture book about Jesus. After all, it was a prison, they told him. Even so, he had new trousers and a sweater and a pair of dungarees. He was lucky, the warden said, because he didn't have to wear a prison uniform like the others, or have his head shaved. For that he was especially grateful.

The cornet he brought to prison was confiscated because it would be too disruptive to other inmates, he was told. In exchange, someone in the woodshop made him a guitar and he received lessons from another prisoner who taught him in the library. The music would always bring back memories, whether the guitar chords or a voice, from long ago before his father became religious, back in the days when his father would take his gun and go into the hills to kill a deer or elk and they'd live on it all winter. They were sad songs. Like the end of the world was coming and there would never be music or a summer night again.

He struck another chord and strummed. Then he could hear the voices of the others calling to him. The voices echoed through the dark. Someone laughed. They called him Fish, because he was new. There was the clang of a door and then the sharp voice of a guard. No one spoke. The boy set his guitar down and listened.

Every morning the others marched past his cell to the exercise yard, to work or to chow. They wore denim shirts and denim dungarees. Their heads were shaved and their faces gaunt and they looked only straight ahead as they marched beneath the guards' watchful eyes. The boy had no contact with them, except at night when their voices floated to him from beyond the door to his cell.

Herbert climbed onto his bed, pulled the black wool blanket over his head and tried to sleep. Long ago, there was blue sky and jacksnipes that took flight, their wings beating so furiously as they rose from the river. He clutched the rough wool blanket. His memory of the outside world was beginning to fade. There was his grandmother's house, his kitten. Where was his kitten now? He had written to his grandmother and asked. She wrote to him all about Jesus but never mentioned the cat.

His mother had written, too, and he cried when he got her letter. She urged him to be a good boy and said he must accept his punishment for his terrible deed. He never heard from his father and he was glad about it. He was glad that they had put him away in an insane asylum. Maybe that way he couldn't hurt his mother ever again. The girls were getting bigger and the baby, too, his mother wrote. He never heard from any of his brothers, but she said they were away working on a farm, except for James Francis. Someone had adopted him and changed his name to Hudson Shake. Herbert thought it was strange that his brother was now someone else's boy, someone who called him by a different name, someone whose own little boy had died and who very much wanted a replacement.

The Mitchells in Shoshone, Idaho, had tried to erase Herbert Niccolls and make him their boy. They gave him music lessons and good food, but he was still the boy from the industrial school. He had wanted to sink into a family, wrap it around him warm and snug like a wool blanket.

The guard's shadow passed the iron latticework of the cell and the beam of a flashlight played across the blanket. The boy remained motionless until the figure retreated through the doorway into the soft light of the other room.

After he had been at the penitentiary a few months, there was a special treat for inmates in good standing. In the prison's auditorium, the Whitman College Glee Club was to perform an operetta for inmates and a few invited community guests. The prisoners had filed in on the floor below and Herbert was the lone prisoner in the balcony. In the middle of the performance, he saw a familiar face. It was reporter and scoutmaster McGrath, who had given him a Boy Scout handbook during the ride to the prison. In the dark, he crept over to him and whispered, "I've mastered all the Tenderfoot knots!"

•

The rolling brown fields flashed by the window as Father Flanagan's train rumbled west. He could see hobo junctions where men who were down and out gathered around small fires near the tracks. They would sleep out in the cold unless they could catch a freight by jumping aboard a slow-moving boxcar.

Flanagan had heard all about that life from the stories the men had told him at the Working Man's Hotel. From his seat in the Pullman car, he could see the underside of cities, the backyards with clothes lines, and the decaying remnants of small gardens, as well as the men and women who picked through garbage cans looking for something to eat.

As the train rocked, there was a soft knock at the door and then it opened. Nate Jacobs popped his head inside. Morris Jacobs, true to his word, had arranged everything. He had even sent his brother along as an assistant. The young man handed him a telegram.

It was good news, he said. Oliver Morris, city editor of the *Seattle Post-Intelligencer*, had arranged a reception for 4:30 p.m., on Friday, at the Washington Athletic Club. He and Mrs. Lamson, the sponsor of the reception, had initially invited thirty, but so many other community leaders wanted to come that Mrs. Lamson suggested a no-host dinner to follow. Of course, they realized that he may be fatigued after the journey, but could he possibly consent? After all, it would be a splendid opportunity to build up strong local sentiment for the cause. Who's to argue with an editor?

Flanagan told Nate to give them his thanks and acceptance. Then he read the telegram over. It was extraordinarily kind of them. The *Post-Intelligencer*'s city editor had even offered to put him and Nate up at the club instead of a hotel. It was an offer A.B. McConnell of the Sherman and McConnell Drug Company had also extended in another telegram sent in care of the Union Pacific Pullman conductor the day before. In fact, several times a day either the conductor or Nate tapped on his door to deliver more telegrams with offered arrangements.

Bozell & Jacobs had not only contacted every influential member on newspapers nationwide but it had also encouraged civic organizations to join the fight to save Herbert Niccolls. At the agency's urging, the Federation of Dads Clubs had written to Hartley, urging him to parole Herbert. So did hundreds of Parent-Teacher Associations, the American Legion, and child-welfare groups from coast to coast. Morris Jacobs had contacted *Time* magazine's Henry Luce, the *New York Mirror*'s Walter Winchell, and New York's Hearst Headquarters, which told the agency to contact William Randolph Hearst in Los Angeles directly.

Oliver Morris had run news stories publicizing the trip, applauding

Flanagan's boys' home training programs in bookkeeping, stenography, gardening, dairying, carpentry, farming, and printing. And he listed Will Rogers, Babe Ruth, Jack Dempsey, Admiral Byrd, John Philip Sousa, David Rubinoff, Tom Mix, Clarence Chamberlain, and many others who endorsed the home. There was a wide variety of persons who represented religious faiths giving endorsements for the home as well, from Omaha Rabbi Frederick Cohn to Episcopal Rector Rev. Dr. Frederick Clayton. Morris had sprinkled in quotes from Walter Head, president of the Boy Scouts of America, who said that the home was "rendering a great service in taking homeless abandoned and wayward boys, regardless of race, color or creed and helping to mold their lives in such a way and manner as to make of them good and useful citizens." Nebraska Governor Charles W. Bryan, too, sang Flanagan's praises.

The *Seattle Times* ran Morris's story and so did countless other newspapers. Flanagan could feel the cause gaining momentum, growing larger and larger and carrying him along with the current. But would the governor relent under pressure? Who was to say where this fight for this child would lead? When it came to protecting children, it warranted being as fierce as the north wind.

He looked out the window as the train rocked through little towns near Shoshone, Idaho. A grove of cottonwood flashed by, then a church, and a school. The bell from the crossing guard exploded with urgent ringing and then faded. He glimpsed children on bicycles. Children bundled in woolen coats carrying books. A boy on horseback riding through the green fields waved to the train, the afternoon sun splashing gold against his face. This—and points west—was Herbert's country. At this very moment, when he should be feeling the kiss of sunlight, the boy was isolated in prison. How very long the days must seem to him.

As the sun set, Flanagan saw the silver ribbon of the Snake River curving through the plains of wheat. The sky was crimson and streaked with gold as the train headed west toward the dawn of a new day. They would be in Portland, Oregon, the next day. Nate had arranged for him to join actor and comedian Will Rogers for lunch and then on to briefly visit with Oregon Governor Julius Meier.

Flanagan looked forward to seeing his friend. Will Rogers had visited the home the year before when he was on a national speaking tour. With all the planned stops on this trip, Flanagan would need a good night's rest. He fatigued easily and had a persistent cough. He would tell Nate to dine without him that evening and have a bit of supper sent in to him.

His arrival in Portland was an understated affair. He stepped into a taxi and was whisked away to the Benson Hotel. Within minutes Rogers came trotting down the marble staircase to warmly shake his hand. The following day, after they had visited Governor Meier, Flanagan was back on the train, heading north toward Seattle. Rogers rode along with him as far north as Tacoma, where he would set sail for Manchuria to become a war correspondent. Before departing he was determined to give Flanagan a gift.

Rogers took a notepad and pen and scrawled down the message that would be sent to newspapers across the continent: "I have known Father Flanagan for many years and he is a very fine man and has a wonderful boys' home. I know that Herbert Niccolls will be a better man if Father Flanagan has him in charge."

On Flanagan's arrival in Seattle, he was astounded to see a crowd waiting at the King Street Station. He slipped into an overcoat and stumbled toward the door, amid passengers—armed with packages, luggage and umbrellas—who were also pushing down the aisle.

Hundreds of people gathered on the platform and spilled into the station. Could they all be here to see him? As he stepped onto the platform, they began to cheer and applaud. A dark-haired woman in a fine fur-trimmed coat stepped up and extended her hand.

Armene Lamson then introduced him to the man at her side, Mr. Oliver Morris of the *Seattle Post-Intelligencer*, who had a car waiting to take him to the Washington Athletic Club where he would have a few hours to freshen up a bit before the reception in his honor.

Morris led them through the station like Moses parting the sea, into a sedan waiting near the curb and then out into Seattle, where rain pooled in the streets and dripped from telephone wires. Out on Elliott Bay a ferry blasted its mournful horn and the seagulls cried and circled. Beneath the pavilion at Occidental Park, ragged men huddled on park benches and gazed at the sedan with vacant eyes.

To save the man, save the boy, was Flanagan's philosophy. Indeed, he would fight for the life of a child. He could no more ignore a child living in prison than he could ignore a child drowning.

•

Seattle was a small compact city with a cold sea smell rising from the fishing boats at the piers and from the farmers' market on Pike Street, and yet it had an emerging sophistication, with its sleek terra cotta Smith Tower, the tallest building on the West Coast, and the regal Frederick & Nelson department store with its popular tearoom. Mrs. Lamson spoke of her work, opening the Free Parental Clinic.

To anyone who knew her, Mrs. O. E. Lamson personified charm and graciousness, and it had kept her and all that she embraced in the papers from the front page to the society columns. Although her name was inscribed in Seattle's "Blue Book," a who's who among society, which included a heavy representation of old Seattle's timber money, she would never be dismissed as merely a captain of pink teas and charity balls. She was a devoted crusader for child welfare, inspired by her own experiences in war-ravaged Armenia.

As the daughter of the head of the Protestant church there, she had escaped the massacres by moving to Smyrna with her family. She had attended American schools in Smyrna, later gone to college in Germany, and finally enrolled in Johns Hopkins University Medical School. She met the handsome University of Pennsylvania fullback and 1905 All American, Otis Lamson, while both were engaged in research projects in Alaska. They married in 1913 and later moved to Seattle where Otis began his medical practice as a surgeon. Armene in turn became the child welfare crusader and the steam that launched civic projects, ranging from the Seattle Civic Opera and the National League of American Penwomen to the Seattle Lighthouse for the Blind. Flanagan sensed, too, that beneath the gilt wrappings of a life of affluence in her home on the shores of Lake Washington, Mrs. Armene Lamson was a driven woman. She had a brilliant mind, was a natural leader, and was the perfect person to lead the campaign to free Herbert Niccolls. When she spoke, the public listened. That was apparent by the fact that reporters had turned to her, as a writer and expert in child psychology, for an opinion on the sentence.

Her involvement in the case began one morning while she sat across the table from Otis at breakfast. As the dawn seeped into the warm kitchen, she picked up the morning newspaper to read about a twelve-year-old murderer being sent to prison for life. It was horrifying but the plight of the boy would do more than just shock her, it energized her. She wrote the governor a letter immediately, and when she read of Flanagan's interest in the case, she wrote to him as well.

When Otis came home from making his hospital rounds that night he found her furiously typing at the desk in their bedroom. She hadn't heard him come in. He walked quietly across the Persian carpet, removed his tie and laid it on his bed. It was a pleasant room, soothing with an unassuming view of the lake. From the window he could see the slate gray lake and the rain shimmering on cedars. He could hear the voices of his three children rising and falling in cadences of laughter and smell the aroma of dinner drifting through the house.

He quietly went to greet his children, knowing that his wife's latest campaign would consume her for a very long time.

•

Now that Flanagan was in Seattle, Mrs. Lamson believed the governor would relent. Surely, the governor couldn't hold out much longer, given the public pressure. There were people who thought Herbert belonged in prison—primarily Hartley supporters. She had been one herself until recently, but it had begun to seem like the once staunch supporter of holding the line on taxes was out of control. He had even lost the backing of his own party.

She hated to tell Father Flanagan that even though she had extended the most cordial invitation to Hartley, he had declined to attend either the reception or the dinner. The governor did send a brief message saying, "Welcome from the people of the State of Washington."

As they arrived at the Washington Athletic Club, Morris and Jacobs quickly whisked Flanagan inside and up to a room in the private club where some of the most prominent Seattle citizens were members. Mrs. Lamson had arranged for Father Flanagan's room to be the best the club had to offer, with a view of Elliott Bay and a large arrangement of flowers.

As she left the priest in the hands of the club staff, she went to the dining room to check on the preparations for dinner. The club bustled with industry as white-coated waiters set tables; the club manager assured her that everything was well under control, but a small worry unfurled inside her. The most critical guest had snubbed them. What if this was all for nothing? What if Hartley never agreed to even speak with Father Flanagan? The manager showed her the list of hors d'oeuvres. It was very basic. The Depression and Prohibition made life so dull. She nodded her acceptance, pulled her coat close, and stepped through the doors held open by the uniformed doorman and into a cab. She had just enough time to go home, kiss the children, make certain Otis was wearing his black suit, freshen up and slip into her black evening gown. It was her favorite—cutaway velvet with a low neckline—and she accented it with a garnet choker, matching earrings, and a fat garnet bracelet.

•

The room glowed amber beneath the chandelier and laughter bubbled like champagne. Mrs. Lamson, in a stunning array of finery and flanked by her handsome husband, swept toward Flanagan the minute he came into the room. Immediately, the priest was surrounded by the crowd. Whenever he needed to be rescued and steered toward another group, Mrs. Lamson was at his side guiding him.

The reception and dinner passed almost as quickly. Afterward he gave a speech, urging continued pressure on the governor on behalf of the "young lad languishing in prison, the boy who had never known a father's protection or a mother's love."

As he told the gathering, "I have come not as a critic but as a citizen to offer my humble home as the solution to this problem. If you have an institution in this state where the boy can be saved for society, then let him go there. If not, I want to take him to my home.

"Of the 3,000 boys we have had there, none ever took another false step. And we have had boys who were much more of a problem than I believe Herbert Niccolls to be. If the good governor would give the boy a chance—he never has had one—I personally will supervise his training and education."

His words were met by rousing applause. Then others came forward and pledged their support and that of their associations. A. E. McCabe, representing the American Legion said that he had wired a message to the governor, indicating that 30,000 members of the Legion and its auxiliaries strongly favored the boy's being paroled to the home. Representatives of eighty-one Parent-Teacher Associations had also pledged their support. So did teachers' associations and school administrators and clergy by the dozen. But what concerned Flanagan the most was the governor's absence. The purpose of the trip was to meet the governor, and yet there was little more than silence from Olympia.

Immediately following dinner, he was due at the KXA radio studio to speak live about his campaign to save the boy. Shortly after that, he would broadcast a message over KOL.

"If I am defeated in obtaining this boy," he said, "it will not be a defeat for me, but it will be another defeat for society. All I ask is that Herbert be given a chance—a chance to use the only thing he has not had a chance to use, his life, the one that God gave him when he was brought into this world."

That night Flanagan fell into bed exhausted, trying to ignore his shortness of breath and the fatigue that made his body feel heavy. The following morning he called and left a message with the governor's secretary. The hours passed. If he stepped outside the club, he was joined by a crowd of followers who trailed behind him down the street to radio stations and newspaper offices where he was to be interviewed. The *Seattle Times*, to his chagrin, afterward wrote an editorial saying that concern about the boy was misplaced. "The boy is better off now than he ever was in his life," the *Times* said. In fact, this was the case. For the first time in Herbert's life, he wasn't beaten, had regular food to eat, as well as structure, warm clothing, shelter, and regular education.

Most of Flanagan's contact with the press resulted in favorable publicity for the cause and he didn't let the *Times* editorial discourage him. He busied himself with writing radio speeches, consulting with Nate, and sending telegrams to the farm with instructions for Father P.A., his brother and acting director when he was away. Had this child recovered from his measles? Was the other's rash chicken pox? He disliked being away from the boys. They needed him and he needed them. He loved them as much as any father loved a child. And here in Washington it seemed that there was no progress—nothing except the rain drumming endlessly against the streets.

Late in the afternoon, after he had returned from tea with Monsignor Ryan at the rectory of Saint James Cathedral, he was jarred from his writing by a knock at the door. The bellboy handed him a telegram. It was from Olympia.

"Will be at Washington Hotel, Seattle, tomorrow after four o'clock. Roland Hartley, Governor."

He quickly called Nate who was visiting Oliver's office in the *Post-Intelligencer* newsroom. He would get his meeting with Hartley! He called Mrs. Lamson as well, and she said that surely this must mean good news. The governor wants to run for a third term and surely he has bowed to the sentiment of the people, she said.

Over a small dinner party at her home that night, they toasted his health and a bright future for Herbert Niccolls. The next day, Nate, Oliver, and a flock of reporters clustered in the lobby of the hotel, while Father Flanagan went upstairs to the governor's suite alone. About twenty minutes later he came down and they looked at him expectantly. The governor had promised to give pardoning Herbert his full consideration and would inform him of his decision.

"Governor Hartley gave me the most sympathetic interview and I am convinced he has Herbert's best interest at heart," Flanagan told the reporters. "He told me he had made an investigation of my school and he understands what it stands for and what I am after. He said he would let me know his decision soon."

In the meantime, Flanagan decided to stay in Seattle for a few more days in case the governor needed him. In the meantime, Hartley would not allow Flanagan to meet with Herbert.

It was hard for Flanagan to bear. He felt short of breath and extremely tired. He preached in two Seattle churches, Saint James and the Church of the Immaculate Conception, and continued to wait. He tried to be optimistic but, in reality, nothing had changed. The boy was still in prison. Several days later, he realized that everything that could be done in Washington had been done. He notified Mrs. Lamson that he would be leaving in the morning for California and would await the governor's decision there.

She protested his plans to depart. The governor hadn't yet reached a decision. Couldn't he speak at more public functions, raise more support for the boy?

He apologized and said he really must leave. Once he was back on the train he gazed out the window. Mrs. Lamson, Oliver and a group of well-wishers had seen him off, and they all looked solemn as the train slowly pulled away from the station. Then he collapsed against the seat. He was feeling so weak. He was going to see a specialist in vitamin therapy in Los Angeles. Perhaps vitamin therapy would help him with his chronic respiratory condition, which had plagued him since childhood and robbed him of the energy he so desperately needed. But most important, while in Los Angeles, he wanted to see William Randolph Hearst. In fact, Nate was already setting it up.

California's seventy-degree November weather was a wonderful relief after the Washington damp. Flanagan breathed easier, relaxed amid the orange groves and walnut orchards not far from the small clinic by the sea. He sent another telegram to the governor letting him know that he could be reached at the Ambassador Hotel and again urged him to consider a pardon. Nate had already left and returned to Omaha. Although the clinic's physician urged Flanagan to stay for a few days for a series of vitamin injections, he was anxious to get into the city to meet with the nation's most influential publisher.

On the day of the appointment, he sat in Hearst's spacious office at the *Los Angeles Examiner*. The publisher leaned back in his chair and listened carefully as the story of Herbert's sad life unfolded. Hearst asked what he could do.

If Governor Hartley declined to help the boy, an editorial supporting the release of Herbert to Overlook Farm would be a great help, Flanagan told him.

Consider it done, Hearst said. How could he not rise to the cause when his own mother was among the founders of what became the Parent-Teacher Association? Hearst asked Flanagan to notify him as soon as he heard from the governor.

As Flanagan was about to leave Los Angeles for Omaha, he once again sent a telegram to Hartley:

I regret that you have not had the opportunity to wire or phone me at my expense as per my telegraphed request. . . . I have 200 homeless boys . . . that need my attention and I do not wish to stay away from them any longer than absolutely necessary. Therefore, I am leaving for Omaha tonight. I hope that you and the board will not keep this poor unfortunate boy behind prison walls any longer so that I may take him to share the joys of Christmas dinner with the other unfortunate . . . boys at my institution. If a doctor is not permitted to reach his sick patient until a disease is incurable, the doctor has no chance. In this case, I happen to be the doctor and Herbert's incarceration in his lonely cell is the ravaging malady that is tearing away his very soul. Please do not make the mistake of keeping this unfortunate boy behind prison bars any longer because a few more months in the terrible environment in Walla Walla will have a devastating influence on the rest of his life. Nothing good can be accomplished by delay of the parole board. I appeal to you as one who has the prerogative to make a useful citizen out of Herbert Niccolls rather than a hardened criminal. The murder committed by this mere child cannot rest upon his twelve-year-old shoulders but must be placed upon the shoulders of a society that permitted such a child to grow up so neglected and unwanted. In the name of all that is sacred and holy on which American citizenship is founded, I again plead with you to come to the rescue of this unfortunate boy.

Ten days later, he sent another plea and as he did so, it seemed as if his words had sailed into the darkness of space.

•

Snow had come early to Omaha. It greeted him as he stepped from the train at the station. Father P.A. met him, eagerly waiting for the latest news. As they lifted the luggage into the trunk of the car, snow swarmed from the dark sky. The flakes dusted their black coats and sheeted the windshield as they drove out of the city into the country. There, the only sound was the hum of the motor and the low, easy conversation of brothers, kindred spirits from the old sod.

The weeks passed and still there was no word from Hartley. The letters, he knew, must be pouring in. The Jacobs brothers had done their best.

"Yesterday, I sent you some dope on the battle that Father Flanagan . . . is putting on to get the pardon of a twelve-year-old murderer," Morris Jacobs wrote to *Time* magazine's Henry Luce. "I'm sending you some more stuff today. . . . I believe this has the possibilities for a peach of a feature because of the nationwide interest in this case."

"Here's a stunt you might pull either in your column or in one of your radio programs," he wrote to Walter Winchell at *The Daily Mirror* in New York. "There's a tremendous fight going on between Father Flanagan . . . and Gov. Hartley."

It was a fight indeed. Flanagan had done all he could. He had done several radio talks and a number of interviews with reporters and had received support from hundreds of good, kind people, including requests to take other children to live at Overlook Farm.

"I have a boy staying with me who is thirteen years old. . . . His mother is dead and so is his father. His stepfather kicked him out of the house in St. Louis, Mo., and he has been tramping about all over the country for several years. . . . I feel that your home would be the place for him."

All over the country children younger than sixteen were traveling alone, ostensibly sent to live with relatives or friends when their families could no longer afford to care for them. But often there were no waiting or welcoming homes on the receiving end. Sometimes a boy ended up at

Overlook Farm, with nothing more than a bundle of clothing tied onto a stick that was carried over his shoulder, hoping that if he got to the farm, he'd be taken in.

Mrs. Lamson had written about it as well. "Vagabond children" showed up at her medical clinic looking for food and shelter. "I sent them to the community lodging house. They came back during the night. They were robbed or subjected to inhumane indignities. . . . The child under eighteen is really a public charge. . . . Your neighboring states could send you such boys."

At the moment Flanagan had limited his home to 200 boys, and he could take additional boys only in extreme cases. Many children he had to place on farms or in foster homes because, with the downturn in contributions that the Depression brought, he could not feed them. He hated turning children away. Farmers were always anxious to take boys in the spring when the crops needed planting but by late fall, when the harvest was over, the farmers, who had pledged to love the boys, would bring them back because they were "no longer working out." It was devastating to the boys. He hoped the home would eventually be able to grow again. He could see 500 children there and maybe even more as additional buildings were added and the staff increased. Some day the farm would be a city of boys, run by boys, a Boys Town. That was his dream.

When the telegram arrived, he eagerly read it, hoping that it meant Herbert would come to Overlook Farm by Christmas.

"The Governor is on his way to Olympia. He will fully advise you later," wrote R. M. Kinnear, of the Prison Control Board.

So Hartley had met with the board. Perhaps now the governor would make a decision. And if the decision was not favorable? Flanagan felt more committed than ever to fight for the boy.

•

Wind howled around the eaves of his office, sweeping snow into deep drifts. Winter had fallen on the farm. The horses in the barn grew heavy winter coats, blew steamy gusts, and stomped impatiently in the stalls. The older boys, bundled in mufflers and caps, squatted on milk stools, burying their foreheads against the cows' soft flanks as they shot streams of warm milk into icy buckets. The younger boys ran through dormitory hallways and squirmed in their seats during their lessons, tired of being housebound as the snow continued to fall and the wind to blow. The postman brought the mail in a horse-drawn sleigh because the truck couldn't get through. The day's mail brought a letter from F. G. Burns in Seattle.

Dear Father, I had a talk with my niece this afternoon. She lives with my sister Amy, who is the Governor's secretary. I asked her how the governor felt about the case of Herbert Niccolls and she said that he was still undecided as yet what to do as he alone would be responsible for anything that Herbert might do of a criminal nature. If he released him and anything happened, public sentiment would condemn him.

It seems the governor considers him a born criminal and hesitates on that account. I would consider this authentic as it was a private conversation between my niece and Amy. . . . No one knows I've written you, not even any one in my own family.

A couple of weeks ago, I sent a message to Amy by my niece to the effect that public sentiment was very strongly in favor of Herbert being paroled to you and that if [Hartley] expected to run for governor again he was losing lots of votes. Amy's answer was that he fully realized that but on account of Herbert's innate criminal tendencies were undecided what to do with him.

I am of the opinion that you will get the boy, but on account of so much publicity and the row in the papers . . . he will take his own sweet time about releasing him.

If the governor doesn't respond to your numerous requests, my suggestion would be to drop the matter entirely at least for the present . . . continued requests will only irritate him more.

Kindly consider this confidential as it is best the governor's office know nothing about my correspondence with you regarding the case. . . . I will probably see Amy at Christmas and will try and find out something definite and let you know.

Flanagan was delighted to receive the letter—an inside source, a link to the governor's office—and he quickly wrote in return, asking if Mr. Burns knew whether the parole board had taken action. Mrs. Lamson had written, too, noting how disgusted he must be with the state. She also inquired about his abrupt departure and noted with anxiety his silence since leaving Seattle.

He flushed with embarrassment. He had been so absorbed in outlining the next strategy in fighting for the boy that he had forgotten to even thank her for her hospitality or the flowers she and the doctor had sent to his room.

I had intended writing several times but I kept postponing it for this one reason—I wanted to be able to wire you the good tidings that the governor would parole the boy to me but, alas, the good Governor has not seen fit to keep his word and now at the eleventh hour, I am writing you this note.

Not having heard from the Governor, I wrote him a nice long letter a week ago yesterday. I hope that through this nice letter, I might be able to get some expression from him. I told him that I knew his heart was particularly kind and loving to children, and that I had known of several cases where he had paroled boys and young men from the penitentiary. I also stated that I would like to be able to send a message concerning the fine spirit of the governor as evidenced by his parole of Herbert Niccolls over our radio stations where we broadcast an educational program every Sunday. It seems though that the governor will not even answer this letter, and I am surely heartsick.

Then he added the courtesies—how he treasured the memories of his visit to Seattle and meeting the many "fine and noble people" so concerned with child welfare, and his delight in meeting Dr. Lamson who reminded him so much of his brother-in-law, a notable Omaha physician. But mostly, he thanked her for the article she wrote in support of his campaign to win the boy.

"It is very fine and very beautiful. I am not going to let up, and I need a lot of advice and counsel from those who have taken such wonderful interest in the case lest I might make some mistake to the detriment of the boy. We all want this boy out of the penitentiary. Whether our home gets him or not is beside the question. I had hoped that we might be able to have him out by Christmas but it does look disappointing now."

Then he added the letter he had received from the man whose niece was Hartley's secretary.

> The writer speaks of occasions where the governor paroled two boys, one fifteen and the other 21. It might be a fine thing if we could get quietly the history of these two cases, as later I may want to use them but not now. Perhaps Mr. [Bob] Bermann of the *P-I* might look them up?
>
> Thanking you dear Mrs. Lamson, and wishing you and your good husband and splendid family God's every blessing for a happy and holy Christmas season and kindly tell my little pal, Armene (Mrs. Lamson's daughter), that I often think of her. I remain sincerely yours.

•

When he had received the highly confidential letter regarding the other cases, Flanagan was intrigued. If Hartley could parole those two youths, why not Herbert Niccolls?

Why not indeed? The cases were worth exploring and his friends at the *Post-Intelligencer* would be certain to help.

How could the governor refuse? The movement to free the child was a juggernaut rolling steadily toward the capitol in Olympia. If Hartley continued to resist, it would crush him. Already his constituents had turned against him and from what the papers said, the governor's support had been waning even before the campaign to pardon Herbert began.

Hartley had been called the "enemy of public education." He was embroiled in a battle with a Senate committee that wanted to audit the books from several state agencies—a right he refused to grant them because he considered the books his personal property. Members of his own party were still angry over his firing the University of Washington president and stripping the university budget. Legislators were angry because he had vetoed a graduated personal income tax and a corporate income tax that was designed to stimulate the economy and help the unemployed and destitute. In fact, the unemployed called him hard-hearted for opposing state unemployment compensation, and families suffering the bite of the Depression were horrified when he said there wasn't any Depression, that men and women simply needed to pick themselves up by their bootstraps. They pointed to the ever-widening gap between themselves and him—with his fabulous mansion in Ever-ett, north of Seattle, its roller-skating rink and garage that was bigger than most houses. The garage was so deluxe that it had a special room for bathing his 1914 Pierce-Arrow and a turntable so he would never have to back the car out. Instead, he would merely spin it around with one hand—the turntable was well designed. The governor who had been elected in the years of bounty was no longer a kindred spirit in times of hardship. Hartley didn't need another fight.

•

Five days before Christmas, a letter with an Olympia, Washington, post-mark arrived in the mail. Flanagan let it sit on his desk a moment, afraid to open it. And then, at last, he plunged the letter opener into the enve-lope and tore it open. Page after page bristled with indignation.

"Because of the youth of this boy, his case attracted nationwide at-tention and furnished opportunity for sensational newspapers to wring the heart strings of highly emotional and sympathetic people. Special writers were dispatched to the ordinarily peaceful town of Asotin, where Herbert was photographed in his working clothes, better to give charac-ter to the exploitation that was to follow," Hartley wrote.

He argued that Herbert's true character and history were not revealed by the reporters who instead portrayed him "as a neglected orphan who had never had a chance. Sympathetic people, particularly those far re-moved from the scene of the crime, were stirred by these subtle mis-representations and persuaded that this boy was being dealt with inhu-manely and that a grave injustice had been done."

Following the trial, after the boy had been delivered to the peniten-tiary "you entered the case, seizing the opportunity to direct nationwide attention to your boys' home, facilitated by the sensational publicity that had [accompanied] the trial. The people whose sympathies had been stirred by the newspaper accounts of the trial viewed your appeal as an act of mercy that no state or governor should deny. These sensational newspapers had almost despaired of keeping the Niccolls case on the front page when you came to the rescue. What a happy situation—Father Flanagan needed the newspapers as a vehicle to supplement his appeals; the newspapers needed Father Flanagan in the role of humanitarian.

"For weeks misleading and false statements went out through the press, from the pulpit and from . . . radio stations, over which you appealed to the entire nation to help get this boy, urging that the governor be overwhelmed with letters. Many people throughout the nation, misinformed by you and the newspapers, responded to this urge. Not a word of consolation or sympathy was extended to the bereaved family of the sheriff who was killed in the performance of his duty—seven brothers and sisters, a wife and four children, entirely forgotten."

Hartley said that he found it deplorable that a man of Flanagan's training would overlook all the facts in the case and that Flanagan, before getting involved, owed that careful research to the officials of the state and the Asotin County officers who had met the difficult responsibility with courage and wisdom.

The fact is that Herbert Niccolls was brought to Asotin in May 1931, by his grandmother, who hoped new surroundings and associations might be the means of changing the course of the boy, who had been involved in serious crimes since eight years of age. This past record was unknown to the citizens of Asotin until the killing of the sheriff.

Contrary to published reports and nationwide radio broadcasts, Herbert Niccolls was born . . . in an average religious farm home, received the sympathetic affection of the average child from his parents, is not an orphan, nor has he been abandoned.

In my judgment, nothing in recent years has taken place so detrimental to the youth of our land as the melodramatic publicity and exploitation which attended your trip to the State of Washington and the request to have this boy turned over to your institution.

Herbert's complex has baffled his parents, other relatives, institutions, and a generous friend who took him from the Idaho Industrial School into a home of refinement and luxury, where he was given every advantage, including schooling, instruction in music and association with two wonderful children. It was hoped that under careful supervision, he would emerge with a degree of dependability that would enable him to again be safe to be at large. All of these influences failed.

Hartley said that he was deeply impressed by the public sympathy for the boy but that it was misplaced. A well-ordered routine fills the boy's day and he has lessons from Walla Walla Superintendent of Schools Dr. W. M. Kern, who examined him and found him up to date in his educational requirements, proving that his lessons had not been neglected.

The case also concerned legal issues, Hartley wrote. Once the boy was permitted to leave the state, his relatives could take him anywhere. It would be tantamount to giving him a complete release. "Legal authority over the boy could not be vested in you or any other agency outside of this state by executive action."

From the indictment contained in your telegram to me from Los Angeles . . . one would be led to believe this state was a wild African jungle with no institutions or facilities for caring for and helping the wayward attain or regain the privileges of citizenship. Our people and institutions rank with the finest in this republic. Our hearts are warm. Herbert Niccolls will never suffer from neglect while he is a ward of this commonwealth.

Herbert Niccolls is not the first boy of tender years to be incarcerated for life in the penitentiary at Walla Walla. . . . In one particular case coming under my observation, the boy was not permitted to associate with hardened or older criminals. I released him from the penitentiary with better than a high school education and well equipped by training to take his place outside. Herbert Niccolls will be equally well cared for.

On a recent visit to the penitentiary, Hartley had visited the boy for two hours, noting that he had gained ten pounds since going to prison and had a well planned routine of study and exercise "under the guidance of men eminently fitted to study and direct him."

In a prison yard, accompanied by only an assigned inmate, Herbert did handsprings and played handball during his thirty minutes of daily outdoor time, Warden Long told the governor. "He's happy here."

"Herbert Niccolls is, at present, unsafe to be at large," Hartley wrote. This case would be the responsibility of the State of Washington. "The chief executive would be derelict in his duty should he undertake to transfer his responsibility to an agency in another state."

•

So there it was. Hartley preferred to allow the boy to languish and instead take shots at Father Flanagan's motives as being purely a publicity stunt to gain attention on behalf of the home. Nothing ever in his life stung so badly.

If the governor would not budge, then war it would be. When it came to rescuing children in need, he would not spare himself. Flanagan was stunned that Hartley could be so ignorant as to believe that Herbert Niccolls had come from a normal home with caring parents. The priest had seen enough families maintain the thin image of respectability to hide a festering hell for a youngster. He had seen homes where violence and want were all too common.

Flanagan also wondered about the governor's reference to Herbert as not being the "first boy of tender years" to be held at the penitentiary. Was he referring to the boys that Mr. Burns mentioned in his letter? Did the state make a practice of illegally warehousing problem juveniles in prisons with adult criminals?

It was only a matter of hours before the phone started ringing. Reporters from around the nation wanted to know his response to Hartley's attack. The governor had made the letter public. Flanagan knew he must respond. He sat down and began to write.

Gov. Hartley was within his honored province as chief executive of the State of Washington when he denied the parole of Herbert Niccolls, the unfortunate twelve-year-old murderer.

But when he deplored my efforts and cast insinuations upon my sincere motives in trying to obtain the boy's release, he stepped into the gutter of ward politics.

Gov. Hartley made the statement that well corroborated experts advised him that Herbert is beyond being saved. As a student of sociology and with fifteen years of experience in the handling of wayward boys, I am interested in knowing from whom the governor obtained this advice.

What a pity and a shame that Gov. Hartley should base his opinion on such evidence when students of sociology are aware that heredity is a minor influence on a child and that environment is the chief influence that determines character.

Herbert's environment, and not heredity, prompted him to do the things that led to the tragic day when he pulled the trigger and killed a peace officer. What Herbert, who is little more than a baby, did and what he is today, is not because of his true heart or mind but it is the result of poor home environment and bad influence on his first twelve years of life.

Flanagan bitterly resented the accusation that the purpose of his campaign to seek custody of the boy was to obtain national publicity for his boys' home. "Father Flanagan's Boys Home needs no publicity. I was surprised that such attacks would come from the executive mansion of the fine State of Washington. To me it sounds like the . . . mutterings of a whipped political boss."

Hartley should be ashamed to disregard the public interest in helping the boy by calling those who wrote letters to him "over emotional and sentimental." Troubled children can have new lives if given a chance, Flanagan wrote. One of the model boys of the home was a boy who had killed when he was only nine years of age.

"I can't believe that it is Gov. Hartley himself making such a venomous and undeserved attack upon me and our institution, but that he has been ill advised; and if he has not, then in my humble opinion he is making Herbert Niccolls a political football.

"What a Christmas for Herbert!"

Newspapers from coast to coast carried the statement. They also carried a story that quoted Prosecutor Halsey and Eastern State Hospital's Superintendent Semple, who likened the boy to "a young tiger after its first kill."

In another story, an Associated Press reporter quoted Warden Clarence Long as saying the boy is "happy as a lark" and doing well. The boy, Long said, was unaware of the fight going on for his custody and that people everywhere had sent the boy Christmas gifts, many more than he can use, Long said. "The lad is gaining in weight, has been getting a daily routine of study, play, sleep and wholesome food and literally hasn't a care in the world."

Flanagan hoped that this was true but would never be convinced that prison was a proper place for a youngster, even one who had made a terrible mistake. There were seven boy-murderers of the 3,000 who had passed through the doors at Flanagan's boys' home since it opened. The fight for Herbert was not over. Flanagan decided that it was time to call Hearst with Hartley's response.

Flanagan clasped the slender neck of the phone, picked up the receiver and asked the operator for California.

•

Three days later as the sun broke through the clouds and webs of ice and snow turned brilliant with light, Flanagan was summoned to the telephone.

It was Mr. Jacobs, a sister said, appearing in the doorway, and it was urgent. For a fleeting minute Flanagan thought Hartley had changed his mind. The governor? he asked. No, Hearst, Jacobs said. William Randolph came through. Had he seen the newspaper? There it was. In every Hearst paper across the nation, an editorial written by Hearst himself in support of giving Father Flanagan custody of the boy.

In upholding the sentence of life imprisonment for a boy of twelve, Governor Hartley said that experts had advised him that the youth is beyond being saved and, when Father Flanagan asked for the boy's release and offered to care for and train him, the governor stated that the purpose of the request was to obtain nationwide publicity for Father Flanagan's Boys Home.

That insult was the small-minded politician speaking the only language that such politicians understand. . . . They cannot imagine anybody doing anything for any other reason.

Father Flanagan has no such motive. He is a high-minded and splendidly worthy man, conducting a greatly needed and very greatly beneficial institution, and it is an outrage that he should be attacked and his motives questioned simply because he happens to disagree with Governor Hartley on the proper treatment of a degenerate youth.

According to the very best sociological and penalogical [sic] thought, it is Governor Hartley who is old-fashioned and reactionary and un-Christian, if not uncivilized, and it is Father Flanagan who is modern and progressive, following alike the gospel of Christ and the light of modern thought and civilization.

While the governor is still floundering in the dark ages of punishment as the only cure for crime, the priest sees the light of modern scientific criminology as a gleam of the light of the world.

Hearst certainly had come to the rescue and it made Flanagan feel better. The children were gathering in the dining hall to decorate a fir tree with red-and-green paper chains and paper snowflakes. He went to join them and lift the littlest one up to place an angel at the very top. He believed it was his privilege to care for them. Flanagan never stopped being able to see Herbert at the farm. He could imagine him as the boys gathered around the tables for grace, as they sat in the chapel and knelt in prayer, as they threw snowballs and made ice angels, as they studied and sang and ran pell-mell through the halls—with a sister trailing after them, telling them to slow down.

Flanagan thought of Herbert in prison at Christmas, far from the candlelight of the chapel, the incense drifting among the smell of evergreen boughs, the colors and scents of the season. At twelve, Herbert Niccolls was alone on the most special day of the year.

•

Armene Lamson sent a holiday telegram to Father Flanagan, wishing him a Merry Christmas and emphasizing that Hartley's attack did not hurt the cause and had prompted a number of editorials in defense. She said she and some of Oliver Morris's staff on the *Post-Intelligencer* were trying to get information about the boys that Hartley had paroled. She also sent her own story, defending him.

"Father Flanagan's interest in this child did not differ from that given to any others [at the home]. He told us: 'They are all children of God, therefore my brothers.' . . . Regardless of how we may attempt to justify our treatment of Herbert, the facts remain that the boy was a helpless victim of circumstances. . . . Even though it may hurt our pride, we owe every effort to salvage this boy."

Oliver Morris had written to congratulate him on his reply to Hartley, noting that the governor had "abysmal ignorance of modern, scientific methods of treating juvenile crime," and that the governor's attitude "has cooked his goose in politics. I don't think he can be elected to anything again. So your visit has accomplished one big good for the state anyway," Morris said.

"On the whole, your effort to get the Niccolls boy has been highly successful. It has centered the attention of the entire nation on the archaic methods of treating child offenders and has made a big man out of you and a very small one indeed out of Gov. Hartley . . ."

Morris went on: "I think, too, that if Herbert's confinement in a penitentiary for a year or so more will not cause you to change your opinion about the possibility of redeeming him for society, that you can get him in due time. Public opinion is with you and we will have a new governor within a year."

One year in prison. Did anyone know what could happen to a child there? If he wasn't raped, he could learn from the worst of criminals. Prison was no place to spend a childhood, even though Herbert desperately needed discipline and structure. No child of twelve was a criminal, and particularly one such as Herbert, Flanagan believed. Herbert never had the chance to know the finer things in life—not possessions, but love and security, a family and a home. He'd never get that living in a prison cell. Those who heard Flanagan's radio address and wrote understood. He wondered why the governor didn't. Even citizens far outside the state were pleased that Hartley's political career was over.

"You have driven Gov. Hartley out of public life," Thomas S. Kennedy, a Washington D.C., attorney wrote. "I doubt if he will receive a nomination for any office in the future. No party can risk such a type as he has shown himself to be."

Flanagan couldn't agree more with a letter that had come from a Des Moines, Iowa, lawyer, Charles O. Holly, who noted, "Every crime that is committed is, to some extent, the crime of society."

The longer the boy remained in the penitentiary, the more difficult it would be for any agency or school to be able to rehabilitate him. Eventually only God would be able to save him. Flanagan wrote to Oliver:

> I think it would be a splendid thing if Mrs. Lamson would write the story of the Herbert Niccolls's case. . . . But it would be most important that all the facts be brought out in his case and not hearsay. The defense attorney, Mr. E. J. Doyle . . . would be very happy, I am sure, to give all those details. It seems the governor and the prosecuting attorney have accused this child of crimes that have not been proven. The commission of those crimes did not come up but have been used since then in statements detrimental to the boy's character . . . as a sustaining argument against his parole. I refer to statements that he put a bomb under the church when the congregation was inside and stole money from the collection. . . . Think of a little twelve-year-old boy helpless and alone and unable to fight back these accusations, and think of the cruelty and the unsportsmanship of a prosecuting attorney and governor making statements such as these.

The truth needed to be made public, and it seemed Mrs. Lamson would be the one to do it. A woman's touch to such a story would make it more of a masterpiece than any he could write.

In the meantime, Flanagan would wait for Oliver and Bob Bermann to find the names of the boys that the governor had paroled—apparently during a kinder day. In the meantime, he would have to let things lie and hope for a more humane chief executive in Olympia in the next year. The papers could do the talking. He needed to look after the home. Donations still were only trickling in and another mortgage payment was due. Would there ever be a day when the home wasn't a slim margin away from closing its doors? Did the world not understand that when you help a child today, you write the history of tomorrow? He felt tired and discouraged. The year was coming to a close. It seemed he had accomplished little.

The night was still and the twigs outside his window were brittle with ice. Frost bloomed on the panes. The clock chimed the hour. The oldest children would be saying their prayers, the youngest sailing through dreamland. The fire in his stove crackled and popped. He poured himself a cup of tea and went to his desk. He would read a few more letters before turning in.

On the top of the stack was a thin blue envelope with the spidery penmanship of someone who wrote with elegance and care. He brought the paper into the lamplight and read it a first and then a second time. The fight to save Herbert Niccolls had made possible what would one day be known as Boys Town.

Mr. and Mrs. Elias Smithier, early settlers of Danville, Kansas, had read about his fight for the custody of Herbert Niccolls and were touched by how deeply he cared for children. He was doing God's work among them, claiming young lives for Christ through gentleness and love, they wrote. In admiration, they wanted to give his Boys Home a gift—240 acres of good farmland.

Then they added, "Merry Christmas, Father Flanagan!"

Chapter 12

GOVERNOR HARTLEY was having his breakfast when the telephone rang. The newspaper was spread across the table and without answering the phone he knew what his day would bring. It was the Associated Press. Hartley snatched the phone from the small table in the hall. What was his reaction to Father Flanagan's statement? Did he say the boy was beyond being saved?

They were damn papist lies, of course, Hartley replied. Then he added, "I was misquoted," he told the reporter. "I made no such statement either directly or by intimation. I said, the jury and trial judge showed discrimination and wisdom in placing this boy where he would be legally restrained, pending further study to determine his ultimate ability to take a place in society. Now does that sound to you like I said he was beyond being saved?"

He had, of course, implied that earlier in the letter. The boy's family history was bleak—insane for generations. No one, short of God almighty could turn that life around, not even Flanagan. He had asked

Halsey, McElvain, and Semple to do a report on the boy's life. What they found should chill even Flanagan.

"This boy has winning ways," Halsey said. "He will appeal to your sympathies, but bear in mind, his politeness, his seeming candor, that he is above the average intelligence of a boy his age, and added to the intelligence, he will lie, steal, commit burglary and kill. A dangerous combination to the welfare of society."

During the trial, the boy had been taken for a walk by a deputy and managed to secret away a rock. He later tore a piece of sheet and made a billy. McElvain said, "I think the Northwest Council of Socialworkers should give more of their time to the good needy children, than to spend so much time trying to get a born criminal into society."

As the experts concluded at the trial, the boy was a born criminal, bad since early childhood. Of that, Hartley was certain.

Flanagan was as tenacious as a burr on a hound, the more the hound scratched the more the burr settled. There was no escaping the subject of Herbert Niccolls. The papers were full of the case, his mail had doubled—if that was possible—and he had received hate mail from people across the country for a case that was simply none of their business.

Last night's *Seattle Times* quoted an editorial from the *New Haven (Conn.) Journal Courier*. It was bad enough that the Hearst newspapers from the *Washington (D.C.) Herald* to the *Los Angeles Examiner* had carried an editorial flaying him for his tough stand on crime, but it seemed astounding that even a New England paper had joined the fray.

With an insane father and a mother fear-stricken because of poverty, without food enough to satisfy a growing boy's appetite [Herbert's] twelve years of experience gave him a distorted view of life. His defense attorney rightly said of those twelve years, 'There was a vacant place in [Herbert's] life and he filled it with his imagination.'

The community probably did not seriously concern itself with Herbert's conduct until he committed murder. It then took the path of least resistance, and sent him to the state prison for the rest of his life.

One wonders why the organized agencies of community welfare did not concern themselves with the case . . . [Herbert] did not become 'bad' all at once. . . . The jury disposed of the child in three hours and as many minutes. But as far as can be found out, the jury had no sentence to pass upon the citizens of Asotin, Washington.

Citizens . . . of every other city and community in the country need to come to the realization that juvenile delinquency does not begin when a crime is committed.

Hartley had only a few years back believed that poverty did have a direct link to crime but when the thought now rose to the surface of his consciousness, he flushed with anger. Trash, that's what it was. He hated the *Times*, more than he hated any newspaper. Ever since Clarence Blethen had humiliated him so badly in 1926 when he started auditing the books of the state Land Commission and complained that the sale of timberlands to private individuals weren't making all the money that they should for the state. Of course, those who wanted to buy the land complained and when Blethen's *Times* asked him about his own background in the timber industry, he told the boys that he had never personally applied to buy timber himself, that he had only acted on behalf of the Cherry Valley Logging Company. In fact, he said he'd wager $1,000, payable to any charity, if anyone could prove that he had applied to buy timber himself. Blethen answered the challenge and published photographs of the application. Somehow the damn reporters had dug up the applications he had filled out in 1910 and 1911 and noted how he had complained about the price of timber being too high. Blethen had topped it all by chortling, "The *Times* asks that Governor Hartley execute his check for $1,000."

He would not be undone by any of them. As if he didn't have enough on his mind. He didn't dare even leave the state for a moment or that long-eared son-of-a-gun Lieutenant Governor John Gellatly might parole Niccolls or approve the income tax. Gellatly was capable of all sorts of mischief. Stealing the Republican nomination was one of them. That's why he made it plain to the reporters who asked, that while he traveled throughout the state, he never crossed outside the state's boundary. If he did, control of the state would temporarily shift to Gellatly. As long as he was the governor, he had no intention of relinquishing that power for an hour or a day.

Now Gellatly, Lands Commissioner Clark Savidge, and State Senator W. J. Sutton wanted him to divulge the results of the Lands Commission audit that had been paid for by $25,000 he had requested from the state legislature. But that wasn't enough; they also wanted him to open the books on the highway department, a state agency directly under his control. As far as Hartley was concerned, they were a pirate crew and he called them that, railing at the idea of a senate investigating committee.

"Anybody can see the books," he told the *Times*. "As individuals they can get all the information they want but as a pirate gang they don't get anything."

He rose from the breakfast table, slipped into his overcoat and hat, grabbed an umbrella and left the mansion for the short walk to his office. It had begun to snow and wet, sloppy flakes tumbled from the gray sky and disappeared into puddles. Western Washington snow was dreary and gray, unlike in Minnesota where snow swathed cities in a mantle of peaceful silence. How he would love silence!

In his office Miss Albright greeted him with a stack of letters from friends and relatives of Walter DuBuc, whose execution was set for April 15. DuBuc would be the youngest to be executed in the state's history. But he had committed a monstrous crime.

He directed her to write one of his usual "I'll give the matter careful consideration" letters, and then to give it to him to sign.

Then Miss Albright handed him another stack of letters, which she had bundled under one heading: Niccolls. When would it ever stop? He was, after all, just one boy. He had met the youth in December. He was a pleasant enough lad, cunning, actually. He presented himself like a little gentleman. The warden had spared the boy the usual head shave given convicts and for the visit, the boy was dressed in dungarees and a sweater, like any schoolboy. In fact, as the boy talked of airplanes and ice cream and all the things any boy might talk about, sometimes it was difficult to place him as the boy who had shot a sheriff, a boy who was a cold-blooded killer.

He couldn't believe that the state's voters would place much significance to the debate come election day. Yes, he would run again. He was already the first governor in the state to serve a second term. He could be the first to serve a third. There was more work to be done. Without him, the Democrats would tax everyone to death and the economy would never get back to where it had been before the crash of 1929.

He called Miss Albright in and dictated a letter to the Senate investigating committee, telling them again that he had no plans to turn over the books. Let them sue! he said. He was, after all, the governor.

•

Even though it was still February and spring a month away, the snow had subsided and the sun beamed down upon Overlook Farm. The boys were restless in the classrooms, dreaming of baseball and tag and the promise of a lazy summer, with the fat bumblebees riding the bouncing blooms of purple clover. What would young Niccolls be doing now? What lessons was he learning? Did they include things no boy should learn—how to pick a pocket, how to steal from shops, the fine art of robbery or worse?

Mrs. Lamson wrote to tell Flanagan that she had completed her story about the boy, turned it in to Oliver Morris at the *Post-Intelligencer*, and then discovered they would not use it. The Niccolls story was past its prime. Morris encouraged her to send it to the *Boys Home Journal*. What a shame that the truth about the boy wouldn't come out in a major publication! As head of the Boys Home, Flanagan had written to Lillian Carse, superintendent of The Children's Home Finding and Aid Society in Boise, Idaho, who had informed him about Herbert's early life. It was true that the family had been desperately poor and the mother had no option but to give her boys to the Home Finding Society because she could not feed them. The mother sent them gifts through the society occasionally and inquired about the boys at least once a year, Mrs. Carse said. She added that Mrs. Niccolls was greatly concerned when she had heard about the murder. She would have come to the trial but she was not on speaking terms with her mother-in-law, Mary Addington, whom she knew would be there.

Herbert had had many scrapes with the law, it was quite apparent, but placing a bomb under the church, he noted, was not one of them. He was gratified to see that there had been good-hearted people who had tried to help the boy, even if they had failed. They clearly did not understand that you cannot take a child from one environment and expect him to function as a child who had been raised in a secure and loving home. He needed help making the transition. He needed the boys' home where there would be others just like him.

What he found disturbing was the *Post-Intelligencer*'s shift from crusading to help the boy to—he could hardly believe it when he read Mrs. Lamson's letter—the possibility that the paper might endorse Hartley, who had announced that he was running for a third term.

Morris Jacobs said he would write to Oliver Morris and find out what was going on. Should Hartley be reelected, it could be a very long time before the boy was released. In Oliver's last letter, he had discovered the identity of the other youths Hartley had paroled. They were Ward Daniels and C. A. Brown, two youths about eighteen years old who were among four bandits who shot and killed Seattle Policeman Volney L. Stevens in January 1921. Stevens had stopped a car with the four inside, and while he was searching a suitcase they had in the car, the youths opened fire and shot him. But before Stevens died, he had fired back, wounding one of the youths. When another police officer came to investigate, the boys took him hostage. They fled to a home, seeking medical aid for their wounded friend and a place to hide. But when they heard the woman calling police, they let the hostage go, stole a rowboat, and were trying to get across the Lake Washington Canal when they were captured.

The four confessed to a long series of auto thefts, burglaries and holdups—mostly in the rural regions outside the city. They were sentenced to prison for life. In 1925, Daniels and two other convicts overpowered a guard and escaped from the penitentiary. They were later recaptured. But in July 1929, Hartley released Daniels and Brown and faced considerable criticism for doing so.

The governor with the heart of stone had freed those thieves who had also murdered a police officer, but he would not free one boy. Flanagan had written to Mrs. Lamson, asking her to get in touch with Mr. Burns, whose sister was the governor's secretary. Mr. Burns should mention to Amy that the opposition was talking about the earlier case, and that it might come back to haunt the governor should it be compared to the Niccolls case. She would impart this new information to the governor who would then have the chance to save himself further embarrassment by releasing the boy. But it all had to be done with great tact. Under no circumstances, he told Mrs. Lamson, should anyone learn that Mr. Burns had ever communicated with him. The good man must be protected.

Although he had maintained a prayerful silence and not plied the governor with any more telegrams or letters nor bombarded him over the radio, he had not given up the hope of having the boy released to him.

Hartley, on the other hand, had not abandoned hope of reclaiming lost ground in the highly public clash and issued the results of an investigation of his own. But only about two pages were devoted to the boy, the rest of the document was aimed at Flanagan. It included copies of all correspondence as well as the governor's response—on the rare occasions that there had been any—peppered with invectives.

"Father Flanagan [is] asking that I transfer a sacred responsibility of mine in the State of Washington to him at Omaha, Nebraska. . . . The Sovereign State of Washington must deal with the case of Herbert Niccolls in a legal way."

And the law had spoken, predicting that Herbert was beyond any saving grace except God's. According to Hartley's report, during the trial, Herbert was taken for walks every day by a special deputy and on one of those days, "he picked up a rock and carried it back to his cell . . . he tore strips from his bedding and made a 'billy' or a bludgeon. This was later found in his cot."

The governor then turned the horrors of the boy's childhood—which Flanagan could well imagine from his years spent working with boys just like Herbert—into a sentimental page from the Children's Hour, maintaining that Herbert was an aberration in an otherwise loving and typical American farm family.

> Herbert's father seemingly thinks much of him and writes him loving letters, as do his mother, grandmother and his brothers and sisters. He writes nice letters in return.
>
> Herbert's mother agrees that Herbert was fed and clothed reasonably well always and had every chance to be a good boy. Herbert's paternal grandmother loved and cherished little Herbert, Jr., as she did her own children. Gave him every thought and consideration possible in her endeavors to make a good boy of him. Punished him when he did wrong. Had him paroled to her twice from the Idaho Industrial School, the last time moving him to Asotin, Wash, where she bought a new home in the hope that she might save him. . . . Let it be understood that the treatment and care surrounding Herbert . . . is not different from that given other juvenile offenders in the institutions of the State of Washington. They are all given what is considered the best that present day civilization and science have produced.

Hartley sent his report to the newspapers and all those who had written to him. Flanagan was astounded. A cell in a penitentiary, the best? Flanagan felt weak and old and battle worn. In many states there had been authorities with beliefs similar to Hartley's, but with time and persuasion, they had relented and let him take the boys. There was a nine-year-old, who had been growing up without supervision because his father was dead and his mother had to work to feed him. The town wanted to execute him because he had accidentally shot a playmate. The boy was now one of the home's best citizens. There was a boy who had shot his father and another who had shot his mother. Beneath the crime of every child, was the crime of a society who neglected him. It was easy to forget to be your brother's keeper, easier still when your brother is a child so easily dismissed—until a terrible tragedy occurs. Whatever would become of young Herbert Niccolls?

If Hartley felt triumphant in his attack, it would not last long. Mrs.

Lamson was already outlining the counterattack, which she would title "An Answer to Governor Hartley's Letter Regarding the Herbert Niccoll's Case." They planned to send it to 100,000 people nationwide just before the Washington State primary election in September.

Chapter 13

IT WAS TEN MINUTES before noon and Broderick was wishing that the interview with the last woman inmate would go quickly so he, Hartley, and the rest of the prison control board could go to the warden's home for lunch. But somewhere in the midst of the woman's frank discussion of her husband's employment difficulties and how it had led her to a life of crime, gongs exploded with clanging. Outside on the stairs leading to the catwalk, men shouted and screamed and running feet thundered on the stairs as guards dashed to the vault outside the door where the tear-gas guns and heavy artillery were stored.

Men knocked over chairs. The woman fainted. Warden Long urged everyone to sit still. Parole Board Advisor and Highway Patrol Officer Garfield Davis had drawn his sidearm and was already out the door, joining the guards running to the top of the wall that surrounded the prison. Long, in the meantime, fought to maintain control in the room and rose to block anyone from leaving it.

First in everyone's mind was the possibility of the escapees making it to the room and taking hostages. The warden ordered everyone back and urged them to let the guards handle the situation. Outside the air shivered with volleys of machine gun fire, and then it ceased. The men inside the room looked at one another wordlessly. But before anyone could move, the firing began again, bullets ripping through the chilly winter day. When silence finally came, the men waited; the minutes crawled by as the warden remained with his back to the door. Someone patted the woman's hand and helped her into a chair.

No one spoke, and in the pale winter light, the room seemed shabby and gray. How many inmates had sat in the chair pleading for parole because of sick parents, sick children, runaway spouses, job opportunities, or a wide variety of other excuses? The board turned most of them down . . . some year after year. Then it was suddenly plausible that some of those very men were loose and storming over the wall, breaking down the door to the board room and crashing over tables.

The door opened and Officer Davis summoned Long. In a few minutes the warden returned and motioned them all to look. Cautiously, the board members stepped from the room onto the catwalk that led around the top of the wall. On the ground below lay two men face down in the dirt, their hands behind their heads. Dozens of guards pointed machine guns at them.

Broderick burst into a hearty laugh, but Hartley and the others scowled and saw little humor. The prisoners had thought they'd try to escape by tying their bedsheets together, with a hook at one end. They had then invented excuses to leave their units to be treated at the hospital. They had barely flung the hook onto the top of the wall, when guards saw them and opened fire. Before anyone had been hit, the rope broke. The first man fell, and the other thought he was wounded and tried to help him. When the guards saw that the escape attempt was futile, they fired again to frighten the men off the wall. Had the prisoners gone over, Long told the board, that would have been another story.

Lying face down on the ground was Robert Landis, a sixteen-year-old murderer, convicted of shooting two police officers in Spokane, and James McCourt. Landis, Long knew, was the ringleader. The sixteen-year-old consistently denied committing the murder and insisted that the police had set him up.

It was common for prisoners to claim innocence and the board members scoffed at Landis and his predicament. Broderick noted that it was the young ones who were the most vicious. "They're young tigers who've tasted blood once and crave for it again. Can't be too careful."

That night, voices whispered through the cellblocks. Bobby Landis was in the hole, solitary confinement in the dark with only bread and water. Herbert Niccolls lay on his bed listening to the talk. At the end of his confinement, the prisoner is broken and no longer a problem, or that's what a guard had told him.

When the sirens shrilled again a few weeks later, Herbert leaped from his bunk and strained to see through the slats of the cell. Someone had escaped. But who? Had they made it? Then he heard the rat-a-tat of machine-gun fire and men shouting—followed by silence. He learned later that James McCourt had tried again, but this time with Jack Steel. They both were sent to the hole and the attempt became merely a ripple in the monotony of the day. Escape attempts were not uncommon; just the month before, two inmates had been caught trying to tunnel under the wall. The most innovative attempts were the subject of speculation for the voices in the night.

Herbert hated the whispers that crept into his cell like vermin burrowing into the tender bud of his dreams. There was a boy just turned seventeen, a bull said. The boy was on death row. He was going to be executed soon. Herbert was wary of the "bulls," so named for the insignia of a bull on the cell lock. Some of the bulls were turnkeys, or guards appointed by the governor and hired at seventy-five dollars a week. Others were just plain guards, who were paid only half wages. Although they did the same work, a turnkey, just like the warden, could be out of a job if a governor wasn't reelected.

Herbert—that's what they called him here—liked the warden. Long had been a sheriff in Spokane a long time ago. The warden said that maybe someday—after Herbert proved himself to be trustworthy—he'd let him come to his mansion to help.

"Trustees," that's what they called the prisoners who worked outside the walls. Some worked on the farm where all the prison food was raised. Others worked in the greenhouse, where all of the fine landscaping plants that surrounded the walls and warden's mansion were grown. Still others worked in the mansion itself. The trustees did yard work, fixed the warden's family cars, and worked as butlers and handymen. The women trustees were maids and house cleaners and did the laundry for the warden and his family.

Anything would be a break from the routine. Although Herbert liked studying in the prison library and had all the books he ever wanted to read, if he were at the mansion, there might be other boys. More than anything, he wanted to break free and run and play and shout and kick the can and throw rocks into the creek. Tears came to his eyes when he thought about it. There was no one here his age, no one to play with. Did Walter DuBuc miss his friends? Walter was only seventeen. But he and his partner wouldn't be around much longer. They're going to hang them both side by side. First time ever in the history of the penitentiary, the bull said. People will come from Seattle to see it.

•

On the night of April 15, Hartley was in his office late. He opened the window to the spring air and the scent of new-mown grass. He opened the file before him and read again the case of Harold Carpenter and Walter DuBuc. They had committed a terrible murder of an elderly farmer. In the last few days, Hartley had been badgered more than ever by DuBuc's family. They asked if he would grant the boy clemency. He could, of course, right now pick up the phone to the prison and call the warden and tell them to stop. He could. But he would not. There had been strong sentiment around Olympia—where the murder victim had family and friends—that the two who did the deed should hang. As the prosecutor argued, DuBuc might not have been the one to bludgeon the man to death with the rifle, but he did set the man up and strike the first blows. The blows were hard enough to kill the man, the attorney had said. DuBuc was a good-looking young man. Blond, blue-eyed, with a husky, muscular body. He was a young man who should have been entering the prime of his life. Instead, he took the life of another.

The parole board determined that DuBuc and Carpenter should be executed side by side. Someone had asked whether it would be cruel and unusual punishment to depart from the traditional method of one-by-one execution in the tower, where the trap door opens and the body drops to a room below. When it does, the body is shielded by a thin drapery, and to observers it is only a shadow.

The execution of DuBuc and Carpenter would be far more of a public spectacle. Let the punishment fit the crime, the board had decided.

In addition to the entire parole board, there were members of the public who wanted to view the execution. In fact, inmate carpenters were ordered to build a scaffold in the middle of the prison yard. Although Broderick urged him to attend, Hartley declined. He had far too many other things on his mind at the moment, his political future being one of them.

He removed his watch and looked at the time. It was four minutes to midnight. The prisoners would be lead to the gallows any moment now. They'd walk into the warm spring air, knowing within minutes, they would leave this life and become one with the earth. As the seconds ticked away, Hartley rose from the desk, shut the window and turned out the light.

In the dark cell block, the whispers carried news of the double execution. The boy listened, perhaps wondering if it hurt to die, if Jesus was there on the other side with open arms—even for murderers—and if someday the bulls would come to take him for hanging, too. Anyone within hearing distance of the scaffold was on edge as the minutes passed. When the trap springs open with the sound of a cannon shot and the body falls, many men drop to the floor sobbing. Some wet their pants. Others curse or cheer. Others are silent. Everyone is affected in some way. Most note the time and imagine the steps: The parson is with them about now. Now come the last words, the black hood.

•

Broderick looked at his watch. The prisoners had eaten their last meal—which most could never keep down—and would be meeting with the reverend now, who would urge them to repent. Under the best of circumstances, DuBuc had difficulty writing and Carpenter wasn't much better. But with the help of the chaplain, they signed their names to a statement, thanking the prison staff for the kind treatment and noting that the chaplain had visited them daily and given them spiritual advice. Then they scrawled across an ink-blotched page: "We are very sorry for the crime we committed and say again it was all a mistake, the excitement of the robbery leading us to do what we had no intention of doing. If we can pay for our crime by giving our lives, we are willing. We hope God has forgiven our sin [sic] and will give us a chance to do better in the life to come."

"Even the hardest ones blubber like babies when it comes to the countdown," Broderick said. He had been invited to numerous "going away parties" at the penitentiary but had always declined, until it came to this one—a double execution. He and Captain Ernie Yoris of the Seattle Police Department, who had seen everything else in police work, got front row seats in the prison yard.

Not long after, Broderick would recall that warm April night in the valley of the Blue Mountains and how a group of twenty, walking from the warden's office, turned the corner by one of the work buildings. There in the prison yard, away from the gaze of the cellblocks, he saw the scaffold, illuminated by four floodlights. Two bone white hemp nooses swayed in a slight breeze. Broderick glanced at his watch. In the moonlight, an owl hooted and dove, talons outstretched into the field beyond. And then there was silence. A few minutes after midnight, Carpenter and DuBuc were brought out. Slowly, they climbed the thirteen stairs to the platform. The minister stood before them and murmured a prayer. DuBuc whimpered and Carpenter snapped, "What the hell is the matter with you?"

The warden asked the boy if he would like to say a few words. The boy stared silently, his gaunt face a composition of hollows and planes in the stark light. Carpenter said the preacher would do the talking for him. Then the black caps were thrust over their heads and the captain raised his arm.

"You try to follow everything, but it's a little too fast for the eye. I was told to keep my eye riveted on one object and I chose the fingers on the left hand of the boy, but I couldn't follow the detail of the plunge any more than I could follow the flight of the soul. With the snapping jerk of the rope's end, the bodies sway and swing circularly—but not a murmur, or a gurgle, nor anything to denote a sign of life. And those fingers never even twinged," Broderick wrote later.

After ten minutes, two doctors climbed the stepladders and placed stethoscopes on each man's chest, listening for a heartbeat. Then Captain of the Guards Hans Damm huffed his way up the stepladder and cut the rope, letting a body fall across his shoulder.

Damm is "a good old soul," Broderick said. "You almost feel sorry for him."

Warden Long declared the hanging well done, both in terms of procedure and retribution. Afterward, he and Broderick went over to the hotel and gossiped until three o'clock in the morning. Later, Broderick went to bed and dreamed—but not of hangings.

Chapter 14

WITH THE EXECUTION OVER, it was gratifying to receive a letter applauding his decision to not stop the hanging. Hartley was smugly satisfied. If his constituents knew how he suffered from his treatment by the press.

"The responsibility in such cases . . . is grave and exacts a service which tries the very soul. There is no rest for me on such a night. My time is put in, until the last moment, studying the affair and the data that is filed in connection with it," he wrote in a letter to a loyal voter. "Those to blame for the controversy in such matters are dishonest, money grabbing, newspaper men, who lie and misrepresent the case, in order to sell their dirty sheets." Miss Albright snapped the steno book closed and left the room.

It was, after all, nice to know that he was appreciated by some of the voters. Hartley wished the rest of the populace would be so wise.

He had filed a lawsuit to stop the Senate Investigating Committee from getting access to the Lands Commission audit or any of the other books under his control, and that had rankled the troops. He was being crucified in the press from one end of the state to the other. The *Walla Walla Daily Bulletin* had a front-page story, quoting from his earlier campaigns when he had been a strong advocate of openness: "It's high time that we got out from behind the bulwark and let the people know the facts about their own business." He had said those words during a special message to the legislature on December 22, 1925. Those were the heady optimistic days when after three tries at running for governor, he had at last won. But things were different now.

The state attorney general had ruled that the Senate committee has full authority to investigate the books, records, and accounts of all state agencies. Nevertheless, he again told Senator Sutton that he would not tolerate the investigation of any department under the control of the governor. They, of course, reeled with shock but before they could recover, he had dealt them one more blow—he denied the senate committee the use of the state capitol committee room.

The *Daily Bulletin* noted that, too, and went on to quote his April 3, 1930, speech: "The honest man in public office with nothing to conceal will not object to an audit of his official records at any time, day or night. When a public official fights a lawful audit of his office you may be sure, he has something to conceal."

He had said those words, but the issue had been a "lawful audit." Now the senate was planning to sue. In the meantime, some of Hartley's constituents were asking if he was planning on attending the national governors' meeting in Virginia in the upcoming month. In fact, several reporters had pressed him on the issue, which concerned Hartley greatly.

As far as he was concerned, an absence would mean that he was abdicating his role as governor and would give "that long-eared, son-of-a-gun Gellatly" a chance to seize control of the chief executive's office, since, when Hartley was out of the state, power was transferred.

"If I go away they can just raise hob!" he thundered. Gellatly was challenging him for the Republican nomination in September. Hartley didn't plan to give him a chance to get a foothold, not for a minute.

•

Near Omaha a brisk wind whipped across the greening prairie. Spring had come and the boys were out tilling the soil, preparing to plant corn, beans, and potatoes. Mrs. Lamson was to arrive by train that evening. Leo Bozell, of Bozell & Jacobs, had financed her trip, both to Omaha and Detroit, where she would address the National League of Women Voters about the plight of Herbert Niccolls. Then she planned to travel to Washington for the National Pen Women meeting, where she also planned to rally support.

After the months of correspondence, Father Flanagan looked forward to seeing her again, and, hopefully, to keep her encouraged. The fight seemed to be wearing on her.

"The governor [is] . . . spreading all kinds of untruths about us all," she had written in her last letter. "He tells that [Monsignor] Ryan did not approve of you. I asked [the monsignor] personally how the governor dared to make such a statement. He could not explain and assured me of the great admiration he had for you."

She concluded her letter by saying that she believed the governor had the Highway Police following her. Flanagan hoped that this was not the case, but it was plain that Hartley had risen from the silence of November to a retaliatory roar. He had received letters from the people to whom Hartley had sent his eleven-page "investigation" into Herbert Niccolls's life, and there was a rippling sign of a turning tide.

There were supportive letters, too, such as one from B. J. Gibson, a Danville, Illinois, father of three boys and a grain broker, who wrote that he had sent Herbert a picture book about Jesus for Christmas. He pledged his support and indicated that he had already written to the murdered sheriff's widow, asking her to also join in the fight to have the boy sent to Omaha. He had written to Hartley as well.

While this help was valuable, perhaps it was time for a different approach. Perhaps it was time to appeal directly to the women of the country. Mrs. Lamson had the right idea when she agreed to address the League of Women Voters and the American Pen Women. Lamson believed that no mother could resist coming to the aid of a wounded child. Bozell had scheduled her to speak at civic groups during her Omaha stop, and it seemed as soon as she had barely arrived, she was whisked away from podium to podium, showering Nebraskans with her charm and sophisticated glitter that left them wanting more.

In Washington, Detroit, and Omaha, the people spoke of her long after she was gone. Newspapers praised her and so did the clergy. The soft-spoken articulate woman with the great dark eyes and refined manners came to symbolize a growing concern for child welfare—and a boy named Herbert Niccolls.

When Mrs. Lamson wrote to Father Flanagan several weeks later, indicating that with the help of Mrs. Newberger, a mutual friend of the Lamsons and the Hartleys, she had managed to schedule an interview with the governor, he was overjoyed. Surely, here would be a way to make the governor give in.

She noted, too, that Lieutenant Governor Gellatly's friends had besieged him with pleas to parole Herbert should Hartley leave the state for any reason. But, so far, Mrs. Lamson said, Hartley was determined to stay in Washington.

•

Nina Hartley had ordered sandwiches and pastries to be brought into the library along with the silver service. It was a balmy spring day and the trees were heavy with pink blooms that with each gust of wind showered down on the clipped lawn like pastel snow. Dr. and Mrs. Lamson, like their friends the Newbergers, were good Republicans—Hartley supporters in the last two elections. But even so, with all the turmoil surrounding the senate investigation and the Niccolls's case, Nina hoped that Mrs. Lamson would not upset the governor.

The women arrived in their best hats and gloves and as they sipped tea, conversation was as delicate as the painted china cups they clasped between thumb and index finger.

The mansion? Yes, it is lovely. The gardens? Fine in spring, with the banks of red rhododendrons blazing beneath the trees. The weather? So pleasant. And the children? Yes the children.

Something must be done for that unfortunate boy, Mrs. Lamson said. Nina Hartley sensed that Armene Lamson was warming up to launch into a full campaign, so she suggested that it might be a good time to go to the executive office to catch the governor before he leaves.

So in her proper leather pumps and matching bag, and wearing her short white gloves and her small spring hat, Mrs. Lamson clipped along the capitol steps about to wage war.

Miss Albright announced her and showed her in. At last, as the door closed behind her, Mrs. Lamson realized with a tremor of anxiety that she was now face-to-face with a man she had come to regard as the enemy, and that a little boy's very life might depend on the outcome of the visit.

The meeting took two hours. As she would write to Flanagan later, she wondered if Hartley was "close to having a nervous breakdown." He paced, his mind wandered, and she fought to keep him on the subject of Herbert Niccolls. He was, of course, inflexible as far as releasing the boy was concerned, but she did win one considerable victory. He would let her visit the boy to see for herself that he was being well cared for. That, she thought as she rose and shook the governor's hand, was a victory indeed.

•

The guard rattled his nightstick along the metal bars of the cell early one June morning, telling Herbert to pull himself together, slick back his hair, and look sharp because company was coming from Seattle.

Now he was wide awake and shoved the black blanket onto the floor, urinated in a bucket, dressed, and waited for the guard to open the cell. The lady will be inspecting the whole place, the guard said, turning the key.

During the last few months, Herbert had fallen into a routine. He woke at 6 a.m., ate breakfast in his cell at 6:45, and at 7:30 a guard took him to the south wall for a few minute's walk, weather permitting. He usually remained outdoors—and under the eyes of the tower guards—until eight a.m. when a turnkey escorted him to the library for his lessons.

The prison library was a small room, musty with damp and the odor of well-used books donated over time by the public. It had one long, barred window that overlooked the prison yard and had a radiator that hissed and clanked.

He sat at a desk beneath the watchful gaze of Mr. C. F. Rose, civilian librarian, who was assigned to monitor every move he made, from the pages he turned in the books to his trips to the toilet. The door to the toilet always remained open and the boy was never allowed inside if other prisoners were in there. The boy, the warden told Rose, was to be guarded and isolated from the main prison population at all times. It would be easy for the boy to slip into "immorality," the warden said, be lured into a darker world of lost souls. Burdensome though it may be, the boy must never be left alone.

"Herbert was not always easy to handle the first year," Rose later wrote in a report to the warden. The boy delighted in seeing how quickly he could disappear when Rose became distracted. He tipped over chairs, threw spit wads, and often wandered away from the desk to the window, which he would push open. He would then shout to the convicts taking exercise in the yard below, calling them names. When caught, he usually lied to extricate himself from trouble. Yet, there were other times he merely stood by the window, his forehead pressed against the glass, his skin translucent in the winter light, watching the sparrows.

Those were the times that tugged at Rose's heart. Despite the difficulty of adapting a prison routine to accommodate a child, Rose had taken a liking to the boy. He took him to the officers' dining room for lunch and had become accustomed to hearing about the world according to Herbert Niccolls. He wondered if any adult had ever spent much time with the boy.

Fortunately, Rose noted, most of Herbert's interests concerned his lessons, brought weekly by Walla Walla Superintendent of Schools W. M. Kern. Rose then assigned educated prisoners, who worked as library assistants, to tutor the boy.

Herbert had an amazing appetite for knowledge, Rose noted with approval. Every day he took new books to his cell to read at night. As the men down the cellblock cursed and whispered, the boy crept through the forest with Longfellow's Hiawatha, rode the plains with Zane Grey, and traveled the South Seas with Robert Louis Stevenson. He saw the fall of Constantinople through the eyes of the *Prince of India* and flew around the world with Jules Verne. Three nights a week he went to night school, where math unfolded before him and tempted him to solve its intricate puzzles. The problems were so easy for him, and he was quicker to answer than all the other inmates, who often scowled and called him "pretty boy" and "girlie."

For the boy, the best part of the day was the time he spent with his "teachers." The first was twenty-three-year-old Kenneth Purcell, who was doing time for robbery. When Herbert said he was in for murder, Purcell told him that it was nothing to be proud of. He took out the mathematics book that Kern had provided and challenged the boy to prove how much math he could do.

The boy was good. Amazingly so, Kern noted when he came to test the boy. He clicked his stopwatch, and then scanned the test scores. His eyes met Purcell's and Rose's.

Kern told Herbert that he had done remarkably well. He was working beyond his grade level, even though Kern doubted that he had spent much time regularly attending school.

From that time on, Rose and Purcell had a new respect for him, and Kern brought harder work. Algebra, geometry, and physics. There seemed to be no stopping him. Rose noted that the boy and his youthful teacher's eyes shined when they talked about mathematics, their heads bent over the books almost like two brothers.

Kenny Purcell had only been in prison six months but he wasn't like the others. He was a delicate young man with dark eyes. His booking information said he had been part of a group of boys who pulled a heist in Seattle. Kenny said he wasn't involved. The judge said he was guilty by association. Kenny had grown up in Canada. The speaker of the house of the Canadian National Assembly and the Canadian war veterans associations had tried unsuccessfully to secure his release. Until his fateful trip to Seattle, he had been a cashier at the Canadian Express, had trained as an accountant, and was a Boy Scout leader. He was a good man, Rose noted. With any luck he'd be paroled before his ten-year sentence was over.

Peter Miller also worked in the library. Inside the walls, he was a model citizen, a European-educated man who claimed to speak five languages. On his intake form, he listed his professional skills as "physician, lecturer, author and scholar." But he had a rap sheet as weighty as his nearly 6-foot 200-pound frame. He could quote Shakespeare and Descartes, calculate the speed of light, identify all the constellations of the solar system, or explain the intricacies of the human nervous system. He moved with amazing delicacy, like a bear in dancing slippers, and his large hands lovingly stroked the worn spines of the books he shelved or checked out to inmates. He would say, How are things, Jake? Heard from your wife lately. Got a book here that you will love. . . . Talk to your mouthpiece, Sam? What does he say about paroling you to your father-in-law's ranch? Well, in the meantime, here's another Zane Grey.

The inmates respected Miller for his gentle ways and his quiet leadership. He had started a fund so inmates being paroled could leave prison with a bit of cash for food and shelter. He worked as a chaplain and had started the prison library. Rose liked to think that only the very best of the inmates were selected to work in the library, and over time he came to believe in their innocence. He had certainly argued that all the way to the Supreme Court on Miller's behalf. There was no doubt about it—Miller had a bum rap this time. If Miller was indeed innocent, then he should be freed.

Where would he be on the outside? Lecturing at a university? Treating patients? Or would he be a type of Fagin who used young boys to steal and rob for him? That's what the newspapers said. There was no doubt that living in confinement forced some men to live more honestly than they would if the choice were theirs.

That's what Rose told Mrs. Lamson and Miss Draham when he was called in to the warden's office to meet with them regarding Herbert Niccolls.

How was the boy's behavior? How was he doing in school? He had been emphatic: The boy was the model prisoner. In the beginning, Rose had caught him in lies and exaggerations committed in the spirit of self-preservation, but the boy had found out that lying got him nowhere. As to his intelligence, Rose told the visitors that Niccolls was an exceptionally bright child and was doing very well in his studies.

The boy doesn't have a chance to get into trouble, Warden Long said, leaning back in his chair. "Then he is not being prepared for release into the outside world," Mrs. Lamson said. If he has no opportunity to choose between right and wrong now, it will be difficult for him to learn that later. "Without learning to make good choices, how can he ever succeed outside prison?"

Outside prison? She still hoped that the boy's life sentence would not come to pass and that he'd be released eventually. The men were silent, and a breeze blew in through the open window. With it came the click and whir of a lawnmower as a trustee trimmed the lawn around the administration building.

Long told her that when Herbert was older—assuming he continued to do well—he could become a trustee. They have more freedom.

But it was not like living in society, Mrs. Lamson responded. There the choices to do good or bad are available every day, every hour. Teaching him about good and evil in this manner is like tying a child's legs and trying to teach him to walk merely by telling him about it, she said. His muscles never get used to doing it step by step.

Rose thought again about Peter. He heard Peter had spent a few years at Sing Sing in 1894 and later spent a year in a workhouse in Saint Louis. He had the battle scars of an old con and an alias, to boot. But in this artificially structured world Peter was a gentle, honorable and honest man.

The only thing that concerned Rose about the boy was his lack of normal emotion, which he and his colleagues agreed was clearly a characteristic often found in criminals.

It is simply not humanly possible to make that boy cry, he told Mrs. Lamson. No matter how much he was scolded or threatened, how bleak the future looked for him, the boy seemed to cope by becoming quiet, as if part of him had flown away with the birds. It is curious indeed and may very well be a sign that he has inborn criminal tendencies, he said, quickly adding that there was no outward sign of it at all.

Even Mrs. Lamson agreed that shedding tears was a visible sign that the boy was capable of remorse. If he was unable to be remorseful, then in the future he might well follow the path of crime again, she knew. Learned experts of the day had written that a lack of emotion was a sure sign of criminal tendencies. However, he is a young man, and young men are especially ashamed of their tears, she told Rose and Long.

•

Herbert was seated at the table in the library when he saw the two women. Mrs. Lamson, the older woman, wore small round glasses, a hat, and a well-tailored blue suit. She walked with the confidence of a colonel on a mission—a rather small colonel in a spring hat. The younger, Miss Draham, clung to her, clutching a straw handbag and smoothing her floral print dress. The seven inmates in the library stared; many had not seen a woman for a very long time.

The women were noticeably uncomfortable in the presence of the prisoners and like roses in frost, held their petals tightly around them, smoothing a skirt here, tugging at a glove there.

In addition to the women were the warden and Olaf Olsen, state director of prisons. The warden looked miserable as the women surveyed the surroundings. They toured the dining room, the hospital, the sallyport, and the cellblock, where they paused before Herbert's cell. It was a warm day and the cellblock was hot and airless, and the stench from the buckets down the row—used because the facility had no indoor plumbing—burned the eyes. The women quickly took handkerchiefs out of their purses and placed them before their noses.

Mrs. Lamson commented on the lack of sanitation and also asked that the cell be measured. Long sent a guard to get a tape measure. The cell was eight feet eleven inches long, five feet ten inches wide and seven feet six inches tall and was part of the wing of the territorial prison built in 1884. Mrs. Lamson noted that the cell had a narrow cot with a black blanket, two shelves of books, a small table, a stool, and the pail "for sanitary purposes." There was no window and the only available light seeped in from the hallway. Then she requested an interview with the boy.

She sat across from him in the warden's office, noting his erect posture, his neatly combed hair and hands politely folded in his lap. She asked him how he liked prison life? He told her that the food was good and that he could read all the books he wanted—hundreds of them—and that he had lots of friends.

He told her about Peter, who was in for life, and the fellows in the cellblock. When she looked shocked, he explained that he wasn't allowed to associate with other prisoners but he did listen to them talk.

She shifted uncomfortably in the chair and crossed her silk-clad legs. Then she told him that a very great man named Father Flanagan of Omaha, Nebraska, wanted to take him to live at his boys' home. She told him, too, that the priest sent his love and prayed for him every night.

"That's very nice of him," the boy said. "Would I get a chance to play with other boys there?" Mrs. Lamson nodded. He gazed past the desk photos of the warden's two sons, past the warden's certificate of appreciation for having served as Spokane County Sheriff, past the American flag in the corner and up the chain of the glass and bronze pendulum light to the pale green ceiling. He willed his tears to subside and then in a voice that broke he said, "Oh, please can't I have one more chance? More than anything, I want to play with other boys."

She told him many people were trying to see that happen. With a slight triumphant smile, she hoped the others were noting that the child was indeed capable of visible sorrow.

•

In Omaha, where the farm was bustling as lessons ended and the boys took to the fields to work, Flanagan anxiously waited for Mrs. Lamson's report. When it came, he hurried into his office and ripped open the envelope.

Herbert, she reported, is "an exceptionally gifted child who has done in the six months of schooling . . . all of the six-grade work and has taken successfully many of the seventh grade examinations."

She noted, however, that his teachers were convicts like the notorious felon Peter Miller, "who had so many sentences no one knows how long he actually has to serve."

Herbert, Mrs. Lamson wrote, "has read a very large number of books while in the penitentiary and is able to give at least 60 in writing by title and author and remembers the general story. In all possibility Herbert has read 2,000 books as he himself stated . . . this was verified by the librarian. I was impressed with the fact that the prison authorities were very proud of this achievement."

She went on:

> Physically, [Herbert] is apparently in good form [and] . . . weighs 89 pounds and is 57 1/2 inches tall." But despite the care they have given him . . . they have contributed nothing to the child's mechanics that control his conduct. . . . In other words, in no way is he being prepared for his return to society.
>
> I asked them individually and collectively if in any way Herbert had given them reason to believe that he had criminal tendencies, or to sustain the assertion made during the trial—and later by the governor—that the boy is a 'born criminal.' They assured me that Herbert has been a model boy, obedient, very sensible, clean cut, polite amiable youngster.

She said that she had begun the conversation with the boy by expressing admiration for the many books he had read and asking him to tell her what books he liked best.

> He told me he likes historical books. He liked 'Caesar best of all' . . . and that he also liked Indian stories, but wished that they were without white men. I asked him why. 'They are always cruel to the Indians,' he said.
>
> When I questioned why he considered this so critically, he said 'after all this land belonged first to the Indians and the white man came and took it from him.' . . . I felt he didn't have the normal admiration of a child of his age for our race and social order. Later on I saw somewhat the same in Peter Miller, who is permitted to talk to Herbert and seems to have quite an influence on the child.

She noted that she impressed on Herbert how important it was to be a "producer rather than a consumer," that it was much more beneficial to do things, write stories and opinions of the things he saw and felt himself, "rather than devour the things done by other people." The comments were made, she noted, "for the benefit of his teacher, the librarian, who is so proud of the reading achievement of this child, but never thinks of giving him opportunity to do things as well as to express his own opinions."

Herbert has, Mrs. Lamson noted, privileges far greater than the average convict, who must wear a uniform, march in line to and from his cell, have his head shaved, refrain from talking while in the workshops, and eat humble prison food without the benefit of knife or fork. The boy's special privileges are the source of resentment among the other inmates.

In fact, even the warden acknowledged that keeping the boy there severely upset usual prison routine. Mrs. Lamson said she would note that fact when she sent a report on her findings to the governor. She would also volunteer to be the boy's guardian, to be responsible for him if only the governor would release him. As she explained, she had been losing sleep thinking about him and wondering how in the great nation of the United States it could be possible for a twelve-year-old to have endured so much. And to think that only four months before Herbert shot the sheriff, President Herbert Hoover had endorsed the White House Conference of Child Health and Protection that provided every child "in conflict with society the right to be dealt with intelligently as society's charge, not as society's outcast."

As Flanagan knew, if given a chance to be Herbert's guardian, Mrs. Lamson would release the boy to his boys' home. On that, as he expected, she remained unchanged. He, too, remained convinced that the boy more than ever would fit in well at the home. The only question was, what was the next step?

•

With the beginning of summer, the heat, whether in the library or the cellblocks, grew worse. Inmates complained more, and grew more restless. Fights broke out. A soft-spoken turnkey went to take a prisoner from a cell to the warden's office, but the prisoner caught him by surprise and punched him in the face so hard that the turnkey fell.

Other prisoners began to yell and threaten the inmate, Why did you do that, you fool? Now the screws will come down on all of us. When the guards rushed in, the prisoner stood motionless by his cell. The guard told him to stand there and not move because he would be back for him.

The guards helped the injured turnkey out of the cellblock. When the guards returned, the largest one removed his nightstick and ordered the inmate onto his knees.

With the first blow, the inmate collapsed to the floor. It seemed like the blows would go on forever. The boy shuddered and plugged his ears to drown out the cries. Then there was silence as they dragged the inmate's body to the infirmary where he would remain for weeks. In the meantime, the cellblock remained in lockdown for seven days. Long believed that it was the most effective punishment. If one erred, they all paid. There were no trips to the library, the infirmary, the workshops, the yard for exercise, nothing except the small cell and the heat and the stench and the hum of flies.

Except for Herbert.

Daily the guards would come for him and take him to the library or out into the yard, where Kenny Purcell played handball with him against the wall of the building. Sometimes the warden would come and fetch Herbert to have him help with the gardening around the mansion, quenching his thirst with tall glasses of lemonade when the noon sun rose high.

The voices of the other prisoners came like hot, dry scratches on the sun-baked walls. The men wept more often now and cursed and then fell into a heat-dazed silence, marked only by the buzzing of insects. It seemed every few days someone was trying to escape, knowing that it likely meant death should the escape fail—which it almost always did.

The tension at the prison was like an electron discharge before a storm. Should the prison erupt in violence, the most vulnerable inmate of all would be in grave danger. The privileges he received made him an easy mark for the others—if they ever got the chance.

While early spring rains had caused Mill Creek to spill over its banks downtown, summer was as dry as the spring had been wet. The wind rushed across the prairie whipping up dust so thick it was impossible to see. Even inside the cellblock with the doors closed, you could smell and taste the gritty air.

On July 9, the storm continued through most of the afternoon, gust after gust of dust swirling in choking clouds. Then about midnight, somewhere in the valley, the wind blew down a power pole and all the lights in the penitentiary blinked out. As the boy lay awake on his cot listening to the howling, he could hear voices outside and machine-gun fire, or was it pebbles hurled against the building in the wind? Then suddenly it was silent, and the dust settled and the stars came out.

The July morning was crisp and fresh as the sun climbed over the Blue Mountains. But following the headcount before breakfast, the sirens began to shrill and guards ran across the catwalk. Ellis Woodward and W. D. Moxley were gone; they had slipped over the east wall and vanished into the countryside.

Sixteen days later, another inmate threw a rope over the wall—and when the guards were not looking, slipped over into the night. No threat of death could keep the inmates from trying to escape that long, hot summer.

By late August, Mrs. Lamson had completed her report, "An Answer to Governor Hartley's Letter Regarding the Herbert Niccolls's Case." It was circulated to the 100,000 subscribers of the *Boys Home Journal* shortly before the Washington State primary election. She told how Hartley had sent an eleven-page document further tarnishing the boy's reputation and invading his privacy. She called the document "the misunderstood and misconstrued details of a sordid life of a child, who, contrary to the Governor's assertion . . . was born into a home of want and neglect."

The governor, she pointed out, has done "a great wrong . . . to a child who in bondage has no voice in self-defense. . . . By broadcasting and immortalizing delinquencies committed in the weakness of a distorted childhood, Governor Hartley further traduces the character and the whole make-up of this child, damning him forever an outcast of society."

She had, of course, noted that she and Father Flanagan had, in respect to the child's reputation, carefully avoided any dramatization of his misdeeds, not as Governor Hartley presumes, "to misrepresent the facts but to make [the boy's] return to society not unbearable by the scorn of his fellow-men."

It does not matter how bad a boy Herbert has been. Our concern is how to make him a good boy. It would be praiseworthy and politically profitable if our Governor concentrated his efforts and the funds entrusted to him to clean out the evil situations and other contributing factors in the criminality of children. Then delinquency or criminality, like any other pattern of behavior, is the child's adjustment to a social situation. Where there is criminality, there is a criminal social situation. Herbert was one of its victims. His crime was the shortsighted solution of his social problem. . . . Not even Governor Hartley can hope for improvement in the trend of behavior of a lad of 12, whose daily routine is composed of just eating, sleeping, occasionally reading and walking about the sallyport . . . or on rainy days a half hour's bunk fatigue in his small barren cell. It needs but a fleeting glance through the voluminous reports of President Hoover's Commission on Law Observance and Enforcement . . . to convince the most naive among us that the chance for reform of an erring and wayward juvenile is null under the existing conditions of all penal institutions. . . . Sooner or later Herbert will be thrown among the older prisoners. . . . It will not be long before his fellow convicts of maturer age and varied experience will point out to him that his criminal act was not well planned, his technique faulty, his feet not fast enough, nor his tongue glib enough to escape the penalty imposed on him by a society, desirous to crush the underdog.

About the same time, *Time* magazine took its long-awaited strike at Hartley, whom they criticized for stripping the University of Washington budget, in effect turning the research university into a liberal arts college while sending his sons to Yale and a daughter to Vassar.

The Hartley machine, as Mrs. Lamson referred to it, was grinding to a halt. In campaigns, he used the Herbert Niccolls case to illustrate his get-tough-on-crime stand. But it became clear that the party was pulling away from him. Newspaper endorsements he had hoped for never came. The Thurston County Court ordered him to turn over all the books, and the judge told him that they were public property, not his alone. And then finally came election day. He bravely stood on a Seattle street corner, waving and shaking hands. Nina stood with him, a deep frown creasing her brow. By the following morning it was over. He had lost the Republican nomination to Gellatly, who would run against Clarence Martin in November.

When Flanagan received the telegram, it was an answer to his prayers. "Hartley beaten. Political machine broken. State redeemed," Mrs. Lamson wrote. He immediately sent a return wire to her with copies to the press.

"Congratulations on your successful campaign activities. Feel sure results will rebound in favor of more humane child welfare work. . . . God above knows of your fearlessness and your sincerity of purpose in daring to oppose such powerful political machinery in the interests of our American children," he wrote.

The governor was defeated by almost a two-to-one margin. As he was packing his possessions and moving from the capitol to his own mansion in Everett, at the penitentiary Kenny Purcell was packing, too. The warden read him the letter. He was to be paroled to a Mrs. M.A. MacLeod of Grayling, Michigan. The young man who had been raised alone by his father learned that his mother, whom he had thought dead, was alive and had been looking for him for twenty years, ever since his father had kidnapped him, fled to Canada, and disappeared. The Associated Press noted that Hartley was moved to parole Purcell by a "mother's tears."

•

That shimmering fall, geese flew past the window of the library. The world burned bright with the haze of gold and the boy tried to think back to a time when he could run free. But the faces of his friends and family had faded like the streets and the neighborhoods. All that remained in his memory of the past was the color blue, a souvenir of the sky, just like the marble—a small world of glass—on the shelf in his cell.

In Asotin, the Watkins children had returned to school. Murphy fished alone now in Asotin Creek. The bands played on at the dance hall at the Little Abner Log Cabin Club and the circus came to town and went. Mary Addington moved back to Idaho. Wayne Bezona still fought John Barleycorn in the foothills of the Blue Mountains.

For Ed Doyle, those fall days would be the last days of his life. The Farmer's Bank Uniontown branch, of which he was a director, had closed, dealing the family and many others in the area a hard loss. In the hours when the hobgoblins from the day rose to steal sleep, he lay beside his sleeping wife, thinking of her, of their new baby son, of all the children who depended on him. He thought, too, of the City of Clarkston that depended on his legal skills, of his clients who turned to him to do "something," to work miracles. But there were no more miracles.

Mary Addington had paid him a visit and given him an order. He objected strongly, but she reminded him that she was the boy's guardian, that she had contributed toward his legal defense, that she was trying to save the boy from sin. Wouldn't he help her save him?

He couldn't even save himself. He wrote the letter she requested and sent it to the penitentiary. Then on October 6, 1932, after a difficult day in court, he said goodbye to his longtime associate Judge Kuykendall, climbed into a V-8, and roared northbound along the two-lane Clarkston-Asotin Highway. Faster and faster the car sailed. The speedometer climbed forty, fifty, sixty, seventy. And then, the Randolph cherry orchard came into view, the leaves shimmering in a haze of gold and falling to the dark, decaying earth.

In a heartbeat it was over. The car veered from the road and slammed into a tree, the impact telescoping the motor, breaking Doyle's legs and jaw, fracturing his skull, and causing internal injuries. He died at the scene.

That year Kenneth Mackintosh retired from the bench after twice being nominated to the Ninth District Court of Appeals. Each time questions were raised about his comments about labor and the Niccolls case. In the Democratic landslide of 1932, Mackintosh's nomination was never confirmed.

In a few years, attorney John Applewhite and Mary Addington would be dead. And day by day, the years would pass in the prison library where the boy would pause during his reading, to try to feed the birds beyond the barred windows.

Chapter 15

I N THE SNOWY DAYS when the sighs of men were muffled in the white
shawl of winter, the boy at his desk and the man by the window spoke
of Shakespeare and Descartes, of sonnets and cycloids, transcendental
numbers and transcendental verse. It would be in those days that the
boy would begin to say "my beloved math" and dream of engineering
planes and of a world unified by reasoning—a world explained in terms
of patterns and probability and numerical sequences, a world with wings
and possibilities, beyond the reach of the parole board.

As Broderick would describe him, Peter Miller was a "Colossus of
Rhodes among Tom Thumbs," and Herbert Niccolls's education was the
better for it, as side by side they forged a friendship founded on the solid
framework of the analytical world.

Miller spoke softly. Other men would come, too, softly padding along
the rows of books and the boy would glance up from his own and gaze
out the window.

To live inside the walls was to live inside the gates of hell, Miller knew.

Here the lost souls were warehoused. Many were poor, most were uneducated. Too often they were threatened with bodily harm and starvation, and even the most passive faced the tedium of endless days with little to do. But it was different here in the library where within the musty volumes worlds unfolded at the turn of the page. He was pleased Rose had suggested that he tutor the boy.

Miller could hardly remember a time when he was free. It seemed so long ago. He had tried to make good. He came out west for a new start, to shake off the shackles of prison, breathe fresh sea air, and see the ragged peaks of the Olympic Mountains floating in the blue-gray horizon beyond the Puget Sound.

Then it happened. As anti-German sentiment swept the country, along with the rumblings of what in five years would be the World War, his broad Teutonic features drew attention. Although he was born in Pennsylvania and was only German on his mother's side, his features, coupled with the fact that he had spent time in a Missouri workhouse and in Sing Sing prison, were a combination that meant trouble. He found himself clapped in the Seattle jail facing a murder charge for a death he insisted he had nothing to do with. The man had died five years earlier in an alcohol-related event, but in order for the widow to claim the insurance money, the death had to be a crime or an accident. The widow hired a private detective to furnish proof, and five years later, after following a series of clues, the Seattle police arrested Miller.

First came burglary charges. He hired an attorney to represent him. But the attorney turned on him and not only elected to testify against him but in doing so claimed that during privileged conversations, Miller had admitted to breaking into two homes and to killing the Seattle saloon keeper.

Miller was placed in a dark cell at the Seattle jail and told that if he didn't confess to the murder, he would be charged with multiple crimes with sentences running consecutively. He would be an old man when he got out of prison, they said. It was summer, the season of light, 1909. He confessed to the brutal conditions in King County and Seattle jails, nothing more, and was tried and convicted of two counts of second-degree burglary after a "half-grown, ignorant and helpless" youth, Willis Taylor, had implicated him. Taylor had been kept in a dark cell in the city jail for fifty-one weeks without a charge, had been beaten, kicked, fed bread and water, and threatened with hanging, for the purposes of extorting this statement. The youth was entirely alone, denied an attorney and at the mercy of Seattle police detectives. Though he was eventually charged with burglary and sentenced to fifteen years in the State Reformatory at Monroe, he was never brought to trial. His plight, along with Miller's, would be the subject of outrage in national legal circles, but to no avail.

In the end Miller was sentenced from twenty-eight to seventy years for two counts of second-degree burglary and one count of perjury, which was added after the Supreme Court dismissed all of the other convictions.

In some ways, the life he had woven from a rich fabric of knowledge in prison was better than any he had known on the outside. There, he had a place of honor and respect. Superintendent Henry Drum and Librarian Rose had written letters to the governor supporting his release. That had been ten years ago. And at last, the door to the outside world would open to him.

The boy stood by the window where a turnkey was crossing the yard in a blast of wind that sent snow swirling about him like a figment from Descartes' dream. That winter the prison was blanketed in the heaviest snowfall in years. Wind howled around the buildings and whistled through the cellblocks. Men shivered in their cells and cursed the weather.

It was a winter straight from Lapland. If the boy had been Descartes he would have crawled into an oven for warmth, later to be swept up in the dreams of an analytical world unified by reason. On February 9, when the inmates were marched from their cells in the morning bucket parade, the turnkey noted that it was three degrees below zero. There had been weeks of heavy snowfall. A few miles to the south in Umatilla County, Oregon, thousands of sheep lay frozen to death and farmers feared for their cattle and other livestock. Even the Plymouth-Umatilla ferries were halted when ice sheeted the Columbia River.

It was on that morning that Warden Long stopped by the library, pausing in the doorway with a handsome, middle-aged man. They spoke softly and the warden nodded in Herbert's direction. Miller attempted to redirect the boy's attention back to the lesson at hand. But then the boy heard the warden introduce the man to Mr. Rose. Everyone in the library paused to listen.

The warden was leaving. Long stood in the doorway, smiling, his hand tucked into his vest pocket, where he kept his gold watch and chain. The warden referred to Herbert as a model prisoner—someone who had read 2,000 books. Proudly, Herbert told them that he had read every one in the library, in addition to the ones brought by Superintendent of Schools Kern. The stranger, James "Marvin" McCauley, told him that that was very impressive. Eleven days later, McCauley, a Dayton wheat farmer, businessman, and grandson of some of the earliest settlers in the valley, became the new warden, having turned down another appointed position in Olympia because he believed he could "do more good" at the penitentiary.

The prisoners speculated about the changes. The high-paid turnkeys appointed by the Republican Long would most likely be laid off and replaced with loyal Democrats, now that Governor Clarence Martin was in office. But what would that mean to daily prison life? A step back to the days of zebra-stripe uniforms and lockstep marches? Back to the Renquist boot—an iron contraption worn day and night on the foot that could shatter bone if an inmate tried to run in it? Miller had seen it all. Be respectful to them. Never challenge them, Miller told the boy. They hold the key to your future.

McCauley, however, brought good news to the prisoners. The shorn heads were ended and the state would start a $107,000 building program that would include new warehouses, a powerhouse, and a modernized hospital. Unlike Long, who believed punishment must include humiliations, McCauley was progressive. He had been a successful Dayton, Washington, wheat farmer until the market crashed in 1929 and he lost everything. When Martin ran for governor, McCauley ran the campaign in Eastern Washington. So when it came time to repay the favor, Martin appointed McCauley as warden.

McCauley believed in reformation and wanted prison to be a chance for men to learn new ways. He took his campaign to Kiwanis clubs, soliciting community support for job training, all the while defending himself against critics who claimed that the changes meant being soft on criminals and crime.

"There is a public curiosity about crime and one always hears about the man who is brought back to the institution. . . . They do not hear about the vast majority who make good," he told the Kiwanis in a speech. "I know personally of hundreds of cases of young men who have had their pride and will-power stimulated to such an extent that they have been able to re-enter society and become useful citizens." McCauley also told them that there was a crying need for segregation to allow some 250 "misfits" to be removed from associating with the rest of the prison population. Although the average age of prisoner is thirty-three, he said, there is an increasing number of youths at the prison. "This shows that greater emphasis should be placed on properly training youth today." The Kiwanis members applauded.

McCauley knew firsthand about young adults. He was a family man with a wife and four beautiful daughters. Although few saw them, their nearness filled the prison like the drifting scent of apple blossoms. In the library, prisoners read about his daughter, pretty pigtailed Nellie, being chosen Walla Walla Pioneer Days Queen and saw her picture in the *Walla Walla Daily Bulletin*, sitting on a fence.

From the trustees who worked at the mansion, the prisoners heard of the girls' beaus who came courting and of grand dinners with the new governor, Spokane wheat farmer Clarence Martin, who had appointed McCauley. The talk around the prison was like the talk around most dinner tables: speculation about the Democratic resurgence, the end of prohibition, Franklin Delano Roosevelt, the New Deal, and hope for the end of the Depression.

The new governor and his wife, Margaret, had been in the governor's mansion less than a month when Armene Lamson contacted the state's first lady on behalf of Herbert Niccolls. According to newspaper accounts written during the campaign, Martin had promised to consider paroling Niccolls, but Father Flanagan and Mrs. Lamson were concerned that the wrong approach would set Martin against the idea of parole like it had his predecessor.

With Flanagan's encouragement, Mrs. Lamson called on the state's first lady, hoping to touch her heart as "a devout Catholic" and an admirer of Flanagan's work with youths.

The visit was much like her visit with Mrs. Hartley, with pleasantries and petit fours, white gloves and white linen. But unlike Mrs. Hartley, who as a governor's daughter was well-versed in the political subtleties of a tea party, Mrs. Martin was a nervous ingenue. Following the visit, Flanagan sent a note to the new first lady.

"My heart is filled with gratitude for the kindness and courtesy you have shown in the sympathetic manner in which you received the good friend of our home.... Mrs. Lamson... expressed most encouragingly the chances to bring relief to that unfortunate child, Herbert Niccolls." Then he asked her support in helping reclaim Herbert instead of punishing him. Several days later, he received a letter from Martin himself, indicating that Mrs. Martin was away. He promised to visit Walla Walla and "investigate the situation" and invited Flanagan to call should he come west.

Unless Martin acts soon, Flanagan wrote in a letter to Mrs. Lamson, "I will have no more faith in him than I have had in ex-Governor Hartley." And he had a deep sense of foreboding—as he packed his suitcase for a trip to Flagstaff, Arizona, where he was to see an alumnus of the home graduate from college—that Herbert would remain in the penitentiary for a very long time.

When several months later, there was nothing new from Martin's office, Flanagan wrote to Mrs. Lamson again.

"Outside of awakening the public conscience, nothing else, I feel, will be accomplished," he wrote. "This is politics. This is why I could never be a politician. I haven't the patience to play the game and I haven't the conscience that it takes for a politician to be successful."

It would have been wonderful for the boy to take his place among the others at the home. He had spent much of his limited time and energy trying to free the boy and now he had to carry on. There were other boys who needed him, others who needed rescuing from similar fates. He would continue to extend the offer to take him, but the boy was in God's hands.

Mrs. Lamson, too, had her own three children and other causes that needed her, including a new juvenile justice law that she created with the boy in mind. House Bill 9 made it possible for juveniles under eighteen who had committed murder to be sent to the State Training School in Chehalis instead of to prison. The bill also called for setting up a civilian Children's Code Commission comprised of members from the juvenile court, state health department, education department, and child welfare experts. She was delighted when it later passed and served as a model for similar bills in other states.

In the meantime, Martin asked Chief Parole Officer Garfield Davis to provide him with a report on Herbert's background. He said that he doubted the accuracy of Hartley's report.

A powerfully built man with a leonine head of hair, Davis looked distinguished in his trim suits and fedora, and he filled the small living room where Mary Addington sat in her worn rocker, penetrating him with a dark, unblinking gaze. Davis had spent his career in the State Patrol and knew every con at the penitentiary. He was unflappable, incorruptible, and a "square-shooter," as Broderick called him, who "couldn't be scared by man or woman"—except Mary Addington.

She had the keen eyes of a predator—large, dark, and watchful—as she pursed her lips and rocked, her face a map of lines. Her seemingly fragile body was tightly coiled as if ready to spring. In the shadowed corners of the room, he heard the scurry of mice as the old woman hissed and rocked, while speaking about damnation and eternal hell and how no one understood her son or grandson, and that the murders were the will of God, and that it was just punishment for the victims. She shows "a marked lack of judgment" and is "very peculiar," Davis wrote.

In Star, Idaho, Davis found Hazel Niccolls, Herbert's mother, a frightened woman who lived in terror of her husband escaping from the asylum and coming to kill her. He noted in his report that she "expressed the deepest sorrow over the act of her son, Herbert, and deeply sympathizes with the widow and children of Sheriff Wormell."

By that April, Martin had not only visited Herbert and enjoyed a long conversation with him after he appeared before the parole board, but had sorted fact from fiction and knew the boy's entire family history.

It was a sad and sordid family tree, with roots in deep poverty. As a farmer Martin knew there was truth to the adage that the apple doesn't fall far from the tree. Yet the boy he had seen had hair neatly combed and wore dungarees and a sweater, was polite as any mother could ever hope her child to be. He suspected that the boy could fit in anywhere. Where was the ragged, gun-toting spitfire who had set fire to a church and shot a sheriff?

According to Davis, Mary C. Addington had been married three times, the first time when she was sixteen. She had nine children, one of them Herbert "Bert" Niccolls, the father of Herbert Junior. She claimed that her husband was a violent man and beat her and the children. However, the residents of Ada County, Idaho, who knew the family, disputed this, he noted. Nevertheless, she divorced the man, married again, divorced again, and married a third time. That third husband died.

When Bert Niccolls was committed to the insane asylum in Imola, California, following his trip there "to save souls," Mrs. Addington was successful in getting him released to her care. After he shot and killed Mrs. Frazier and was taken to the asylum at Orofino, Idaho, Mrs. Addington moved there. She began working as a maid in a hotel and launched another campaign to free him, eventually moving to Asotin. "While she has tried to convey the impression that her reason for moving to Asotin was to establish a home for her grandson, amid new surroundings upon his release from the training school, it is the consensus of people who are acquainted with her scheming that her move to Asotin was part of her plan to secure the release of her son from the insane asylum," Davis wrote. He added that perhaps she had hoped to convince Idaho officials to release the man, so she could remove him from the state and from Idaho's responsibility.

Mrs. Addington, Davis noted, was raised by religious parents and had been affiliated with a number of churches, among them the Methodist Church South, the Church of Christ, the Church of Truth, and the Pentecostal Church. Mrs. Addington is what is known as a "holy roller," Davis wrote.

According to Davis's report, Herbert "Bert" O. Niccolls was born at Montrose, Colorado, in 1893, and lived there until he married Hazel Gillespie in Baker, Oregon, when he was twenty-one. Hazel had a happy childhood as the daughter of a building contractor and was seventeen when she married Bert, after a three-month courtship. For the first few years, Bert worked in logging camps as a blacksmith and at other logging-related occupations until he and his young family moved to Star, Idaho, in 1918. He was known to be "a religious enthusiast" and not overly industrious, but he provided the necessities of life, often by hunting game.

Davis related how after Bert's second commitment he was "classed as a paranoiac and dangerous to be at large." When informed that his son had killed the sheriff of Asotin, the elder Niccolls was said to have said that "there is nothing I can do." When he was subpoenaed to testify at his son's trial, he tore up the notice, threw it on the floor, and said "I should worry."

Bert Niccolls's maternal grandmother was insane and confined to an asylum at Blackfoot, Idaho, where she died. Two of his paternal uncles were inmates of insane asylums, Davis wrote. In all of them, the cases of insanity were "accompanied by homicidal tendencies," he added.

Even for a progressive, the family history of mental illness and violence was shocking and hard to overlook. On a spring evening Martin set the report down on the desk in his new office and thumbed through the pages. The letters advocating for the boy's release were beginning.

"It's the modern theory that juveniles don't have the same ability to form criminal intent as do adults," wrote King County Superior Court Judge Everett Smith. Those who have twelve-year-old boys will know how reckless and irresponsible they can be and "just the other day I observed my 10-year-old grandson . . . swaggering around with . . . bravado. . . . There are not many steps between him and the boy of 12 with a real gun, who from inadequate training . . . takes a notion to commit some crime."

Martin pored over the letters and the report, refusing to interrupt himself, even long enough to notify his wife of his whereabouts. He was a conscientious man, except in family matters. He knew of his wife's tears but no longer was moved by them. They had become part of his routine, like the chiming of a clock or the turning of a calendar page, marking years while signifying nothing.

Yet he preened over his appearance, his tiny mustache, his sleek hair, and dapper suits that made up his public image. And he was aware, too, of his standing in the party. It could be politically advantageous to parole Herbert Niccolls and become Flanagan's hero. But it seemed more risky when the boy's family opposed it. Should that hit the press, it could be political suicide for him and give him an image of being soft on crime. He read Davis's report again.

Mrs. Addington, Davis said, is strongly anti-Catholic and she vehemently opposes any move to take the boy from prison to live at Boys Town. In fact, she insisted that the boy's attorney contact the penitentiary and advise them that any attempt to move him would be fought. Even the boy's mother added that he should remain incarcerated until he has paid for his crime. Martin shook his head. It was a sordid tale. No wonder the boy got into trouble. It was in his genes. And the case was one that should not be decided quickly, no matter what Flanagan and his supporters thought.

Mrs. Addington's request via attorney Doyle had mystified Warden Long when he received it. But it stunned McCauley when it was passed on to him. The boy had done well under the current arrangement but it was disruptive to prison routine and McCauley worried about the boy's safety. He was only too aware of the sexual appetites of incarcerated men and the boy's small frame and tender age would make him easy prey. Eventually, it would be difficult to justify keeping him out of the main population. It would be a blessing to have him paroled to Father Flanagan. It would be one less thing to worry about. And he had plenty of those.

Even the guards were talking about how Mrs. McCauley packed her bags and left in the middle of the night, how the warden followed her past the guard towers at the gate, pleading with her to return to the house. She had been despondent since arriving at the mansion and when she left, she vowed never to return. However, she was back within days and once again the mansion rang with the cannon fire of heated arguments and accusations.

When summer arrived, Herbert worked for McCauley as he had worked for Long's household. He liked the new warden, who always had a kind word and an easy smile but who also seemed troubled as he brooded at his desk, staring out the window at the summer flowers. Herbert's spade rang out as he tilled the soil. The girls' laughter drifted from open windows and the fountain in the courtyard splashed. He wasn't allowed to speak to them and Mr. Rose advised him to not be caught staring at them either. But it was difficult not to. He caught glimpses of swirling petticoats, heard the click of high-heeled shoes, saw the slash of bright lipstick on a creamy face, sniffed the breeze for a hint of perfume that was as heady as the fragrance of flowers. He had caught glimpses of women when the prison baseball teams played, and the women from the wing outside the walls sat in the bleachers and cheered the men on. But the McCauley girls were the only young women he had seen since coming to the penitentiary. He wondered if Jean Watkins ever thought of him.

Planes droned overhead, scribbling chalk against the blue sky. They were magical machines to him, sleek and silver, rising like birds, capable of carrying him far away into the softness of a cloud-padded heaven. Did the other prisoners dream of the future, too? He seldom thought of them; they were so much different from him, with his privileged status, lunching with officers, being tutored, and kept separate from the rest. He had overheard conversations and knew they resented him more each day as their suffering became greater.

While McCauley had made changes, many of the routines continued. Each morning prisoners marched two-by-two silently from the cellblocks to the cafeteria for meals, to prison industries like the license-plate factory, the laundry, the tannery, or the tailor shop, and were never allowed to speak throughout the day. Although there were new buildings under construction, it would be a few years before a new cellblock was added. Most cells remained cold in winter and unbearable in summer. During June, July, and August, the temperature was consistently over 100, peaking on July 15 at 104 degrees. Men fainted and the stench from the open buckets burned their eyes and made them gag.

The 1,500 prisoners were crammed two to a cell and the weaker of the two often succumbed to the whims of the other. Herbert did not like the muffled sounds in the night and the occasional sharp cry.

On July 28, Ollie Lee Stratton was hanged for murdering a Port Townsend man the previous year. As always, prisoners heard the cannon-fire snap of the trapdoor springing open and later the roar of a truck shortly after midnight as someone went to collect the body. Later Stratton would be buried in the graves flanking the prison—Cellblock 9 they called the area, where each grave was marked with a number rather than a name.

As the heat of July and August wore on into September, there were more and more furtive glances between prisoners, subtle movements in shadows, like the scent of a storm before the clap of thunder. Five men tried to escape in two separate incidents—one was killed by the guards.

The frightened public demanded increased security at the prison, Martin asked McCauley at the fall parole board meeting: "Is this what prison reform brings?" The public wanted to know.

•

Fall came in a sheet of gold, bringing with it the first brushstroke of frost. The boy knew it had arrived when he awoke before dawn and shivered beneath his blanket.

November brought rain in biblical proportions and just when it seemed the earth could absorb no more, it began to snow. Dizzying drifts spiraled from the heavens. The parole board was snowed in and staying in the hotel downtown. They arrived for the meeting, stomping and blowing like draft horses, peeling away mufflers and gloves set to dry near the radiator, filling the room with the scorched smell of wet wool.

Shortly before the meeting, Miller told the boy of his news. His brother in Mexico had offered him a business opportunity in a smelter if he could persuade the board to free him. He, of course, wanted to return to Seattle and clear his name but his supporters—primarily attorneys who "hated to see the law abused"—urged him to leave the area. If he didn't go to Mexico, he could go to see another brother in Melbourne, Australia. And if not there, other destinations called to him. He spoke many languages. He had money saved from years back. Anything was possible.

Peter Miller had been up against the parole board many times since arriving in 1913. Each time he had hoped and each time he had been disappointed.

At the November 1933 meeting, he appeared again. He gazed about the room coolly, as if the board members were mere children, and when asked about his accomplishments he noted that he had read ten thousand books during his lifetime. Broderick did not dispute it. "It was evident that he had absorbed everything in them but the bindings," he wrote later. "He discoursed on every conceivable subject with deep understanding."

When Miller asked the board for permission to go to Mexico City, he also amazed the board by showing "a fine knowledge of the Castilian language," Broderick said. And after making the demonstration, Miller stood waiting. The radiator creaked and popped, papers rustled, a chair scraped against the floor and one of the board members cleared his throat. This time instead of the usual rejection, the board members approved his parole.

Miller was stunned. He had spent twenty years in prison and was now nearing seventy. Slowly, he walked from the boardroom into the prison yard, snow falling lightly as freedom with all its possibilities unfurled before him.

Yet the prospects also concerned him. So much was left to be done. Who would represent the men's concerns to the new warden? As the icy breath of winter sailed through cellblocks, rage fueled dreams of revolt. Who would be there to dispel anger, to tell the men that violence begets violence and ask them to give the new warden a chance? The tendrils of anger crept from the license-plate factory to the tailor shop, entwining all in its path. He had seen it in the prisoners' eyes. If only they would wait. But their desperation grew in summer's sun and the winter's cold, until now violence and hatred were ready to spill over the boundaries of self-preservation and common sense. What would happen to the boy should the prisoners riot? They hated the youth for the privileges they lacked. In the four towers were guards armed with machine guns. Any rioters would be cut down. No one would be spared, and their hostages would die as well.

It was December, the day of Miller's departure, and in the library the boy sat at a table reading and Rose was at his desk. The librarian stood and shook Miller's hand. The boy stood also. For the first time Miller noticed the growing down on the boy's lip, the lanky young body and the voice that wavered between boyhood and manhood. A young man was emerging from the angry child and his wild heart was now being filled with calm reason and a passion for knowledge.

Herbert watched from the window as guards led Miller away to freedom. Snow quickly erased the heavy footsteps as Miller crossed the yard, the snow covering his bare head. Flakes swarmed from the heavens, the wind sending them swirling higher and higher until there was nothing but the howl of the wind.

Chapter 16

I**T WAS ONE P.M.** and the back-to-work call from the chief turnkey's office rang through Cellblock 1. Levers clanged. Cell doors flew open and the steel runways echoed with dozens of marching feet. Two-by-two the inmates returned to the prison industries. Assistant Chief Turnkey Williams watched them pass. They were orderly, compliant. He returned to his desk.

As the hands of the prison clocks crept closer to 1:50 p.m., the veteran guard on the catwalk studied the gray sky. There was an uneasy silence around the prison yard. Perhaps he thought of the still eye of a hurricane—the blessed respite in the midst of Armageddon and the collapse of the orderly world—as he again glanced at the shadows around the cellblocks. He saw a flicker of motion. Was it a piece of paper scudding across the lawn in a puff of wind?

It was cold and the grass was dotted with islands of melting snow. He completed his patrol, opened the door to the guard station, and blew on his hands to warm them. He then poured coffee from a Thermos and removed two chocolate-chip cookies that his wife had wrapped in wax paper. The afternoon was so still he could hear the ticking of his heart.

In the library, Herbert Niccolls was doing his lessons. Mr. Rose, whose job was also to censor the mail, laid another stack of letters down and sighed.

McCauley sat in his office staring at the pile of paperwork on his desk. He had returned from lunch at the mansion and he had a pain in his gut. Stress, the doctor said. There were 1,500 men crowded into a prison built to hold 700 but the public questioned his plans for prison reform. Then there was the matter of his wife. She had left again and was now back. But for how long? He didn't approve of divorce—it seemed like failure. Yet the calm of loneliness seemed better than the domestic storm. Indeed, it was calm. He glanced at the clock.

In the workshops the men paced and watched out the windows. About 300 prisoners had just entered the exercise court outside Cellblock 5 and they, too, stretched and walked slowly around the yard, shivering in the cold, except for a group of six. With furtive glances, the six edged toward the heavy steel door of the cellblock and eased it open.

They were lifers with no possibility of parole, and the gamble for freedom came easily. For the last two months they had crafted a plan, carefully synchronized to make it possible to take over the bulls inside the cellblock without the ones on the wall ever knowing. Then it was a simple matter of using the hostages as human shields—the more vulnerable the better—and they could force their way out the gates.

The conspirators disappeared inside the cellblock one by one. When the last of them was out of sight, a man at a window in the shoe shop let a handkerchief flutter to the ground. It was the signal that the man in the barbershop was waiting for and he, too, passed on his own signal.

•

Officer Burnett was watching the men in the yard when he heard the door to his office open. He whirled around in shock and demanded to know what the men thought they were doing and then ordered them back into the exercise yard.

Pulling a chain from his pocket, one calmly told Burnett that they planned to lock him up. Burnett's hand moved toward his hip and as the man with the chain struck out, Burnett's nightstick cracked against the prisoner's forehead. The prisoner reeled and stumbled. Then as blood trickled down his face, he rose and screamed for the others. Suddenly, wrenches, pipes, a club, and a knife appeared in a surge of flailing arms. The first riot in the prison's history had begun, and when it was over eight would be dead.

Burnett was the first injury. As he sprinted toward help in the cell-block lobby, a prisoner with the crude knife made from scissors used in the tailor shop, slashed across his belly. Burnett was almost to the lobby when the mob caught him again. Their arms rose and fell. Men cursed. Flesh split. Blood spattered. Turnkey George Binder ran to the door and was stunned at the carnage and ordered the men to stop. Binder was well liked in the prison and the mob told him to stand back, but Binder struck out with his fists. He in turn was struck with a chain and when he stumbled, another hit him in the head with a wrench. Finally, he and Burnett, were locked together in a cell. Guard Addington, who was not a big man and nearing sixty, rushed in. He too was struck over the head and slashed.

Guard Jackson was talking with Guard Hubbard, who was leaning nonchalantly against the wall near the alarm box in an office, when four prisoners walked in. Jackson stared at one of the men's caps. What was the matter with it? he demanded to know. The prisoner, who had hidden a homemade knife beneath the cap, apologized, removed the cap, and in a flash, whipped out the knife and ordered Jackson and Hubbard into the corner. Jackson grabbed a blackjack from his belt and struck the man with the knife in the forehead. But the man stepped back, unfazed. Before Jackson could strike again, someone had slipped a wire around his neck and he was jerked backward; the wire tightened.

Jackson struggled to breathe and could hear the roar of his own heartbeat, the dull thuds of fists splitting flesh, a sharp cry, and the flash of a raised arm with a knife. As if in slow motion, it came down toward Hubbard. Jackson tried to throw himself between the attacker and the guard, but was jerked back. Then the arm went up again. This time the knife was meant for him. He could do nothing but stare in horror. Suddenly an inmate stepped between him and the man with the knife.

What the hell was going on? It was Bobby Landis, notorious now for his own escape attempts, Landis who was shouting, Landis who was saving his life.

Then Jackson slipped into unconsciousness as they dragged him into a cell and locked him up with Hubbard, who was bleeding from stab wounds to his shoulder.

The lucky break that ultimately would bring an end to the escape plot came when an inmate, long believed to be a stool pigeon, rushed into the cellblock screaming that he was about to be killed. The mob turned as the man dove beneath a table. Addington moved toward the door to the clothing room and took the key from his pocket. But the mob had again turned to him. He struck out with a club. Addington staggered toward the door and inserted the key in the lock; the door opened with a creak. He squeezed inside, clicked the lock and unsteadily climbed to the barred windows overlooking the prison yard. He kicked out the glass, took the police whistle from around his neck and began to blow. Again and again the whistle shrilled across the quiet courtyard.

The No. 1 Tower guard scanned the building. Just then his phone rang. It was the guard from No. 4 Tower. "Hear that whistle? Sounds like trouble."

After years working in the prison library, Mr. Rose had developed a sixth sense about danger, sensing it as easily as he could catch the scent of an impending thunderstorm. But on this afternoon, he went to the window. He heard the whistle. Again and again. Then it was still. Too still. Unnaturally so. He placed a call to the administration building. There was no answer.

What happened to Herbert Junior during one of the worst riots in the penitentiary's history is uncertain. Rose, who was fond of the boy and entrusted to care for him, could have ordered him to hide in the one place he'd be unlikely to be found—a mail sack. Or he could have been locked up with Rose and his assistants, or he could have become a victim of sexual assault. There were numerous reports of ongoing sexual assaults at the prison, some Lamson and Flanagan had heard about. Given the inmates' jealousy and resentment over Herbert, he certainly would have been vulnerable during the riot, especially when the inmates were looking for human shields. One thing that is known—when the rioters entered the library, Rose sat quietly sorting the mail. He calmly looked over the top of his glasses as the men rushed through the door.

"What do you think you're doing here? You'll never get away with it."

They scoffed at him, waving knives and telling him that they were going to lock him up. Rose, a veteran employee who was not easily frightened, leaned back in his chair and sighed, looking at the stacks of mail. They again ordered him out from behind his desk, threatening to "rough him up."

"Well, in that case, let's get on with it," Rose said. "But my assistants are coming with me." The men were shoving them down the hallway and into cells when Rose shouted, "You boys leave my mail alone if you go in there again."

As the cellblocks exploded, outside several hundred men in the exercise yard continued to calmly walk, unaware of the chaos. Meanwhile, the mob dashed down the hallway, locking up inmates hesitant to join in. Then the mob rushed into the chief turnkey's office where Williams sprang from his desk in shock.

He ordered them to put down their weapons and reached for his nightstick, but not before he was clubbed with a pipe. Some of the men took the keys to solitary and freed the men there, giving them the opportunity to join in the fray. As with the majority of inmates, most declined. Meanwhile, Williams was held at knifepoint.

They wanted the warden. They held a knife to Williams's throat and ordered him to get on the phone and tell the warden someone had been hurt. Williams lifted the receiver and dialed. The men waited expectantly but there was no answer. Just then the phone rang and Williams was ordered to answer it.

The warden wanted to talk to Guard Jackson. Jackson was removed from a cell and brought to the phone. If he tried anything, one inmate whispered, pressing a knife against the guard's stomach, "I'll spill your gut."

When the tower guards told McCauley about the whistle, he knew something was wrong. Then he learned that Chief Engineer S. B. Bowen and a parole officer had gone behind the walls and never come back. He feared that they had been taken hostage, possibly along with the women visitors in the cellblock lobby. When Jackson answered the phone, McCauley told him that if things were all right, to walk outside to the front of the building. Although Jackson had replied calmly that everything was routine, he never walked out. In order to stall the mob and give his guards enough time to get in position, McCauley continuously placed calls to the cellblock but refused to answer when anyone called him. He hoped, too, that the mob would eventually be forced to move into the open, where the guards had a better chance at subduing them with less risk of harm to the hostages.

After the inmates made several more futile tries to entice McCauley to come to the scene, one of the ringleaders glanced out a cellblock window. On the catwalk surrounding the prison, an army of guards with machine guns had suddenly appeared. An inmate shouted to the others but when the ringleader looked out the window, there was only one guard in sight.

The ringleader shouted at the others. Were they crazy? All the bulls in the place were locked up and the rest of the prison guards didn't even know. He gave an order to wire the captured guards together to form a human shield. Many were severely injured and bleeding as they moved into the afternoon light—Jackson, with a wire around his neck, and Williams were among them. When Williams stumbled off the sidewalk and fell, nearly pulling down several others, one of the inmates stabbed him in the leg, warning him not to try it again.

Slowly, the band shuffled across the prison yard until they were within a dozen feet of the wall. The army of armed guards stood up and the band stared into the muzzles of dozens of shotguns and rifles.

"Open up the gate, or we'll kill every bull here," the ringleader said.

A tower guard replied that it would not open and that if any of the officers were hurt, the rioters would pay with their lives. Let them go now. Lie down and surrender, he shouted.

The mob cursed and yelled as the guard on the wall again ordered them to lie down. Slowly, the group began to move backward toward the cellblock. None obeyed the command to lie down. Suddenly, Williams, who was leading the human shield, stopped and refused to move. The inmates behind him prodded him with knives but still he resisted. The guard on the wall again repeated the command to lie down.

Suddenly, a shot rang out and everywhere there was confusion. Orders were given and ignored on the wall. And in the yard, the mob began to scatter. Hostages freed themselves and bolted, except for Jackson, who was held with a wire around his neck. Three inmates gathered behind him. More shots were fired. More commands were given to lie down. Two men fell; others ran toward the wall, or the cellblock. A bullet slammed into a man, standing behind Jackson. Then another bullet slipped between Jackson's arm and side and buried itself in his captor's shoulder. One of the guards, Briggs, became confused in his flight to freedom and ran toward the shops, but was grabbed by four fleeing convicts. More bullets were fired. Briggs collapsed. An inmate dived through a basement window. Another leaped through the doors of the cellblock and then collapsed from a bullet wound. The parole officer and chief engineer came to the door of one of the shops and as they did a bullet whizzed past, striking and killing an inmate, who was not involved in the escape and standing ten feet behind them. Another inmate popped his head outdoors to see what was happening and was struck and killed by a ricocheting bullet. Another inmate in one of the shops held a mirror out the door, hoping to watch in the reflection, when a bullet struck it, shattering the mirror and leaving a piece of glass impaled in his hand.

When the shooting stopped, the lawn was soaked in blood and covered with the bodies of the dead and wounded. Briggs and eight inmates died that day. One man in solitary was taken to the field where the dead lay only to identify the body of his son. When spring came that year, many of those who had rioted were still in solitary, listening to the drumming tattoo of the rain. When it subsided, the summer heat began.

Throughout the prison, there was a dark and uneasy silence, the silence of despair, but for Herbert Niccolls, at fifteen, there was an anxiousness to sail across the sky into the future. Dr. Kern from the school district arrived once a week through the end of June for lessons but it wasn't the same as when Peter Miller had been there. Now there was only Mr. Rose to talk to and he was busy most days. The press still arrived, but not as often. When they did now, they asked the boy what he wanted to become. They seemed to believe that he would one day be paroled. But at the prison, there was talk of ending his special status and putting him with the other inmates. A life sentence, after all, was a life sentence.

Chapter 17

THE GREAT NORTHERN trundled through the Cascade Mountains and across the Eastern Washington prairies for eight hours before it came screeching and hissing to a halt at a crossing a quarter mile from the prison. Passengers opened windows and looked back, questioning the delay. While in the prison car, men stumbled to their feet, their chains clanking. A guard walked the length of the car, thumping his nightstick against arms, legs, and shoulders, barking orders to stay in line. Another guard pulled open the door to the car and stepped out. The night air was warm and the heat from the unusual 100-degree days radiated from the rails. He nodded and motioned to the guard inside. One by one the chained men stepped out, among them James Ashe, journalist, literary agent, and prisoner.

He was a small-boned man with a shock of chestnut hair swept back over a broad forehead. He had olive skin, the kind of dark eyes women found appealing, and the smooth-skinned hands of a gentleman. Like a character from some of the books he represented, he spoke with a slight accent that hinted of old-moneyed Boston homes or the British aristocracy. He was educated at Oxford, provided with ample funding for his education and maintenance, and had served three years in the British Army during the World War. Until he ran afoul of Mrs. Sara Shannon, he had always been regarded as a well-heeled gentleman, more likely to be reclining in a smoking jacket in a posh club than to be unwashed, unshaved, and wearing tattered jail clothing on his way to a state prison.

"The frails," he heard another prisoner complain, blaming his predicament on women. He could echo the sentiment, except "frail" was not something he'd call Mrs. Shannon.

•

The Seattle police detective asked him at the time of his arrest if he fancied himself a ladies' man. Pretty boy with fancy manners, he had called him. Then the detective struck him with the nightstick until there was nothing fine-featured or delicate left. Even his precarious claim to social standing had nearly disappeared. But he clung to the image of his former self like a man on a life raft.

He was born in Holyoke, Massachusetts, the illegitimate son of a British aristocrat. But despite being financially well provided for in his youth, he was only too aware of being on the outside looking in, never quite able to belong to anyone or anything except when he drank. That's when he saw his image reflected a hundredfold in crystal chandeliers in the Olympic Hotel Spanish Ballroom and in the silver trays of hovering waiters. When he was among them, he was the sun in a galaxy of adoring planets. But the image quickly dissipated like champagne bubbles and once again he would find himself adrift and alone.

He moved well in polite society, wherever it was—Dallas, Los Angeles, Boston, Seattle, Tampa—and found it easy to charm women. While working in a Tampa advertising agency, he met and married pretty Verna Princeton, a Tennessee belle. He bought her an automobile, toured the coast with her, stopped to see her family, and then drove up the Atlantic coast. They stayed at charming hotels, dining and dancing, and then traveled to Maine, where he completed a real estate transaction, netting an easy $34,000. With the proceeds, they flew back to Palm Beach, then to New Orleans for the Mardi Gras, where they caught a train and continued on by parlor car until they reached Los Angeles. They settled there amidst the glitter of Hollywood. They met movie stars and went to the best parties. After making contacts in the business world, he started Canterbury Publishing. He bought his Verna a stylish muskrat coat and expensive bracelets and rings, and for a while they were happy.

Then her mother moved in and Verna was no longer his alone. He was jealous. She was angry. They fought and, seeking a change to revive their flagging marriage, they moved north. They bought a weekly newspaper in Bend, Oregon, turned it into a prosperous daily, sold it, and moved to Seattle where he planned to work as a literary agent. It was a community of old-timber money, a solid fortress of respectability, if one could only gain entrance. Mrs. Shannon, a wealthy widow of a pioneer Seattle doctor, seemed to have the ticket for entrance.

James Ashe had contacts in the literary world and, while kissing their hands and gazing into their eyes, sipping cocktails and listening to their heartbreaks, he wove a net of business arrangements that ultimately brought his downfall. He found himself spending more and more in order to "keep up appearances," as he told Verna. But the money wasn't coming in like it had in the past. For the first time in his life, he was worried about having enough to eat and pay the rent.

Once when Mrs. Shannon invited him to her hotel apartment to discuss her book, *Helloise*, over cocktails, she noted in court testimony that he inexplicably left with the bottle of gin, a can of soup, and some apples. Nevertheless, more invitations followed and somewhere it seemed the focus of what the money was for became lost.

Mrs. Shannon called him incessantly, his secretary testified at the trial, and he made excuses to avoid her. It was the last straw for Verna, who moved out and returned to California. Not long after, Mrs. Shannon complained to police he had defrauded her of $16,000. He was arrested and charged with larceny. He had his fans, though. It wasn't to his benefit, however, having the courtroom filled with them—women who called him "Jimmy" and doted on his Back Bay accent.

The first trial ended in a hung jury. The second trial immediately followed and for months he languished in jail. It had been hellish—the brutal beatings, the solitary confinement. And then the guard with the nightstick. He had done unspeakable things to him. He told his attorney, Albert Rossellini, his only friend, and he noted it on his prison intake form. In the end, the jury found that he had defrauded Mrs. Shannon of $5,000, not the $16,000 she said she had paid him to fix a literary contest she didn't win. The jurors recommended he be leniently sentenced. But the judge instead declared him to be the "worst kind of scoundrel" and sentenced him to five to fifteen years in the penitentiary.

•

There he was on a hot night, stepping from the prison car, a guard nudging him in the back with a nightstick. He walked slowly, the chains at his ankles keeping his gait short. His hands were chained to a band at his waist. Not far away the prison, its dark silhouette ringed with lights, loomed on a hill. It filled him with terror, as it did other prisoners on the "chain." Even though it was only June, the day had been dry and hot and the temperature had dropped little. A gust of wind sent the dust swirling and a tumbleweed cartwheeled past. The bone-white moon blanched the prisoners' faces. The guards ordered the men to walk two-by-two. The iron gate to the prison creaked open. It was as if he had at last come to the entrance of hell.

The train creaked and groaned as it pulled away from the crossing, its whistle shrill in the night.

•

Mr. Rose was finding his duties as mail censor, librarian, and now teacher a tedious endeavor. It was not that the boy was especially difficult, but it did take considerable time out of his day to instruct Herbert Niccolls. When James Ashe was assigned to him as a library assistant, the soft-spoken literary agent seemed to be a natural tutor for the boy, who shook hands with him like a perfect gentleman. The warden himself suggested Ashe for the job. With his slight build and refined ways, Ashe would never fare well mixed into the rest of the prison population. In fact, he had already developed a wary nervousness and a strained, gaunt appearance.

The first day the boy noticed how Ashe fidgeted, rubbing the back of his neck and often appearing to hold back a floodgate of tears. While he could teach the boy mathematics, his skills at writing and literature were his strengths. Ashe was surprised to find himself in the boy's company—the boy he had heard so much about. Until now, he believed the Herbert Niccolls of the newspapers to be tougher, older than this fragile slip of a boy, not unlike he himself had been at that age, with his fine-featured face and dark hair. Herbert would be a handsome man some-day. Not that it would do him any good. It would be a detriment as long as he remained in prison.

Ashe spoke often about Hollywood, where he and his wife had opened Canterbury Publishing. There were parties on seaside terraces and in grand hotels, fragrant orange groves, and the kiss of the sun on golden sand. Anything was possible in Hollywood. Mortals became gods and goddesses and there were more of them than the stars in heaven.

Ashe told the boy of cowboys with magnificent horses and saddles twinkling with silver and how he knew so many stars—the saucy Clara Bow, the petulant Mary Pickford, and Douglas Fairbanks. Who would have ever thought there would come a day when he, "Jimmy" Ashe, would find himself destitute and his family inheritance gone. Though everyone, of course, lost fortunes in the crash of 1929.

Financial matters had put a stress on his marriage. But when Verna's mother moved in, it was the beginning of the end of the closeness the couple had known. Moving to Oregon only increased the distance be-tween them. She missed California, the warm, sunny days. She missed the Egyptian Theatre, shopping at the department stores on the boule-vard, and the breathless excitement that crackled in the air.

"Come to Hollywood and change your life," was the motto of the day. On a hillside north of town in bright white lights the word "HOLLY-WOODLAND" lit up the night like a gilded invitation to a new life.

The thought of movies with sound amazed Herbert. Ashe told him how the audience wept when they heard Al Jolson speak in *The Jazz Singer*, falling on his knees and crying "Mammy!" Herbert heard the voices himself when they started showing movies with sound at the prison. He found it astonishing to sit in the auditorium and hear the thunder of horses' hooves, the whooping of attacking Indians, the sigh of lovers. There was a vast world beyond the walls, a world of adventure far more exciting than the predictable, controlled world of prison where the choices were so few.

Herbert longed to visit Hollywood. Someday if he made good, perhaps he'd be free. Then, like a bird, he'd fly over the walls. From the library window he could see beyond the guard towers to the tops of trees afire with gold. Ashe told him there was a world out there where a man could be anything he wanted to be—provided he lived right. And then Ashe fell silent.

•

In the recreation yard, leaves rocked on a breeze, drifted to the frosty earth. Inmates enjoying a brief respite chatted with one another and smoked cigarettes—the blue tendrils of smoke curling in the chilly air.

Ashe also was assigned to teach English at the prison's night school and work on the *Agenda*, the prison magazine. Every day he read inmate manuscripts, circling the words of their dreams, slashing their time-skewed vignettes of home and the holidays with the hard line of proper punctuation.

They wrote of sleighs, snow, and grandma's house. But not the boy, he wrote of flying machines and time travel. He had no homesick pangs. While others suffered, the boy thrived. The methodical life of education, exercise, and regular meals within the confines of rigid structure of the prison suited him. No longer was he able to break free, tumbling into the dark time and space where his impulsive acts had no boundaries.

While Herbert seemed content with prison life, Ashe, on the other hand, spent hours writing to his attorney and to friends, asking them to persuade the governor to grant him clemency. He had been in prison only five months but it seemed like a lifetime. The first thirty days—his "fish time," as the time when the new inmates, or fish, were kept isolated was termed—were especially hellish. He was sent through the shower with the others and deloused. The fine woolen jacket he once wore was only a distant memory and in its place were a denim shirt and trousers.

If he had been inclined toward pretentiousness before, he was more so now in this wide landscape of despair. He spoke properly, primly, trying to grasp at the hem of what had been his life as a gentleman as it swept past into history.

Now, he was in the prison library with a young boy who was ready and willing to absorb any knowledge that he wanted to share. His influence was considerable. Gradually, Herbert's language shifted to mirror Ashe's and the slang was gradually replaced with phrases like "indeed, I shall," and "certainly." He stood erect like Ashe, too, and copied his manners. It came naturally. Herbert's mother, after all, had raised him to have good manners, the one thing that was free, she had told him.

While he and Ashe got along well, sometimes, in the middle of a lesson, Ashe would suddenly stop and become speechless, his eyes brimming with tears. One day the tears no longer came and he knew then that the tender spot where passion resided had become cold and hard. The chill of December swept over him.

•

Since the riot in February, deep, broken, bass notes of desperation linked the inmates. Through the infestation of black widow spiders in June, the stabbing death of an inmate that same month, the heat of summer, executions, and the scandal—a prison clerk who had been charged with theft was sentenced to the very institution from which he pilfered—the days passed with little more significance than another tally mark on the wall.

The prisoners knew of the arrival of winter when they awoke to find ice crystals in the buckets and could see their exhalations linger in the frigid air. Christmas was coming but it made no difference to most. The lucky received letters or visits. For the rest, it was just another day in the cold, standing in lines—lines for food, lines for work, lines to chapel—being a number, not a name.

For some, the years passed with little change, every so often an appearance before the parole board, where they listened to the governor's grumbling while they stared at the floor respectfully, cap in hand, not daring to hope that this time the door might swing open. But what would the outside world bring—so many changes for those who'd been isolated for decades.

As Christmas day of 1934 came around, McCauley had a surprise of his own in mind. Workers spent days stringing wires through 1,500 feet of metal conduit in the cellblocks. Utah Orthovox Magnetic speakers were installed. And in the boardroom, there was a maze of black panels, powerpacks, transformers, tubes, control buttons, switches, a twelve-tube bridging amplifier, and a microphone. Those who had been in prison for a long time had never heard the magic of radio. As the installation progressed, no one was sure what the warden had in mind—until Christmas Eve. That's when, shortly before lights out, there was a scratching noise, a whine and crackling, and the cellblocks filled with glorious sound as "Silent Night" rang through the prison.

Chapter 18

MEN WERE DYING in record numbers across the nation as trapdoors of numerous gallows slammed open, marksmen in firing squads took aim, and prisoners were electrocuted and gassed. In 1935, 199 people, more than any at any other time in the nation's history, would be put to death in the United States. In Washington, only one man, Hong Yick, a Chinese laborer convicted of murder in King County, was executed that year, but in the next several years, as many as three or four would be put to death each year.

The Depression was at its peak. Bruno Hauptmann had a date with "Old Smokey," the New Jersey electric chair, for kidnapping and murdering the Lindbergh baby. United Auto Workers struck at the Chevrolet plant. FDR explained his proposed Work Relief program. The Resettlement Administration moved poor families to planned Greenbelt towns in Wisconsin, Ohio, and Maryland, and the U.S. Supreme Court declared the National Industrial Recovery Act unconstitutional.

As for Herbert Niccolls, he was old news and the publishers told Armene Lamson this when she again tried to raise public awareness about his plight. Instead of featuring Father Flanagan's entreaties to free the boy, the headlines spoke of the Midwest drought and crop failures that were causing people to starve to death and move from their prairie homes, heading westward. There was the rumbling of war as in Germany Hitler became chancellor, abolished essential freedoms, and flexed his might. What was one small boy in the midst of such turmoil?

The bishop ordered Father Flanagan to take a three-month sabbatical in Rome after it became plain that Flanagan was so weary and worried about his home's survival that his own health, which was never good, was in jeopardy.

Speculating that Flanagan would now be back from Rome, Mrs. Lamson wrote to him, the governor, and McCauley. To her relief, Flanagan wrote back. He still wanted to see Herbert, "even at this late hour," adding that "Martin is no better than Hartley."

"He likes to play politics apparently, but why they don't play politics with others instead of a little boy [who] has been sinned against. . . . It seems that old man Satan has something to do with this—he doesn't want this boy to be saved."

Her letter prompted a quick response from Martin, who insisted all was well with Herbert. She felt reassured and yet a trace of suspicion would always linger whenever she thought of him. He was very young. How easy it would be to take advantage of him. She wished Martin would parole him to Boys Town.

Martin, however, had other plans. A regular visitor at the penitentiary, he had taken a liking to the boy and discovered that they even shared a birthday, June 29. McCauley also was proud of the boy's advancement and had brought him to the mansion more and more to work. Herbert shoveled snow, polished cars, and gazed, when no one knew he was looking, at the warden's daughters, drinking in their musical laughter.

•

High winds swept through the valley that March, sweeping the topsoil into a flurry of dust that made visibility almost impossible. It seeped into the cracks and crevices of houses and blew into cars. It swept through the prison dairy, the tannery, the cannery, and the barber shop. It spiraled and blew in the door of the administration building, swirled around the guard towers, and crept into the cellblocks, where dust floated in the shafts of light from the barred windows overhead. And it caked the windows of the warden's mansion, veiling the outside light in layers of silt. Mrs. McCauley had left again after a domestic storm that rivaled the one outside. McCauley remained to console his daughters.

If ever there was a time when McCauley needed a compassionate friend, it was then. Never had the public been so dissatisfied with his leadership and his plans for prison reform than after the riot. Day after day, the newspapers carried scathing stories. Every favor—such as letting the prisoners have more items in their cells than they had ever had before to the dismay of the guards—was now trumpeted to the public as unwarranted leniency. He had stopped the old practice of shaving the prisoners' heads. He let prisoners talk at work and at meals. They no longer had to walk with their arms folded across the chest.

He had thought that these changes would result in improved behavior—so few of the men were really problem prisoners. But it hadn't. What it got him was disrespect. The prisoners had saved the juice from their breakfast prunes, taken it back to their cells and fermented it, making the potent alcohol they called "pruno." They hid other contraband items and made weapons at their assigned jobs and used them to try to escape. The Spokane newspapers detailed it all, calling him a naïve and ineffective leader.

If ever he needed a star, now was the time. Nationwide, penitentiaries were grappling with the same question he had—what to do with juvenile offenders. The national Children's Bureau had started insisting that young people needed to be treated differently by the courts and the prison system than their adult counterparts.

McCauley couldn't be more pleased with Herbert Niccolls. But the question was how to keep him challenged? He was bright and in no time would need college material. McCauley agreed to make an arrangement with Washington State College in Pullman for correspondence classes, knowing that there would be others, both in prison and out, who would say that he was once again coddling a criminal. In the meantime, he had another execution to plan for.

•

That spring snow fell in April, dusting the white blossoms of the cherry trees and the swelling buds of apples and pears. On the night of the April 2, the mercury sank to twenty-four degrees in the valley. Farmers awoke from sleep to frantically light smudge pots, hoping to ward off the killing frost. Most were unsuccessful and lost their crops and their income for the year to come, and they joined the others who were broke and hungry as the Depression deepened. In October, snow came again, the earliest snowfall on record, accompanied by frost. In the dark valley, smudge pots once again burned like glowing orange eyes in the dark and wraiths of smoke rose and danced in the cold, still valley.

In December came the prison's Annual Revue. For weeks, the strains of banjo music, tap dancing, and a cavalcade of notes from the prison orchestra floated from the auditorium, a teasing reminder of the world outside. But two days before the performance, the sirens blared, signaling an escape, and the prison was locked down.

Eight had escaped from the new Cellblock 6 shortly after the night locks were thrown open at six a.m. All the escapees were serving long sentences, most of them for robbery. There had been tunneling attempts beneath the walls before but none had been successful until now and McCauley's administration was to blame. He surveyed the gaping hole in the A Corridor.

The escapees had removed some of the reinforced concrete flooring and dug a forty- to fifty-foot tunnel beneath the walls and the six-foot concrete footing buried beneath. Tons of dirt had been removed and disposed of down the cellblocks' plumbing—a luxury that some of the other cellblocks still didn't have. It must have taken a year to dig, McCauley theorized. How could they have undertaken such a large operation so covertly? How could three of them— Richard "Shotgun" Thompson, T. H. "Tubby" Johnson, and Clarence Miles, all who had made escape attempts previously—not been watched more closely? Miles had two escapes alone and had vowed that there would never be a prison that could hold him.

McCauley knew that any minute now his phone would ring and it would be the governor wanting an explanation of how the escape happened, how there had been such a security lapse. Unless the escapees were rounded up quickly, innocent citizens were at risk.

McCauley called the *Daily Bulletin* to advertise a fifty-dollar reward for each. By nightfall, all but two of the eight had been caught.

Despite the escapes, plans for the revue continued, the current of excitement sweeping through the prison. It opened December 11 to a full house of not only inmates but members of the public as well, with inmates singing "The Scat Song" and "Mammy, I'll Sing About You," à la Cab Calloway and Al Jolson, respectively, and tap dancing to "The Hen House Blues."

With two missing prisoners, an angry governor, an unhappy wife, and the general discord that permeated his household, McCauley wasn't in the holiday spirit. There was the usual extra work for the staff that Christmas brought: sorting out the extra mail and packages and removing contraband, such as the pair of roller skates one inmate's family had sent and the pair of skis another inmate had received, much to the amusement of his fellows.

Each wing had a designated day to write letters and afterward a designated inmate collected them and took them to the library. There Mr. Rose censored them, recorded them, and sealed them in envelopes before they were taken to the post office and stamped with the P.O. Box 520 return address. Each inmate was allowed to write fifteen letters weekly, which was more than what most usually wrote. But during holidays, the letters coming in and going out multiplied vastly.

Even Herbert received a letter. His mother had written, urging him to "be a good boy." And he had been, under Ashe's tutelage and Mr. Rose's guidance. Herbert's success was the one achievement in McCauley's tenure as warden of which he was especially proud.

The crowd was milling out of the auditorium, and the prisoners were filing out and being ushered into cellblocks. A few members of the public who had attended walked past the guards at the checkpoints and once again entered the world of freedom.

What did McCauley know about freedom? Lately, it seemed he had been oppressed by duty with no way out. Even his household trustees seemed to hate him. One woman had sliced all the collars and buttons off the shirts that she was supposed to wash and iron. Then she stormed back to her quarters, knowing her trustee days at the warden's house were over.

Ice covered the pool at the base of the mansion's fountain and glazed the tiers where on summer days water cascaded in a tinkling, rushing serenade. The windows of that magnificent old brick home, too, were frost-glazed, despite the amber glow of light from within. A trail of smoke drifted from the chimney. Perhaps he would sit by the fire, pour himself a drink and hope his wife was in bed asleep. Then at last the day would be his, to brood and to deny the pain in his gut.

Chapter 19

FATHER FLANAGAN was sitting on the porch wrapped in a blanket when two young boys came bearing a bouquet of spring flowers. He had been ill again. Seriously so. The children were allowed to visit him only in shifts, two or three here and there, each whispering to him that they were praying for him. He leaned forward in the chair to listen closely to the soft words, to pat a shoulder. The last few years had been difficult. When the crops had failed at the farm—as they had throughout the Midwest during the drought—the home had been perilously close to closing. But here it was two years later, still open; children were still being fed—although sometimes not much.

He had written to Mrs. Lamson about Herbert Niccolls. What had happened to the boy? How was he faring in prison? A mere child in with the worst of humanity. Governor Martin had done little. Sure, Martin had seen the boy and struck up a friendship, he had been told. But he had not paroled the boy to Boys Town so that he might have a chance to grow morally.

Flanagan had heard that Hartley was trying to run for a third term. It seemed all the energy put into the Niccolls campaign, all the editorials, the letters, the radio speeches—all had been for nothing. He knew well that the longer a boy was in bad company, the harder it was to turn his life around. Intervention must start early, the earlier the better, to save the flower from being lost among the weeds.

That's what he told his audiences wherever he spoke, from the radio stations of Seattle to an address he gave before college students in Flagstaff, Arizona. He told them, too, that gangster films were bad for children, especially poor children. He had seen a change in the movies, from the sentimental, where right prevailed, to those where criminals were heroes.

Darryl F. Zanuck's *The Public Enemy*, produced before the Production Code Administration imposed censorship, was the worst. It depicted a poor boy who gained underworld prestige and power and lived the high life by becoming a vicious criminal. *The Public Enemy* ushered in a new kind of film that was darker, with more sex and violence than ever before. And nothing could have been worse for the Herbert Niccollses of the world.

"Police authorities stress the possible evil influences of such films which encourage hungry and bewildered youths to go out and do similar things in real life to get money and relieve their miserable conditions," Flanagan had said. And misery was everywhere in these days of acute unemployment. Everywhere the hungry marched into state capitols to beg legislators for government help. They set up camps, nicknamed Hoovervilles, at the edge of towns. Union members battled for pay and benefits with the owners of factories, farms, and coal mines. And all manner of racketeering plagued the nation's highways as travelers were waylaid and money extorted from them as payment for being allowed to pass.

In the meantime, Boys Town had incorporated as an official village with its own mayor and post office. Poor though it was, for boys it was a sanctuary in the middle of chaos. Knowing his home for boys was now an official town with roots and a future gave Flanagan satisfaction. Perhaps now, Boys Town would survive him.

It was summer, sizzling and windy, with great rolling tumbleweeds skittering down the road in front of the warden's mansion like a runaway carnival ride. The circus had come to town and trucks rumbled up and down the road near the prison, the advance man announcing the coming of the show in the big top—Big Sadie, 500 pounds of wiggly-jiggly love, and her husband, the 7-foot-5-inch Boris the Russian Giant. There were lions, tigers, and bears, too, tamers in top hats, elephants wise and wonderful, acrobats, jugglers, magicians, clowns, and dazzling bareback riders in sequined costumes.

Herbert could hear the parade, so close and yet part of that forbidden distant world. He returned to his spade and the garden and the rhythm rang through the afternoon. From inside the house came the sound of sobbing. It was a familiar sound, though before he had always associated the sound with his mother.

McCauley had congratulated himself on the fact that the two inmates missing after the escape were found the next day in Spokane and returned to the penitentiary. But on July 8, nine inmates assigned to the prison cannery were caught trying to tunnel out of the prison. One was a lookout as others dug with shovels taken from a construction site near the laundry. With seventy men busy canning peas and beans and milling about the loading dock, depositing the dirt beneath the cannery platform was easy. Guards, however, had suspicions. When it came time for the inmates' weekly baths, they had noticed an unusual amount of fine dirt on seven of the inmates when they stripped. Guards began investigating and found two men busy working deep in a seven-foot hole that they had begun three days earlier. At the rate they were going, they expected to be outside the No. 3 Tower wall in several days.

The nine were placed in solitary confinement, but in the cellblocks inmates wondered how the plan could be improved. McCauley knew that there would never be a day when someone wasn't planning a bid for freedom even though success was against the odds.

The new cellblock was open and housed 240, Herbert among them. He decorated his cell with pictures of boxers clipped from magazines.

Unlike the rest of the prison, the new cellblock had running water, air-conditioning, showers down the hall, and vertical bars that let in more light than the flat latticework of steel in the old section.

Then at 11:07 p.m. on July 15, prisoners fell from their bunks and woke up in a roaring, quivering darkness, as if hell itself had opened its jaws beneath their feet. Herbert, too, awoke to a rumbling sound and a rocking that tossed him from bed. For a minute, the floor bucked. Books flew from the shelves as if a giant beast was rubbing itself against the building. He heard lumber creek and plaster crack, heard the groan of iron bars. Then the sirens began to wail and he heard cries. As suddenly as it started, it was over. Then moments later the earth bucked again. Although he was locked in, he could sense the panic that swept the cellblocks as men tried to escape falling objects. They feared they would be trapped alive in the decaying, crumbling buildings.

The McCauleys were returning from town when the earthquake hit, rocking their car and causing it to careen to the side of the road as the street before them rose and fell like the tracks of a carnival ride. Behind them, in Walla Walla's business district, the buildings swayed and rumbled. Men and women in their nightclothes raced out of houses. Pendulum clocks in the second-floor office of the post office stopped. Dogs everywhere began to howl. Drawers and doors at the Immigration and Naturalization Office in town flew open, and the contents were tossed about, as though they had been ransacked by ghosts.

In the mansion, the timbers groaned. Cracks shot up plaster walls, forking like lightning bolts, and from the fireplace sparks flew as a log left burning tumbled onto the carpet. In the master bedroom there was a shudder, a loud crack—like the sound of gunfire—and then the entire ceiling, supported by heavy timber beams, collapsed onto the bed. And still the house shook and swayed.

When it was at last still and the McCauley family reached their home, McCauley raced up the driveway and flung open the door. Dancing flames swept through the living room, across the Oriental carpet, up the walls, filling the house with smoke. He raced to grab the garden hose and called for the guards. Together, they doused the flames. When at last it was over, his wife and daughters stood in stunned silence in the doorway.

The smell of smoke burned his nostrils and seeped into his skin and clothing. He surveyed the damage. The china cabinet had toppled and dishes flew everywhere. The chandelier over the dining room table still quivered, its prisms tinkling. In other rooms, the ceiling was bowed and about to collapse. He heard his wife's cry and raced upstairs to find her staring in horror at the timbers on the bed. Had they not lingered in town that night, had they returned early and gone to bed, they would have been killed.

He then did a quick survey of the rest of the prison, which was not substantially damaged. No one was injured. The most significant casualty was the mansion. The home—with all its history, festive dinners, visits from governors who had spent hours in front of the fireplace talking politics before retiring to the special guest suite—would have to be torn down. McCauley bundled up his family and drove them back into town to deposit them in a hotel. In the morning, he would have to do something about housing.

The paper the next day was full of news about the quake. The seismologist at the Carnegie Institute said it had centered along the eastern borders of Washington and Oregon and was not only a backlash from but rivaled the quake that had devastated Helena, Montana, the year before. Citizens compared the earthquake with the one that occurred in Seattle on Christmas Day 1914, or another that occurred in 1931, or the 1906 fire and earthquake in San Francisco.

The strength of the quake was anyone's guess. The seismologist at Gonzaga University in Spokane was unable to determine it because the seismograph needle shook loose from the drum. Most citizens, however, reported little damage.

The earthquake brought a surprise benefit. Wells nearly dry were suddenly brimming with water. At the Walter Maxson ranch, the family awoke to find that overflowing well water had saturated the front yard. And Mill Creek, which meanders through Walla Walla, was suddenly filled to the top of its banks with rushing water.

Meanwhile across the nation, the drought was killing crops and thousands of people were dying, if not by starvation then by suicide. The newspaper was full of their stories. As the Depression deepened and fortunes were lost, the world seemed bleak and hopeless with a never-ending stretch of dust and tumbleweeds. By September, homeless men who had traveled from the Great Plains states showed up at the city jail begging for food and shelter.

It was then that a small tornado swept into the valley, racing across the wheat fields in a black fury, and then lifting once again and disappearing into the clouds. The hardship didn't prevent Walla Wallans from celebrating Columbia Days, in recognition of the city's pioneers. Nellie McCauley, one of the warden's daughters, became Miss Columbia, the festival queen.

In the meantime, work began on a new warden's house, made of red bricks and with a porch—not grand at all, but solid, comfortable. In no time the family had moved in. But Mrs. McCauley was unhappier than ever and the more estranged husband and wife became from each other, the more McCauley relied upon his daughters and they on him, as they sought shelter from their mother's wrath.

McCauley watched as one by one the suitors came—nervous young men who had to pass beneath the shadows of the guard tower to pick the girls up on dates. As his wife's involvement in their lives declined and she became more and more despondent, McCauley hired a cook, a woman with a daughter who was studying voice at nearby Whitman College.

The girls became friends easily, and McCauley delighted in seeing Oregonia "Ora" Farrar in the kitchen, baking bread and pies and cooking roasts on Sunday. He began to count on her for advice.

•

It was shortly before Christmas when the accident happened. His favorite daughter was spinning before him in her new dress, beaming in anticipation of the high school dance she would attend. She teetered on her high heels, and her hair that fell in soft curls was brushed back away from her face. The sight of her made McCauley weak-kneed as he recited the rules and gave his usual admonition: if her date wasn't a gentleman, he'd be hearing from him. If McCauley could give his daughters one thing, it would be happiness.

It was raining, a fine mist that sparkled in the light from the guard tower that swept the perimeter of the prison. It seeped into a person's bones and sent old and young alike to hover near their fires with their fingers curled around mugs of hot tea or coffee, or anticipating snuggling into down comforters floating to sleep in islands of dreamy warmth. The exceptions were those in the dreary, cold cells or those who were young and warmed instead by the fire of first love.

The young man was anxious, as his car bounced along the road and screeched to a halt near the tower where the guards watched him carefully. He could see their silhouettes. He was unsure of what he was supposed to do. How was he to get to the home beyond where his love was waiting? He straightened his tie, glanced in the mirror, and patted his hair in place. Perhaps if he ran, he could avoid a confrontation with the guards. He picked up the boxed corsage from the front seat. The prison loomed dark and forbidding. As he opened the car door, he was captured in a blinding beam of light.

"Freeze! Don't move or I'll shoot!" someone yelled. "Raise your hands!"

Clutching the white box, he slowly raised his trembling hands. It seemed like forever as he stood at gunpoint in his white dinner jacket.

Inexplicably, he bolted from the light and sprinted up the driveway toward the warden's home. He heard the volley of shots begin, heard the wind whistle as the rounds slammed into the dirt behind him. One hit the boxed corsage and sent it flying. Then he felt something rip through him, send him flying through space into blackness that was soft and permanent.

For the McCauley household, it was one more tragedy, and it would push Mrs. McCauley over the edge. She hated life next to the prison and hated her husband for bringing her there.

From his cell, Herbert no doubt heard the shots and wondered if it was another escape attempt, an increasingly familiar occurrence. His memory of the outside world was fading. He could only sample it through the books strangers sent him. Because he had become famous in his own way, he had not been forgotten as most prisoners were—including ones not much older than he.

Although he didn't know them, people—some of them very well known—fought for his release. The notion of a child spending his days in prison was troubling to a good many citizens, most likely because Father Flanagan, with the help of his media contacts and public relations firm, would not let the public forget about the barefoot-boy murderer.

•

The killing of the young suitor was the last straw for Mrs. McCauley, who packed the next morning, left the house, and filed for divorce. The girls remained with their father, and eventually the young man's death—which was quietly kept out of the papers—was no longer spoken of.

As for Herbert, he was growing up. He had grown taller and was now wearing wire-rim spectacles, which would always give him a bookish look. He was now older than some of the new inmates. How much longer could he be segregated from the main prison population? The inmates and some of the guards hated him for the favoritism he received. McCauley refused to put him in with the others, where he thought the boy was not likely to survive. And as long as he was warden, that was the way it was going to be, he told anyone who challenged him.

In the meantime, he took Herbert to his home to work and often brought him into his office just for a chat. With his good manners and keen intellect, Herbert would fit well into any office or on any high school campus. No one would have believed he had ever spent time in prison for murder. The parole board that had the power to parole even those serving life sentences had suggested placing Herbert with an elderly farmer, recommending that he take the farmer's last name so he could leave the negative publicity attached to the name Niccolls far behind.

Herbert needed less publicity, McCauley knew. Superintendent Kern and the parole board had all said so, but Herbert had become a living symbol of the fruits of poverty, a token juvenile delinquent who was a living example of the prison's ability to turn a life around, or so they hoped. McCauley used Herbert as an example when he spoke to the Kiwanis Club, defending himself when critics claimed he—and Governor Martin—were soft on crime and punishment.

Most prisoners became better for the experience and left to go on to productive lives, McCauley told critics. The biggest challenge was to keep prisoners busy. Although the prison was a nearly self-sufficient, walled city, with its own tailor, shoemaker, dairy, and other industries, there were still too few jobs for the increasing prison population. Day after day inmates sat in the small dim cells, staring out through the squares of the iron latticework and looking forward to a glimpse of the sky while going to the dining hall.

Herbert was almost like a son to McCauley. And McCauley was almost like a father to Herbert. There were games of checkers and talk of what Herbert had learned that day, talk of the future, and of what Herbert would like to do with his life should he be paroled. Herbert loved the visits, a reminder of life beyond the walls. McCauley encouraged him to keep learning and doing well, in the event that someday he would be free. Herbert worried about what would happen should the warden leave? Would his special status end and he be placed in the cellblock, at the mercy of those who had been less fortunate for years? The guards said it was no longer fair to keep Herbert segregated and privileged while the other men suffered. But McCauley waved their concerns aside. Herbert was special—he had an exceptional intellect that amazed his teachers, McCauley believed. What a waste it would be to stop his education now. But McCauley's good intentions were short-lived.

Chapter 20

IT WAS NEW YEAR'S EVE, 1937, and for weeks the prisoners had secretly gathered pots and pans from the kitchen and anything that could be used for making noise, hiding them in their cells. Early in the evening, the warden broadcast his usual New Year's greetings, urging the inmates to make the next year better than ever, using the time in prison for personal growth. Warden McCauley told them that they could make as much noise as they pleased but not to damage the property. He warned them that the following morning not a single cup or wash pan should have as much as a dent in it. Then he returned home.

At nine p.m. the bedtime whistle blew, but it was ignored. Cheers and the sounds of the celebration at Times Square drifted over the airwaves as the New Year was greeted on the East Coast. At ten p.m. there was a loud pop—a champagne cork exploding far away in Chicago as party-goers sipped the bubbly, kissed, and danced cheek-to-cheek. Then music once again sailed like silver arrows through the cellblock. As the clock ticked on toward midnight Pacific Time, the men became restless and paced in their cells.

Then the Rocky Mountain Time Zone slipped into the new year. The soft-voiced announcer from KSL in Salt Lake City was on the air. "You are listening to the sweet music of Gan Jarber and his boys from the beautiful Mountain Inn here in Salt Lake City. Join us while we give old Pappy Time a boot in the seat of his trousers and drive him from these peaceful hills. There he goes! Greetings everyone!"

Amid the boisterous shouting from Salt Lake, an orchestra played valiantly on. With one hour until midnight on the West Coast, inmates rolled from their bunks and dug out the hoarded noisemakers from under mattresses, benches, and ventilator shafts. At last the hands of the clock showed midnight and the cellblocks exploded with sound. There was clanging and cheering, whistling and shouting, as another year was ticked off. The din reached a crescendo and then slowly subsided as the radio faded and the lights went out; the new year was enfolding all in a mantle of sleep. Herbert was alone with his dreams, edging ever closer to becoming one with the adult prison population.

Nineteen-thirty-eight brought another political victory for Clarence Martin, who spent $12,638 on his campaign for an office that paid $6,000 annually, far less than the substantial income from his milling company in Spokane. For the second time he trounced former governor Roland Hartley—who accused him of being a big spender and a big taxer.

The voters apparently liked what Martin's first term had brought, but despite his successes, nothing seemed to adequately reverse poverty. It wasn't just in his state, it was nationwide. Just before the election, 500 "non political and nonpartisan" women marched to Olympia to complain about price-fixing, monopolies, blockades, bombings, and other violence that prevented farmers and businessmen from bringing products into cities. "Business, industry and payrolls have become the victims of these racketeers, forcing hundreds, often thousands of breadwinners out of work," they wrote in a petition to Martin. They urged prosecution of the lawbreakers, reminded Martin that the power to stop crime lay in his hands, and urged him to live up to his oath of office and fulfill "the solemn pledge to safeguard the rights guaranteed to all by the Constitution."

The following day he ordered the State Patrol to establish stations on the highways to help farmers get to market. But the old-age pensioners remained unhappy with him and complained because the state kept $7.50 a month out of their $30 monthly pensions.

As any experienced politician knew, the after-battle glow of political victories never lasted long. And in Martin's case, the regal governor's mansion had its share of domestic strife as well, although peace appeared to reign when President Franklin D. Roosevelt came for a visit. Roosevelt first visited Spokane, meeting with the U.S. marshall in charge of security—Wayne Bezona—who had left Asotin not long after John Wormell's murder. Roosevelt visited the Grand Coulee Dam and then the governor's mansion in Olympia, noting there wasn't any home quite like it in Albany.

In the meantime, brief news stories gave glimpses of another side to mansion life: "Mrs. Clarence D. Martin . . . was recovering today from a bruised, blackened eye, scratched face and bruised knee as the result of a fall on a slippery street. . . . The governor said she might be able to attend the inaugural ball Wednesday."

In July 1940 she was hospitalized for a broken wrist that the newspaper said also happened in a fall. Within two years, Margaret Martin, even though she was a devout Catholic, divorced her husband of twenty-six years. Governor Martin remarried a short time later, but within several years his second wife also left him, claiming "extreme cruelty."

Whatever shortcomings Martin may have had in his personal life, to Herbert he was the ideal mentor. Whenever Martin traveled to Walla Walla he visited with Herbert.

Reporters also occasionally visited Herbert and stories appeared in newspapers from the *Spartanburg (S.C.) Herald Journal* to the *Oakland Tribune*. For Herbert, the year passed much like the others had—his only view of the world was through the books in the library that kept alive his dream of designing airplanes. For the other prisoners, there was too little to do. When not employed in prison labor, they spent much of their days crowded two to a cell.

McCauley was proud of the fact that the prison was better than it had been in Warden Long's days, when the National Penal Society had criticized the prison for keeping men in the small cells for twenty hours a day, for providing them with no relief from Walla Walla's extreme temperatures, and for having poor ventilation and little light. With the exception of the new cellblock, most of the cells were still like cages, with 80 percent of them covered with flat, iron bars. While those grim circumstances received little protest or concern from the public, McCauley was able to expand prison industries, remodel some of the facilities, and add activities, all the while coping with 1,537 prisoners—the largest prison population to date and more than double the population the prison was meant to house. But he was managing—and even keeping the daily expenses to fifty-eight cents per man—less than other institutions in the state.

Indeed, the prison was almost self-sufficient and even had surplus to sell. Thousands of pounds of farm and garden products were grown, including potatoes, corn, tomatoes, lettuce, and onions. Despite his successes, it seemed ever since he had come to the prison, he had had to defend himself for his "liberal," policies. He wanted to make a difference, wanted to be humane. Yet he and Governor Martin, who had appointed him, were both criticized. McCauley always stepped up in defense.

"Examination of the records will show the percentage of prisoners released by Gov. Martin is less than the percentage of prisoners released by any preceding governor," McCauley told the *Daily Bulletin*. "Also his releases are less than the governors of the majority of other states in the union."

Time and again McCauley had to answer questions about when Herbert might be released. "When we are satisfied that he will do well," he told those who asked. McCauley was acutely aware that men the same age as Herbert did not have the same privileges. But Herbert, McCauley believed, was a grand experiment and one he hoped to be able to repeat. He would like to build an entire unit just for prisoners like Herbert, who were young or not hardened criminals.

"After he finishes high school I probably will keep him where he is but will put him to work in the shop where he can become accustomed gradually to association with other prisoners," McCauley told a *Post-Intelligencer* reporter.

"Of course, freedom means more to me than anything else," Herbert added. "But if I ever get out I want to be an aviation engineer. . . . I would like to prepare myself for the work while I'm here."

More than anything, he wanted to fly, but his eyesight was poor and the lenses of his prison-issue spectacles were thick. In the meantime, Herbert appeared before the parole board again and again. While thousands of supporters would support Herbert's release, those in Asotin—who had been vocal opponents of any such plan—loudly protested, as they always did whenever the subject came up.

•

Meanwhile, there were the usual escape attempts, executions, and parole hearings. James Ashe's eyes were infected and the prison doctor did little with them. Finally, he lost the sight in one eye all together. Even the guards knew Ashe was walking the thin edge of sanity.

George R. Perry of the J. G. White Co. of New York City wrote to Martin, asking for Ashe's release. Perry also wrote to the parole board and the prosecuting attorney hoping for their support. Perry, an engineer, said he would give Ashe employment working on the construction of a power plant and electrical system, the dam and locks across the Amazon River near Manao, Brazil. He offered to pay Ashe all expenses, plus $140 a month if only Ashe could be released by October.

"He has lost the sight of one eye, and Dr. Gowen of Walla Walla states that the sight of the other eye is being seriously imperiled with his present incarceration," John Schaefer, secretary of the parole board wrote to Martin. "It is the feeling of some of the officers at Walla Walla that this man will go insane if compelled to serve the full balance of his sentence, as he is constantly worrying over becoming completely blind."

King County Prosecuting Attorney Gray Warner also wrote supporting Ashe's release, noting that his testimony for the state in the jury-tampering charge had led to a conviction. But still the parole board hesitated, and Ashe waited.

No longer did he talk about Hollywood in his bittersweet way, or about Oxford, or his mother, who, he said, was Lady Ashcroft, a British aristocrat. He stopped scratching out poetry in his dim cell, even though that had once helped keep him sane.

Whether it was the prisoners or the guards, everyone had mocked him. He was a rare specimen in the prison—a blue-blood with an Oxford education, while most of the others had never even gone to high school. Herbert Niccolls was different, though. Every day Ashe saw him maturing, mirroring his language, his mannerisms.

What would manners and education get Herbert in prison? The most dangerous thing of all—envy. It was the subject of the one and only poem Ashe published in the *Agenda*, and it factored in the press accounts of his trial. Once he no longer had the shield of wealth, they were determined to strip him of any dignity. Herbert was already the subject of envy from those who would victimize him, given the chance.

On an October day when the chill of winter bore heavily upon Walla Walla, and the siren song of sultry South American jungles gave him hopes that he dared not have, Ashe stood before the board, waiting, waiting, waiting as they read through his file. Then one looked up and peered over the top of his glasses, giving a nod that meant freedom. A suit of clothes was waiting for Ashe outside the board room. Perry, his future employer, met him at the visitors' entrance. The gates opened, and then they were gone.

•

By June 1938, Herbert had completed more than enough studies to easily pass the final examinations, and he was awarded a diploma from Walla Walla High School, even though he had never been inside its doors.

It was the first high school commencement exercise ever held inside prison walls. The ceremony took place in the prison chapel and included music by the prison orchestra and an address by the prison chaplain. Herbert's teachers and a select group of inmates attended. In addition, there were reporters and photographers. Herbert was photographed in his shirt and tie, standing erect and accepting his diploma from H. H. Helms, Walla Walla County school board chairman.

The event was noted in newspapers throughout the state. The barefoot-boy murderer moved farther away from the life he once knew. He was now a scholar with a diploma and dreams of a future.

Armene Lamson noticed the story in the *Seattle Times* and sat down at her typewriter to write to Father Flanagan, who was preparing for MGM to come to Boys Town to film a Hollywood version of the town's creation, after they completed their film-related business on the West Coast.

"It occurred to me it would be a very fine opportunity to see Herbert Niccolls and the governor. I am sure he will be very grateful for such advice as you would be able to give," she wrote. "We have a very fine governor—his wife is an ardent Catholic—and very friendly to you."

Then she wrote to Martin, and as she had first done seven years earlier and had continued to do many times since, she asked for Herbert Niccolls's release to Flanagan's care.

This week's newspaper carried the news that Herbert Niccolls received his high school diploma at Walla Walla and that Father Flanagan may come to the coast to assist in the production of some moving picture story of his great work with boys at Boys Town. . . . As you know both Father Flanagan and I have silently watched the development of this unfortunate boy and would like to be of assistance.

I am sure it would be very fortunate if this great man with so much experience could be asked as to the next step in enabling the State of Washington to finish successfully the rehabilitation of this young man. . . . It is certain that a young man with intellectual ability such as Herbert who has read so much of the affairs of the world would never be satisfied to be isolated on a farm until his pent up curiosity is satisfied. Won't you let us be of service?

Martin reassured her that Herbert was doing well where he was. But he, too, wondered what to do next with Herbert.

•

Herbert wanted to fly and busied himself designing and making model airplanes. If only he could soar into a sky that was as blue as the glass marble he kept in his cell. But like many prisoners, he was restless, having too little to do. Often he sat in his cell, trying to read, trying to write as the flies tapped against the bars in his cell in the new Sixth Wing, where—unlike the other inmates—he roomed alone.

In August, *Seattle Star* reporter Stuart Whitehouse came to write a story about the unconventional high school graduate, and Herbert told him of the void in his life now that high school was finished.

"I could easily—and sometimes it is a temptation—learn the criminal trade. Of course, I am comparatively isolated from other prisoners but it would be possible. That I do not want—emphatically! When I leave, I want to turn to a normal life. That is my prime ambition," Herbert said.

Whitehouse suggested he try writing. It seemed like a natural extension of Herbert's love for books, and the prison magazine, the *Agenda*, always needed contributions. A pro-prison publication—censored to have nothing but praise for the administration—it chronicled a variety of aspects of prison life, with topics ranging from the dairy, the laundry, inmate baseball teams and boxing matches to essays about the chapel. Herbert became an occasional contributor.

He wrote about the prison post office and the holiday mail—what was allowed and what was forbidden. During Thanksgiving and Christmas only, McCauley bent the rules and allowed friends and relatives of inmates to bring them socks, suspenders, cake, candy, shelled nuts, fresh fruits, whole dates, and figs, but nothing else. To Herbert, Post Office Box 520—which served 1,600 people—was a channel through which flowed a wide range of human emotions, that were no doubt foreign to him.

"Vows of eternal allegiance between separated sweethearts . . . cheery, newsy missives from friends . . . notices of business triumphs—or failures . . . announcements of births, and letters of congratulation . . . announcements of deaths and letters of condolence," he wrote. All in- and outgoing letters were opened and censored. All of the forbidden items—bathrobes, pajamas, razors, Monopoly games, chess, Hop Ching, checkers, and various toys—were returned to the sender.

The article was his first and he sent a copy to Whitehouse, who told the *Star*'s readers that the barefoot-boy murderer was becoming a writer.

Herbert never missed a chance to see a movie, sitting in awe in the prison auditorium. There in the flickering shadows were windows to the world: rebellious heiress Claudette Colbert jumping ship and ending up with Clark Gable; Bette Davis turning from spiteful southern belle to self-sacrificing nurse as Henry Fonda battled yellow fever; the swash-buckling Errol Flynn saving England from treachery. Herbert was now used to movies with sound and loved them all as he loved books. They filled the empty spaces of his life that others filled with visitors.

With the exception of official visits from the governor or the occasional journalist, no one visited Herbert. His grandmother was dead. His attorneys were dead. The man who wanted to visit him the most—Father Flanagan—couldn't do so because there was no hope that he could take Herbert with him to Boys Town, which was becoming internationally famous.

That September, MGM's *Boys Town* movie debuted at the Omaha Theater, with Mickey Rooney playing a star role as Whitey, the troubled teenager, and Spencer Tracy playing Father Flanagan. While the press predicted that the movie would fill the Boys Town coffers, ironically Flanagan reported in October that the home had received only $5,000 in donations—less than the year before. Scraping for funding would continue as the number of boys seeking a home there increased tremendously. Flanagan found himself more and more often on the fund-raising trail—traveling city to city with his message: "There is no such thing as a bad boy."

That fall, Herbert began taking correspondence courses through Washington State College in Pullman and later through the International Correspondence Schools, which eased his boredom.

McCauley, whom he had relied upon as a friend, was seen less around the prison. The prison chapel and warden's home were the site of a wedding and reception for Ora's daughter, Wanda, and her musician fiancé, Karl Diettrich. It was common for trustees to be used as servants at any time, and weddings were no exception. Trustees parked cars, set out the four-foot-high poinsettias, the china and silver, prepared the turkey and ham—all raised at the prison—as guests from Seattle and the college's music department came for the festive event. Once again the warden's home was filled with laughter, fine food, and good spirits, with Governor Martin often visiting, as well as other dignitaries from around the state. The guests could almost forget the guard towers looming just outside the door, except for the nights when executions were scheduled.

In April 1936, McCauley asked Karl Diettrich if he'd like to observe an execution. Diettrich hesitantly agreed. At midnight, Barney Fleming, twenty-nine, from King County, the first of three inmates to be executed that year, would be put to death. The condemned man walked to the scaffold and climbed the ladder. A black hood was placed over his head, and then the noose. A member of the clergy asked him if he had any last words. The scaffold sprang open with such force that in Cellblock 6, the new unit where Herbert stayed, the sound resounded like cannon fire. Prisoners there often wet themselves from the trauma.

During the first seven years of Herbert's sentence, fourteen men were executed. Since he assumed office in 1933, McCauley had presided at all of the executions, ready by the phone until midnight, should there be a last-minute call from the governor granting a pardon. The clock always ticked away the condemned man's final hours. It also ticked away what would be the short span of the warden's life and, in the process, the time Herbert had left in a precarious role as a prisoner of privilege.

Chapter 21

WHETHER BECAUSE of McCauley's illness or Martin's increased interest in Herbert Niccolls, gradually Clarence Martin assumed more of the task of planning for Herbert's future. But what that future would be was the subject of a vigorous debate. Martin was impressed by Herbert but wasn't going to stake his political future on his being successful outside the walls. Nevertheless, Martin asked an associate to contact the Boeing Company on Herbert's behalf. Perhaps if he was out on his own for a while and took some vocational classes, the personnel director said. The parole board suggested sending Herbert to the Civilian Conservation Corps, where hundreds of young men worked on public-service projects in a structured environment. It was an idea favored by W. M. Kern, who had now retired from the school district but still had an active interest in Herbert's case.

"The years since Herbert arrived at the prison have seen very pronounced change in him and all for the good," Kern told Martin. "One of Herbert's primary handicaps is due to the fact that he has not been able to associate with normal boys of his own age, a serious barrier to his general education and development."

"Yesterday, I visited Herbert again and was strongly impressed with the notion that a temporary parole, for the summer, and enrollment in our local CCC camp would be a splendid and helpful experience for him. . . . Enrollment in the CCC camp should prove highly beneficial in a number of respects: Association with young men of his own age; the discipline of camp life; ability to make his way in organized community life; self confidence and the ability to earn and save; and finally, and of supreme importance, the ability to serve. . . . Would Herbert prove trustworthy and return to the prison when his parole expired? I am convinced he would."

Martin discussed the idea with the parole board and, even though the camp had benefits, he wanted more for Herbert. He still clung to his idea of placing him in a home of a gentleman farmer—someone, like McCauley, who would treat Herbert as his own son. Kern was annoyed that Martin refused to consider his idea.

"Mr. Wilkins wrote to me some days ago to the effect that you and he had agreed that Herbert should be paroled, at the proper time, to some interested and kindly disposed farmer who would make him a member of the family, give him a name and educate him." Kern told the governor: "You will recall that I suggested a temporary parole; had mentioned the CCC Camp at Goldendale. . . . There are certain reasons why I am strongly inclined to favor a few temporary try-out paroles for Herbert. There are certain factors or conditions in Herbert's case that may have escaped your attention and not had the consideration they merit."

Then he returned to the well-used argument of Herbert's heredity predicting his future.

"He is a constitutional psychopath which, in this case, indicates de-generacy due to impaired heredity," Kern said. "I cannot take time . . . to give the evidence upon which he based his findings. While I do not pretend to speak for him, he would doubtless tell you that Herbert has no moral sense; is a menace to society; that neither education or religion offer any hopes of effecting a cure; that he is destined to become a 'repeater' in penal institutions; that nothing you and I can do will change the results."

The Herbert Niccolls Martin knew was nothing like the young man Kern—who had supervised the boy's education and visited him weekly for the past seven years—claimed to know.

"I hesitate to subscribe to the idea of enrolling him in the CCC camp. It seems to me that he should be placed more definitely in a home . . . until he could have become more adjusted to the outside environment," Martin told Kern.

Kern suggested giving Herbert a job teaching delinquent youth, who were jailed at the boys' reform school in Centralia for crimes like theft and incorrigibility. He suggested letting Herbert join the ROTC. With Hitler marching through Europe, the United States might need pilots at any time if it did as Britain hoped and entered the war. He mentioned that Herbert might be eligible to enter the Coast Guard. But with poor eyesight and a felony conviction for murder, those options fell through. And for Martin, Kern's words played over and over again like a scratched record.

"He's a constitutional psychopath . . . a menace to society."

Others who knew Herbert and believed in his rehabilitation also paused when they thought of what he could be like outside the controlled world of the prison.

"Even though Niccolls has been away from the other convicts, he sees all of them every day," wrote John Schaefer of the parole board. "He is the type who wants to go places and see things. He is like a bird, who wants to take wing and fly. That is why he would like to become an aviator . . . remember he stole several cars when very young, even before he knew how to drive an auto."

The Boeing Company politely refused to take Herbert, suggesting that he first take vocational courses to see how he fared outside of prison.

Mrs. Lamson and Father Flanagan never doubted that the best thing for Herbert—even at the late date—still would be Boys Town, which was receiving more attention than ever before.

In March, Spencer Tracy won an Oscar for his role in the movie *Boys*

Town. A replica was given to Flanagan. Tracy had inscribed it with the words, "To Father E. J. Flanagan, whose great human qualities, kindly simplicity and inspiring courage were strong enough to shine through my humble efforts."

Days later, four boys, three sixteen-year-olds and a fifteen-year-old, stole a car in Seattle and were on their way along the Sunset Highway toward Snoqualmie Pass when a service station attendant in North Bend noticed that they were fidgety. He called the police who blockaded the highway. The boys said they were heading to Boys Town.

That month, Flanagan's board of trustees announced it would help 200 more boys and, in a $635,000 building project, would enlarge the town to include four new dormitories, a dining hall, an enlarged heating plant, and a sewage disposal system. At last more contributions began to trickle in—along with celebrities like Bob Hope, George Burns, Gracie Allen, Babe Ruth, and Lou Gehrig, who were among many to visit. Boys Town was becoming a household name.

Meanwhile, Herbert knew nothing of Flanagan's continued interest in him. And true to Herbert's favored status, he was kept busy at the prison, teaching classes at the school when he wasn't studying. He learned to bind books in the bindery, something that pleased him so much that he created a special volume of Sir James George Frazer's *The Golden Bough*, and at McCauley's suggestion gave it to Henry Broderick, who still held great influence over the board.

The book was covered in black leather and had a red-silk binding. It had hand tooling, including Broderick's initials, and it resembled a sixteenth-century volume. Broderick, who kept it on the desk in his Seattle office, delighted and marveled at the rich calfskin cover, the neatly stitched binding in the Douglas Cockrell tradition. Broderick was moved and showed the book to visitors, not only for its beauty but for its symbolism—the remaking not only of the book but of a young life.

Herbert bound another book for Olaf Olsen, the state's director of prisons. The young man became such a proficient bookbinder, a skill that was taught by another inmate, that the officials suggested he teach it to others and write about the binding process for *The Agenda*.

There is a vast difference between a bound book and a cased one, he explained to *Agenda* readers. "Rudyard Kipling was one of those rare men of the pen who wrote not only quantity, but quality," Herbert wrote. "A great number of his most noted writings have been collected in the book *A Kipling Pageant*. I had seen the book before but it had been merely one of the many books I see daily in the prison library."

But now, the book's drab, military-inspired uniformity was gone. "This book was bound! . . . Each side of heavy oak, the back covered with vari-colored horsehide. . . . A well decorated book, no matter how elaborately it may be worked, is an undeniable addition to the most exclusive library, for the volume serves to break the monotony of room design, as well as offering the beauty of an object of art to the appreciative eye," he wrote.

He held a finely bound book of his own creation between his slender hands. Beauty and art were topics far from his beginnings, as a child who knew nothing of either but a great deal about violence.

McCauley read Herbert's writing, listened to his speech. The daily reality dueled with the phrases long associated with Herbert's name: "A constitutional psychopath . . . impaired heredity."

Where prisoners were concerned, Herbert couldn't have been farther from his old family ties, McCauley knew. Herbert's mother wrote at first, but never came to see him. Instead she hid in southern Idaho, terrified that her husband would again be released from the mental hospital, and that this time he would kill her. Bert Niccolls never wrote to his son, nor did the other members of the family, who were scattered throughout the state. It would be many years before Herbert knew what had happened to his brothers and when he finally did learn, they wouldn't know him. Their paths had forked long ago and Herbert was no longer the frail, malnourished child who had killed a man. He was slender, educated, and sophisticated. To some, he was the shining star of the prison. To others, he was self-important, a braggart who had been coddled by the administration for years. They thought that a young man who was sentenced to life should be serving it among the rest of the prisoners.

Had it not been for John Wormell's death, what would have become of him? He had received a fine education, for which he'd always be grateful. But had he not been in prison would he have ended up as mad as his father and some of his other relatives? Would there ever be a time when he could step away from the past and claim only his future? He walked erect and spoke perfectly, as if a stray word would cause him to teeter from the narrow beam stretched over the canyon he had once lived in, that deep, sorrowful darkness. Somehow—thanks to the sacrifice of one man's life—he had managed to crawl free.

Yet, he wasn't free at all and might never be. It was a frightening thought, especially as he heard about McCauley's illness. Cancer, the guards had said. Herbert was worried about where he would be without the warden's protection. There was always the governor, but Martin had been governor since 1933 and still had not paroled him. Some guards and prisoners told Herbert that it would never happen, that it would be political suicide for Martin to appear soft on crime when no one in Herbert's own family championed his release, and before her death, his grandmother had openly opposed it. Still, Martin continued his interest in Herbert and in June wrote a letter, wishing him happy birthday.

Herbert wrote back, updating the governor on his progress and being optimistic. "Thank you very much for remembering my birthday. My, but I was tickled when I came in from construction work and found your letter waiting for me—it reminded me that our birthdays are synonymous in date. Thanks again for remembering me."

Many things have happened since you and I started counting our birthdays together, haven't they? Just one year ago I received my diploma from high school and for the last year have devoted myself to writing, aviation, radio, book-binding, and other things. I've already reaped the benefits of my writing in a small measure. For the last few issues, I've been fortunate in having the editor of our *Agenda* accept stories from me. Not much is it? But it's a start!

And the aviation mechanics course sent to me by the International Correspondence Schools is growing increasingly interesting. In writing, I learned that a narrative hook was a sentence or paragraph designed to catch and hold the reader's attention. The International people seem to think that their students need narrative hooks, in their courses, for my lessons have consisted of mathematics, laws, formulas and so forth, dotted occasionally with advanced booklets on motors, electrical data, etc. Lately, I received a hook from them which was aviation carburetors. I suppose most students do become jaded over booklet after booklet of math, laws, etc.—but the narrative hooks are unnecessary in my case— I'm already half way through! I hope to use this course as a firm ground for what I'd like to be—an aeronautical engineer. When I first became interested in aviation, I was thrilled at the thought of flying—but that has passed by. Of course, I intend learning to fly, but I want to design! A chance conversation turned me from flying to designing—when my acquaintance began talking about 'skin friction,' 'stress analysis,' 'strain on longera [sic] and ribs' and other technical studies of the aeroplane, I became quite interested. I had studied trigonometry, and here was a chance to use my beloved math!

I studied radio as a hobby for a couple of years, and that, I saw gave me an advantage if I wished to study aviation—I wouldn't have a lot of radio to mess with, for I already have the basic principles—in fact, I've built radios. I have a good book on aviation, and I've learned a few bits of information from it—and I've a few ideas of design of my own that I'd like to work out.

Then, too, for a real hobby, I've learned to bind books in a craftsman-like manner. It's a fascinating study, this binding, and I feel very much repaid for the time I put in on it . . .

Well, goodbye, until I see you again. And thank you again for remembering my birthday—the birthday we share in common.

Martin, meanwhile, had a plan. "Is there any way that a test and study of this case can be made?" he wrote to Dr. M. W. Conway, superintendent of Eastern State Hospital for the insane. "This young man is now twenty and has been confined about eight years. It seems to me that if any chance is to be given him, it must be undertaken very soon.

"You might think this over and return the correspondence with memorandum as to any suggestions that you might have. I will no doubt be having a conference on this case sometime next week."

·

It was in the air, sure as the change of seasons. It was the scent of freedom, the dream of life beyond the walls. He had caught glimpses of it when he worked at the warden's mansion, looking up from the flower bed to see the fields disappearing into the blue-shadowed foothills. Now, the guards, too, were talking about it and the other inmates as well, and they seemed bitter with envy.

Robert Landis was only sixteen when he was sent to prison and had been trying for parole ever since. He had saved a guard's life during the Lincoln's Day Riots of 1934. Didn't that mean anything? It did to the guard, who wrote on Landis's behalf. His parole wasn't opposed by the Spokane police, who arrested him, but the parole board insisted on prisoners admitting their guilt before parole would be considered. Landis insisted he was innocent.

"I know that you will agree with me that the incarceration of a boy of tender years in a penal institution where those accused of promiscuous crimes are also incarcerated is not in keeping with approved methods of dealing with humanity . . . and that a prolonged and aggravated continuation of the incarceration . . . is not conducive to a rehabilitation," wrote Pat McCarran, a friend of the Landis family and himself a politician.

Landis had a brother who was an attorney with the Federal Deposit Insurance Commission in Washington, D.C., another brother who was a Chicago businessman, and a sister who was a teacher in Los Angeles. All pledged to help him find a job and assist him in any way. Still the doors of the prison remained shut to him and would until 1951. By then Herbert's life would have changed dramatically again as he walked the delicate balance among those who resented him on a path to a place Ashe had once told him about.

·

On a November morning Herbert left the prison with Wilkins for Eastern State Hospital near Spokane. There was considerable rancor among the inmates. He was now older than many of them, and they did not enjoy the privileges or the segregation he had. While they stood in line for breakfast or chapel, Herbert walked through the yard as James Ashe and Peter Miller had done before him. He looked to the warden's home, where there was no sign of life—no congenial warden to invite him into the office for a last-minute chat, no flashes of color from his daughters, as beautiful and out of place as tropical birds. With every step the old life was fading.

What would this new world be like? He could hardly remember what it was like to be on the outside. What would he do without the predictable order that had become so familiar? Could he please his new supervisors? He was someone in the prison pecking order, but who would he be outside the walls?

"Boy lifer gets first air ride leaving prison," trumpeted the *Daily Bulletin*. Accompanied by the head of the parole board, Herbert climbed into an airplane. Martin had arranged for his dream to come true. The propellers spun and began to roar. The plane trundled down the grassy runway and suddenly lifted up, climbing higher and higher, circling over the prison. Far below, Herbert could see the walls, the guard towers, the warden's house. He could see the tree-lined streets of the town and the golden hills beyond. The plane sailed through a cloud and emerged again into the blue—a sky as perfect as the marble Murphy Watkins had given him.

The flight was "the greatest day of my life," he told reporters when the plane landed in Spokane. There he met Martin, who took him into the luxurious Davenport Hotel, where Herbert experienced his first elevator ride. Photographers captured Martin helping Herbert into a coat, telling him to face the future unafraid and to win freedom for himself and for the sake of "other young fellows who are hoping for another chance in life." And then he and Martin were off to the hospital at Medical Lake, where Herbert would spend the next year being analyzed by psychiatrists.

It was an imposing red-brick building, regarded as one of the finest mental hospitals of its kind in the nation. There were all kinds of new convulsive treatments for the ill—insulin, metrozal, and electroshock—

that helped keep the patient population manageable and sometimes restored sanity. Herbert would have a job there and undergo counseling.
As Martin turned him over to hospital authorities, he told him, "Herbert, I'm counting on you not to fail me."

Martin—who told reporters there were no plans to pardon Herbert
even if the psychiatrists say he had overcome "abnormalities evident at
the time of the crime"—was harshly criticized by many. The process of
moving Herbert from prison alone sparked the concern of the towns-
people of Asotin. The town council passed a resolution opposing Herbert's release, citing the witnesses' comments at the trial that Herbert
had "a definite strain of criminality which the psychiatrists . . . warned
would remain with him throughout his life.

"The making of a hero out of this boy who killed a good man would set
a very bad example before the youth of the land." It was signed by Mayor
Joe Forgey and City Clerk C. W. Carlile.

The Asotin Chamber of Commerce also passed a resolution protesting
his parole that was signed by Chamber President William Anderson and
Edward Bucholz, its secretary.

Martin wrote to both the chamber and the council, saying, "if and
when the matter of release of this young man is given to us for final
determination, will be glad to consider your own attitude."

Releasing Herbert would have a "very bad effect" on police officers,
since the victim of the killing was an officer, B. H. German, a former
parole board advisor, wrote to Martin.

"We have gone to very great extremes in this country in our leniency
toward people who violate the law, and although there has been a very
persistent . . . move for the past 170 years to lighten the punishment of
a criminal, at the same time crime has increased at a very alarming rate,
and I cannot help but feel that our extremely lenient attitude toward
crime is one of the big factors in bringing this about." He called paroling
Herbert potentially a "serious error," adding that it was about time the
pendulum of leniency "started swinging in the other direction."

There were possible supporters, too, including Clarkston Mayor A.
Ray Johnson, who asked Martin if he could visit Herbert at the hospital.

Martin encouraged the mayor and other city representatives to make the visit. In all, four from Clarkston went to Eastern State Hospital. They visited with Dr. Conway and Dr. Miller, the head officials, dined at the hospital, watched patients play baseball, and toured the greenhouse where they had their photos taken. After lunch they were taken to see Herbert and they came away beaming.

"We surely enjoyed the attention shown us," Johnson told Martin. Herbert "showed us . . . his work and seems very happy. . . . I was very impressed with his actions and he seems to be so happy to know that we wanted to see and talk to him. . . . We are of the opinion that the boy has a future if given a chance and we do not believe there is anything wrong with the boy."

Mrs. R. L. Berlinghoff of Lewiston, Idaho, the daughter-in-law of Lilly Frasier, who was killed by Bert Niccolls, added her thoughts, as well. "A person shouldn't say anything. . . . But the grandmother was the cause of lots of their trouble," she said. She added that she and her husband believed Herbert should be given a physical examination and if found to be all right, he should be released. "We know he has good in him."

Martin gave the letters to his secretary to file. He had taken a bold step, gambling on Herbert, who could make or break him. He wanted to run for a third term. Should Herbert, once freed, become a menace to society, Martin's chances of becoming the first Washington governor elected to a third term would be nil.

•

Almost two months after Herbert went to Eastern State Hospital, McCauley collapsed in his office and was rushed to the Walla Walla hospital, where he was diagnosed with liver cancer. He remained hospitalized through Christmas, his daughters gathering around his hospital bed, while outside flurries of snow spread a gown of sparkling white over the sleeping town. His friends came. Martin sent his best, and Ora, whom he had married three years earlier, sat at his bedside. Reverend E. T. Allen, the prison chaplain, came and asked God for healing. Then on December 27, McCauley went into surgery. The outcome was not good.

It was a quiet New Year's Eve at the prison as inmates wondered what

McCauley's absence might mean to their future. McCauley had been fair. He had allowed privileges his predecessors never had. Lifers could remember the days of the lock-step marches. They could remember being punished for small infractions by being placed in the "hole," where they would live for thirty days in total darkness with only bread and water. Without McCauley there certainly would be no raucous New Year's Eve celebrations or musical reviews and movies. No one had done more to make the prison humane than McCauley.

On January 7, James Marvin McCauley died. Seven hundred came to the funeral in Dayton, McCauley's home town, where soloists sang "The Old Rugged Cross" and "The Garden." And the prison chaplain eulogized him as a man who "had won the love and admiration of all, and his integrity and ability had made him invaluable to all with whom he was associated."

As they had in the past, reporters referred to him as the "liberal warden," who had made relations between the inmates and administration the best possible, and they praised the improvements he had made in prison conditions.

In Olympia, Martin was saddened by McCauley's death. Back in 1933, he had wanted to appoint him to a position in the capital in gratitude for his help with the campaign, but McCauley convinced him that he wanted to make a difference where it was needed the most—in prison. McCauley would be difficult to replace. But in the meantime, Martin had a legislative session to preside over and a campaign to run. He hoped that by November he would be the only governor in the state's history to be elected to a third term. Hartley had reentered politics and was running again. The September primary, however, brought an end to both Martin's and Hartley's hopes. Martin lost Democratic party support. In his remaining months as governor, there was still unfinished business. Herbert was one of them.

As the year of Herbert's stay at the hospital wore on, he continued to excel. At the hospital he worked in the library and learned to drive a car. The chief hospital librarian took him to Spokane, to familiarize him with the city and also to see movies. Yet, midway through Herbert's stay, Dr.

Conway told reporters that he was not "yet ready to say what disposition will be made of the case."

Herbert "seems happy here and he is well liked. He gets along with people and he is a model patient so far as his behavior is concerned . . . I told Gov. Martin we should have him here at least a year before we made any recommendations yet regarding his parole."

As the end of Martin's term drew near, he knew it was time to act. On January 7, 1941, Martin granted Herbert a conditional pardon. News photographers shot Martin helping Herbert—wearing a suit, white shirt, and tie—into a topcoat.

"It is needless to say that I appreciate this chance to learn to stand on my own feet and make my own living," Herbert told the reporters. "I'll do everything I can to make good, with the help of my friends."

Martin said Herbert has proved himself to be worthy of the trust placed in him. "He has been an excellent student while in prison, and I have every confidence that he will establish himself as a useful member of the community.

"During the years I've been in office, Herbert and I have become mighty good friends. You see, we discovered that our birthdays fall on the same date, June 29, and so we have something special in common.

"The doctors have given Herbert full clearance. They say there is nothing wrong with him, physically or mentally," Martin said. "I know it will not be easy for him, after being in prison since he was twelve, but whether he makes good is up to him."

Chapter 22

HE ARRIVED IN SEATTLE on a dreary January day with a few dollars in his pocket. He checked into the redbrick YMCA on Fourth Avenue and was assigned a room at four dollars a day. Even though he had been to Spokane, it didn't prepare him for Seattle. Here, the buildings were taller and the streets rambled up and down the hills. And there was all the sky he could possibly want—gray flannel, deepening into black-velvet winter nights, pink-and-blue sunrises over the Cascade Mountains, and vermillion sunsets over Puget Sound. But he was small among the towering buildings—the hives of industry and commerce—and was stunned to see so many cars shooting past.

Unlike at the prison or the hospital, no one was watching his every move. There was no warden, no visiting governor to encourage him, no librarian to invite him to dine with the officers, no press hovering over him, celebrating every hallmark of his prison life, creating and reinforcing his celebrity status. Here in the city, he was invisible. Who was he, now that he was no longer prisoner No. 13973?

Martin had arranged a job for him at a machine shop. It was menial work and nothing like the challenge of mathematics or designing planes on paper or building radios. Nor like teaching English and math to other prisoners during night school, as he'd done for the past few years. No one seemed to know who he was. Didn't they realize what he could do? That Herbert Niccolls was the shining star of the prison? Known for his intellect?

Headlines announced his parole, and the *Post-Intelligencer* included an editorial applauding Governnor Martin. "It is impossible to deal intelligently with human problems by wholesale methods. . . . Unless the offender is regarded as an individual and strict interest is taken by some other individual, it is impossible to determine whether the case is one that offers the hope of rehabilitation or calls for the sternest repression. . . . The attention that Gov. Martin has been able to give to Niccolls's case should provide a worthy example for those who will follow him in office—and for many other citizens."

The *Seattle Times* sent a reporter to interview Herbert and for a while he was happy in his familiar role in the spotlight, explaining his wonder at the new city.

"You must remember I've been shut away since I was twelve. Things that are commonplace to others are new and unknown to me," he said. "At Medical Lake (hospital) I learned to drive a car. I'm sure nuts on automobiles now.

"But here in Seattle, everywhere I turn is something new. Such a little thing as a meal ticket. I've never seen one and now I'm going to have one. I'm eager to know what one looks like. Just think, I'll be able to order whatever I want to eat!"

Over time fewer newspapers reported on the story. He was no longer the frail but charming boy who taught himself the Tenderfoot knots in his prison cell, nor was he "the young tiger" ready for another kill. Instead, he was friendless and bewildered. No one seemed to care that he was friends with the governor. For once, he was stripped of an identity. When he did tell others about his friendship with Martin, it created animosity between himself and his coworkers. Still, nothing could diminish the pleasure of being free.

He walked the streets of Seattle in awe, riding the elevator of the highest building west of the Mississippi, the pale terra-cotta Smith Tower. He pushed the elevator button and the gleaming brass doors opened. A pretty girl seated at the controls, closed the grillwork, and asked him what floor. He didn't know. He wanted to go as high as possible. She smiled at him and pushed the button to the observation deck and the Chinese Room.

There were so many beautiful women in Seattle. They wore silk stockings and high-heeled shoes and hats that matched their coats. They had neat wavy hair or long glossy tresses. They worked in offices, rode the streetcars, dined in cafeterias, sipping coffee and laughing with friends. He saw them walking arm in arm with handsome men and he didn't know how he would ever talk to one. He hadn't had a conversation with a woman since he was a small child. Jean Watkins and her sisters were probably the last. He could barely recall any of their faces now, so much time had passed.

He strolled through the elegant, red Chinese Room and walked around the observation deck. The city unfolded before him and beyond that lay Puget Sound, the ragged peaks of the Olympic Mountains to the west, and to the east the snow-covered Cascade Mountains. A plane soared over head, off to magical destinations—places he had only read about in books. How far he had come. But how far did he still have to go to rise above the drudgery of the machine shop, where no one knew him and no one cared, where he was disliked for his careful speech, his gentlemanly posture, his dubious claim to fame?

"Do you know who I am? I'm the famous Herb Niccolls." That was quoted by Assistant Parole Officer W. H. Stillman to the Board of Prison Terms and Paroles a year after Herbert's parole.

To his dismay, one day Herbert was called into the supervisor's office and fired from the job that Martin had gotten him at Seims-Drake Company. He knew that Martin would be very disappointed; he had risked so much, and now there was every likelihood that the parole board would demand that Herbert return to prison. This time, he'd be in with the others. There would be no special privileges.

"He loafed on the job and with a feeling of superiority strutted among employees causing dislike. . . . It was said that the parolee likes to tell persons of his record. He is catching up on this by paying $5 a week for a $4 room. It was said that *P-I* reporters want to use his name with stories, such as 'first Christmas out of penitentiary,' with picture showing him at a banquet for the occasion. He doesn't drink but is hypnotized with his own self importance."

Stillman's report was damning but Martin took it in stride. Not only did he instruct the Seattle parole office to leave Herbert alone and not require him to report, but he called on those who owed him a favor. In no time, Herbert was working in a bakery. It was hard, heavy work. There were racks of bread and flour sacks to lift and trucks to load. But it was steady income and it meant freedom.

•

Then one day Herbert was reconnected with his past. The man standing before him was Wesley, his older brother, whom he hadn't seen in fifteen years. They shared a joyful greeting but found themselves staring at each other, looking for the child each had been.

They knew nothing of one another's lives; Wesley never knew until Herbert told him that he had grown up in prison. On Herbert's twenty-first birthday, Wesley gave him a camera so Herbert could photograph the amazing sights of his new world. That summer they hiked the 6,340-foot Mount Tumac north of White Pass in the Cascade Mountains, where Wesley had a job as a fire lookout on the extinct volcano's cone.

When they came to a place where the face of Mount Rainier seemed so close they could almost touch it, Herbert took out his camera and shot a photo, and they rested a while.

"What was it like?" Wesley asked, as the shadows grew long.

"It saved my life," Herbert replied.

As darkness fell, the men spread out blankets. The stars came out and they were brothers again, and for that brief time, all was right with the world.

•

Then came the attack that would change the nation's path—and Herbert's. Japan bombed Pearl Harbor, and although the United States had refused to join the war as Hitler and Stalin carved up Europe, now it rose to action with an indignant roar.

Some 300 alumni from Father Flanagan's Boys Town were in the service, including one who had been on the *U.S.S. Arizona* when Pearl Harbor was attacked and who was missing in action.

On the home front, the shipyards were hiring. Herbert moved to Tacoma to work for the Todd-Pacific Shipyard as a tabulating machine operator in the accounting department. He moved into the home of his maternal aunt and uncle and began working the graveyard shift. It was a workingman's town with a bustling port. Tugboats chugged in and out of the harbor, towing mighty ships, barges, and timber. A wood-products factory belched a sulfuric odor that drifted for miles on the wind, and there were harbor bars known as much for their brawls as their beer.

In his dingy office with the scuffed wooden desks, Herbert tabulated the accounts. From the window, seagulls could be seen pinwheeling above the barnacle-crusted wharves. Herbert made a good salary—$280 per month—and it allowed him to buy a car, which he later sold to buy another. Then he sold that one and bought yet another. With his income came a new sense of freedom—the liberty of cash.

Shortly before Christmas 1943, the new governor, Arthur Langlie, asked the Board of Prison Terms and Paroles for Herbert Niccolls's parole status. Unlike other former prisoners who had to comply with strict regulations, such as restrictions on owning a gun, buying a car, or changing residences without a parole officer's permission when they were on the outside, Herbert was exempt from the usual requirements because of specific instructions to the board from Governor Martin. When Martin left office, the parole board once again felt it needed to manage Herbert.

"We have heard informally that Niccolls is not keeping a good parole and that the wide publicity given him by the previous administration has given him the idea that he is a noteworthy individual who is not to be held to the same rules of behavior as other men," A. M. Murfin, chairman of the Board of Prison Terms and Paroles, wrote to Langlie's secretary.

Langlie ordered an investigation, and two months later asked the board to work out a parole arrangement that would give Herbert the same reporting duties as anyone else. Martin protested and demanded that Herbert be left alone and not be interviewed. But that was a demand Langlie and the board ignored.

In the meantime, Herbert met with district parole officer George Fahey at the Pierce County Courthouse and agreed that monthly visits to update the board on his progress would be advantageous. Fahey noted that Herbert "drinks moderately, smokes, enjoys the acquaintance of people he believes were highly respectable." He noted, too, that Herbert was bonded by the Hartford Mutual Indemnity Company to $15,000 and expects to be bonded for an additional $15,000 when he takes over the administrative accounts.

Although Fahey found nothing amiss, Frank Haggerty, an employee of Eastern State Hospital, had a different opinion. He wrote to the parole board that when Herbert was a patient at the hospital, he found him to be "very boastful in relationship with the employees, somewhat deceitful and guilty of petty thievery of personal property of . . . employees." He encouraged the board to write to Dr. Conway at the hospital and tell him that Herbert was not adhering to the conditions of his release.

One month later, Herbert wrote to Langlie himself, referring to him as "my esteemed governor," asking that he be released from his parole requirements. He was being inducted into the army.

"It is a matter extremely vital to me," he wrote, "for, being just an inductee will not be my tag—no, I will be, unconsciously or not, discriminated against because of my parole."

He wanted to erase the past, rewrite history, and he argued his point.

I have done as well as any, and better than most, I truly believe, in readjusting myself to normal life after being released from Walla Walla. I can bring forth witnesses in my behalf to testify to my character. . . . I know of no one who, I can honestly say, has anything against me. My record is clean. My break with the past has been a complete and total severance with any persons or organizations of whom I would be ashamed to acknowledge acquaintance.

I feel that I would have a much better chance, and be a better man for it, if I felt that, after leaving the Armed Forces, I were my own master—free in every sense of the word; able to vote, to live where I wished—to enter into business for myself, to make of myself a truly useful citizen—not just another "ex-con" or "parolee." That is why I respectfully petition you to grant me a pardon.

The pardon never came. Langlie replied that he had many requests from young men with prison records who were entering the military service and he had a policy of declining to grant pardons under the circumstances.

Although the pardon was denied, a draft deferment was granted because Herbert's work at the shipyard was more vital to national security than calling him into active service. So he continued to enjoy his status as an up-and-coming executive with a comfortable lifestyle.

With McChord Air Force Base and Fort Lewis just outside Tacoma, soldiers were everywhere, either going to the war or coming home from it. And the radio was full of war songs. "Don't sit under the apple tree with anyone else but me," crooned the Andrews Sisters. Then they sent dancers into overdrive with "Boogey Woogey Bugle Boy."

The war and all its passion rushed past Herbert—working in his gray office with his numbers and his tabulating machines—like the planes that drifted overhead, carrying with them his dreams of long ago. Despite his failure to land a job in aviation, he still thrived. He learned to dance, to charm the ladies by lighting their cigarettes, buying them cocktails, and offering them chairs. They crowded around him like butterflies, drinking in the honey of his charm. He had dark wavy hair and the same engaging manner that had won over the governor and prison warden and others who had fought for a better life for him.

By 1944, he was living in a basement apartment in the stately home of Navy Lieutenant Commander A. Bloom in northeast Tacoma. He had a view of Commencement Bay to the west and the islands beyond, and he was only a few miles from the office. As the years passed and he fit more into the workday world of a bachelor in the prime of his life, the prison years grew distant. In April 1945, the parole board sought to refresh that memory and sent him a warning letter, notifying him that he had not reported to his parole officer for several months and that if he did not, he would be placed on a list of those considered for return to prison.

He made contact and was once again in good standing. But he was faced with a new problem—the end of the war. The bustle of activity in the shipyards was slowing as the need for great battleships declined. By August, he was notified that he would be laid off in a month. But he did not worry. He had so impressed the representative of Remington Rand—the company that made the tabulating machines—that he had a standing job offer should he ever need work.

Herbert quickly petitioned the parole board for permission to leave the state for an interview at Twentieth Century Fox. He took the train through the hillside vineyards and fields of onions and rice, and finally entered a valley filled with orange groves and, beyond, the famed Hollywood sign on the hill. Ashe had told him about it, the city of dreams, the symbol of the richness of America, where a man could be anything if he worked hard.

Taking a job at the studio meant getting permission to be free of parole supervision. Herbert's request went down the bureaucratic chain from Governor Mon Walgren's office to the State Board of Prison Terms and Paroles. On September 19, 1945, Herbert was granted a release from parole supervision—but not the pardon that would erase the past and restore his civil rights.

He packed up the car and traveled south toward the sun.

Chapter 23

Hollywood, 1946–1983

THE AIR HELD the barely perceptible nip of late winter. Dry leaves flew past him like pages from the script of his life. How amazed he was when he arrived in the city in 1945. It was a place like no other, a fantasy world of palm trees, nearby white-sand beaches, beautiful bronze-shouldered women in the thinnest of sundresses, with sunlight dancing on blond-streaked hair. Living was easy, and the pace was relaxed as the sun-drenched afternoons turned into balmy evenings. Herbert Niccolls dined in palm groves and on patios, sipping martinis, listening to the crash of waves on the shore. He marveled at the thick white linen, the silver, the efficient, understated service at the Brown Derby, and he danced at the Palisades to Tommy or Jimmy Dorsey—doing swing steps and the jitterbug. He became a regular at the Musso & Frank Grill, the chophouse on Hollywood Boulevard where Humphrey Bogart, Charlie Chaplin, and a slew of writers, from Ernest Hemingway to William Faulkner, dined and drank. He saw the footprints of stars newly placed in concrete in front of Sid Grauman's Chinese Theatre, and fell in love with the Formosa Café, home to the glitterati from Warner Brothers Studio across the street, with its red vinyl booths.

He loved the art deco Pantages Theatre, site of the Academy Awards ceremony. Hollywood with all its tawdry glitter of dreams made and lost was a city like no other. But it was the great studios—the estates of the dream-weavers—that captured his imagination. Anything was possible in their worlds-within-worlds. Here the famous kissed and cursed, laughed and loved. They swung from vines in jungles, had shootouts at sundown on the western sets, rode the Orient Express, walked the streets of New York, dined with sheiks on the Arabian desert or explored the sea—all without ever leaving the studio back lots.

The grandest of them all was Twentieth Century Fox. While Herbert's eyesight worsened and the lenses of his glasses became thicker, what he once dreamed of doing in the air—sailing into a boundaryless world through flight—he now sought to do by writing. He wrote science fiction stories for *Argosy* and other magazines and began experimenting with writing screenplays. But his primary income came from translating the affairs of Fox studios into the language of numbers.

On his first day at the studio, the head of the tabulating department, Galvin, "Woody" Wood, showed him to a desk in the basement-level office, where fluorescent lights beamed down on the humming machinery. He was introduced to his coworkers and asked to join the studio Square Dance Club, the Reelers. He quickly fell into a routine—cards fed into the interpreter were punched at 96,000 holes a minute, then into the collator, where information about the profits from the studio's creative endeavors were translated into punched patterns.

It was math, logical and reliable. When nothing else in the world made sense, he could count on that universal language. Slowly, the studio moved ahead into the computer age as the gossip about the industry bubbled at the studio commissary, where all sorts of employees gathered in a democratic assembly in the buffet line for French dip, chicken-fried steaks, and banana-cream pies. Diners came in from the back lots, Stages 1 through 19, from the New England Street, the New York Square, the Melody Ranch, the lagoon, and the jungle. They were costume designers, lighting technicians, advertising executives, and landscapers.

Nothing amazed Herbert more than stepping from his office into what appeared to be a peaceful neighborhood where leafy trees—spray-painted the night before—flanked trim houses. It was here, at the call of "Action!" where children rode their bicycles down the street and smiling mothers in gingham or floral aprons called them in for dinner or lunch, or kissed the cheeks of smiling husbands. It was American life as it was supposed to be.

Hollywood also appeared synthetic, a mirror of life, without a heartbeat of its own. With its meringue-carved Rodeo Drive, shops with designer clothing and chi-chi restaurants flanked Arts and Crafts bungalows, Frank Lloyd Wright moderns, Italianate villas, ranch-style haciendas, and mammoth, pillared mansions, all juxtaposed against one another like movie sets. Who was he—the ex con—in this sugar-crusted place?

Once he had settled into this glamorous new world how could he reveal his past? L. Ron Hubbard seemed to have the answer. Hubbard believed that religious fervor caused neurosis and psychosis. He was strictly antireligion and anticommunist, and he waged war against the psychiatric profession. Hubbard once lived in Washington State; he'd been a Boy Scout, loved aviation, and in the 1930s had written screenplays and pulp science fiction. Hubbard and Herbert Niccolls had much in common, and they became acquaintances in the early days of the Scientology movement.

Over and over, Herbert tried to reach the state of "clear," where his mind was free from the debilitating memories of the past. But he had plenty he wanted to forget. He went to Scientology classes, repeated them, and underwent "auditing" to tally the memories he wanted to shed. The harder he tried, the worse the memories became, until he turned to nightly boilermakers to hide from them.

Despite the studio's successes, times were changing. The golden days of Hollywood were dying. The truth was in the cold logic of numbers. Fewer people were going to movie theaters. They were staying home and watching the new medium called television. Politically, the post-war nation had changed as well. As Joseph Stalin aggressively carved up war-torn Europe, Cold War fears and suspicions were rife in the United States. From the nation's capital to Hollywood, government agents looked, and found, signs of a communist plot woven like a thread through the cultural tapestry of America.

The House Un-American Affairs Commission became active—after remaining quiet throughout the war. Even the studio employees' magazine, *Action*, told readers how they too "could fight the bomb." As panic in the industry roiled around him, Herbert settled into a comfortable life. He lived in a modest home near the University of Southern California and enjoyed his freedom. No longer did parole officers play a part in his life. He was far away from prison, from Asotin, from Idaho, and from all of what his life had once been. Others may have had critical views, but he loved America. It was a place where anyone—even a convicted murderer—could rise to prominence through hard work.

His brother Paul came to live with him for a time and later Wesley, after he was discharged from the service. Herbert took them to Macambo's, Ciros, or Friscati's to see who was with whom. As always, Herbert slipped through the crowd, almost invisibly, firmly believing he would never marry.

It was easy for Herbert to throw himself into his work, always willing to stay late, always eager to find ways to make the operation run smoother, always intrigued by new technology that would make computing more efficient.

•

Long after Herbert left prison, Flanagan unsuccessfully tried to locate him and then let it drop. Flanagan was about to consider another Washington case—that of Joseph Maish, a sixteen-year-old who was sentenced to hang for murdering a young girl. He was thirty minutes from climbing the ladder to the gallows and had eaten his last meal—two cream puffs—when Governor Mon Walgren commuted his sentence to ninety-nine years in prison.

At about the same time, the citizens of Las Animas, Colorado, asked Father Flanagan to accept a twelve-year-old alleged killer, James Melton

Jr., to Boys Town. The boy was accused of killing his sister.

And the requests went on and on.

"It costs so little to teach a child to love, and so much to teach him to hate," Flanagan told his followers. "There are no bad boys. There is only bad environment, bad training, bad example, bad thinking."

•

Although Flanagan, who died in 1948, did not succeed in freeing Herbert Niccolls, his campaign to free Herbert no doubt kept the lad from being forgotten, as happened to so many other incarcerated youths.

Until the day of his death, Flanagan was working to help children, paying $25,000 bail for the release of a sixteen-year-old sentenced to life in prison for killing his stepfather, taking in a twelve-year-old who killed the father who had whipped him once too often. Flanagan unsuccessfully tried to save young sailors Maurice Simniok and Joseph Lemmon, who had killed a Mississippi sheriff while they were AWOL and on a crime spree. He continued to preach that the best way to curtail juvenile crime was to prevent boys from growing up in poverty.

•

For Herbert, studio life continued, much like a large family. At the hub as a Fox booster was the employee-run Studio Club, a social and fund-raising club for charities and employees in need. The club sponsored black-tie dinner-dances and square dances, as the studio square-dance club grew from 30 to 200, reflecting the dance's popularity throughout the country.

In the meantime, the studio's *Twelve O'Clock High* opened with a gala black-tie affair. Some 2,000 spectators stood before Grauman's Chinese Theatre that evening as searchlights swept the sky and a sixty-piece Air Force band played in the forecourt of the theater. Seven Air Force generals along with some eighty top-ranking film celebrities were there, as sleek as prize Afghans and as cosseted as royalty.

The studio's bowlers wrapped up the year's competition with (Gregory) Peck's *Polecats*, leading by five. For a man with no family there was always someplace to go, some studio-related event to make Herbert feel included, and he became fiercely loyal to Fox.

Then one day Herbert received a letter from South America from James Ashe. Ashe had sent it to the prison, which sent it to the parole board, which sent it to his maternal aunt in Tacoma, who eventually sent it on. There it was in his mailbox—the past touching him in this new life. It wasn't the first time. Asotin's Judge Kuykendall occasionally wrote and Herbert responded with details of his success. But any contact reminded him that he would always carry the stigma of his past with him, as inescapable as his shadow. And although he had "audited" his own past—step by step taking himself back through his life to some of its most painful memories as his Scientology teachings prescribed—he was never able to rid himself of the lingering sadness and fear to achieve what Scientology called the state of "clear." Shortly after receiving the letter, he moved to an apartment closer to the studio.

As the studio moved from the socially conscious films of the 1940s and early 1950s to frothy musicals in order to compete against television, Herbert researched the latest developments in computers and began teaching programming at the University of California, Los Angeles. But he still longed to soar into a world without borders through the flight of imagination. He wanted to create for the screen.

They had often used him to review scripts because of his language skills. He pitched some of his screenplays to Fox but without success. He made plans to start his own production company. With his characteristic charm, he cultivated contacts in the industry—people whom he hoped would someday be investors. It would be many years before he came close to launching it.

The face in the mirror he saw in the morning was confident—a young executive with plans for moving up. Anything was possible, until he thought of the past. When he was restless in the evenings, he'd walk the streets of Hollywood, feeling the warmth of the streets beneath his shoes. Behind doors were so many secrets, so many lies, so much wealth and glamour, disappointment and poverty. One could so quickly teeter-totter into the other.

•

By the end of 1955, Joseph McCarthy was losing ground. As the Soviets launched Sputnik and the Cold War continued, anticommunist films flourished. Despite their low-budgets and thin plots, they capitalized on public fears and amounted to little more than propaganda. One of them starred Roy Rogers, who along with his palomino Trigger, donned an asbestos suit to fight enemies of the nation.

Niccolls had a Cold War entrée of his own—a screenplay about his friend Stephen Apostoloff's escape from communist Hungary. Apostoloff and Niccolls co-wrote the story that had a title poignant to both, *Journey to Freedom*.

The film was directed by Robert Durtano and was produced by Republic Pictures. The bright red movie posters showed the hero with his gun drawn, and behind him was a blonde nurse in a slinky green dress with a slit up her thigh, a costume more provocative than any Eve Brent, the female lead, ever wore in the film.

•

One night a friend invited Herbert to stop by his house for a drink. There was someone he should meet, he was told. She had blue eyes and brown hair. She was a petite woman who aspired to be a writer. She was beautiful. She was an Oklahoma girl—genuine and kind. He fell hard, but she was already married.

He took her out for a drink. How genuine her laugh was, her conversation so spirited, and those eyes. She had left her husband in Seattle and wanted a new life. But Herbert was forty-three and set in his ways: a drink after work with friends from the studio, a quick bite to eat, then home to read books on computers and the latest technology. He would have a boilermaker for a nightcap, and then sink into his easy chair to watch television until he drifted off to sleep.

Now there was someone to disrupt that routine, to make him think again of the past. He would have to tell Patricia, risk seeing the veil of distrust fall across her face and have her walk out of his life forever. He paced. He smoked cigarettes and, finally, as she looked up at him expectantly, he told her.

"What does it matter? You were just a kid!" she said.

At Patricia's acceptance, Herbert couldn't marry her quickly enough. He whisked her away to Mexico for a quick divorce and then married her and settled into a comfortable routine in a bungalow in Culver City.

He tinkered with inventions, patenting a typewriter carriage return. He took Patricia out for cocktails and dinner. He knew it would only be the two of them. A partial hysterectomy had rendered her incapable of bearing children. They would grow old this way—dining out, going to movies, reading books.

The studio was teetering on the edge of bankruptcy, Hollywood itself was changing, but they had each other, and one day Patricia had news that would change Herbert's life forever. He was going to be a father.

He grabbed her and danced her around the room and then raced out to buy cigars. "You'd think you invented fatherhood," she told him. But the doctors had grim news. Carrying the baby to full term could put her life at risk.

"They want me to have a therapeutic abortion," she told him one night. "I won't do it." Instead, she rested in bed often and avoided any strenuous activity. Then on a spring morning, she felt the first pains and was rushed to the hospital. Sometime later, a baby boy was born. Herbert held the baby in his arms and named him Jonathan.

Over the years, he brought his young son to the studio and showed him the sets—the opulent New York street scene for *Hello Dolly* and the Korean War vintage military compound used for *M*A*S*H**—and he took Jonathan to elaborate employee picnics, where members of the costume department dressed as characters from *Planet of the Apes* and swooped down, capturing children.

Despite his success at the studio and his delight in his son, there was a lingering sadness in Herbert that would never diminish. The sadder he was, the more gregarious he became, attending parties, giving toasts, building up the egos of others and getting little in return. As his brothers would someday explain, no one heard and no one saw the boy inside as he called "drinks for the house," picking up tabs that were far more than he could afford. As the parties and his lust for boilermakers and highballs continued, his savings dwindled.

Time after time, he ended up in auto accidents when he was under the influence of alcohol; fearing involvement with the police or the insurance company, he simply paid the damage out of his own pocket, offering any amount in order not to involve the authorities. And despite his good income, the family could never afford to move from the modest Hollywood apartment where his son spent his entire childhood.

Yet, he found refuge from his unhappiness when he was with his son. After Patricia was hospitalized for nearly a month due to complications from multiple ulcers, he took Jonathan out to Big Bear Lake to talk to him about his mother's precarious health.

There were tears, hugs, and quiet time by the lake and fishing. Patricia eventually recovered. The time at the lake started a tradition that would continue. Whenever father and son needed time together, Herbert took Jonathan out to the desert or the mountains for long talks and snowball fights, but he never shared anything with him about the past. It was a subject locked away and shrouded with shame.

In the meantime, Herbert's city was sliding away from the place it once was to a center of urban decay. Scruffy young men with tattered clothing and long hair sat in doorways. And even the starlets didn't seem as beautiful or elegant. The romance and glamour had gone, along with good manners and dignity.

Tattoo parlors and souvenir shops began to line the streets where the famous once dined and danced at posh nightclubs, places where million-dollar movie deals had been made and dreams were lost and found. Whenever he saw angry young boys on the street, he'd stop to talk to them, to offer them money, a home, help.

•

Throughout the years, Herbert continued to be the gregarious host, a gentleman with courtly manners.

"Such lovely manners," his grade-school teacher had said during his trial.

"Well-mannered," echoed Mr. Rose, the prison librarian, the warden, the Pomeroy sheriff, and Governor Martin.

"He wasn't happy but he tried to make people think he was," Wesley said many years later. Herbert reunited with other family members, but most of his siblings remembered little more than his name. He occasionally saw his mother, who later moved to northern California. Throughout his entire incarceration she had never visited him and her letters had been rare. Jonathan remembers occasional holiday dinners with her, describing her as a stern woman who could stop her grandchild cold with a raise of an eyebrow.

His brother Hudson recalled Herbert as being successful and gregarious, a fixture at Twentieth Century Fox and an enigma to the rest of the family. The boy who had once hid food in the turkey house and wore burlap sacks over his feet as he walked to school in the snow because he had no shoes now wore nice suits, had brought Tennessee Ernie Ford home to dinner, and worked with movie stars.

He had attained more than anyone in his family and they looked at him—with his connection to the movie stars—in awe as he cruised around Hollywood in his green Mustang. By the mid 1970s, Herbert was nearing retirement with nothing to show for his years of work. The once sleek, modern apartment was showing wear and becoming as run down as the neighborhood.

Herbert tried to bring in more money and returned to the idea of starting a production company. He began with two partners, but when one partner died, the plans for the company were set back.

In 1977, Herbert was nearing sixty and concerned about retirement. He had spent money as fast as he made it. He met a multi-level marketing guru, who promised great riches for an initial investment. The scheme seemed to make sense. Pat Boone endorsed the product. The first investors recruited other investors, who recruited others, with a percentage of the profits being passed on up the line. The product to be sold—insulation—seemed like the answer to the energy crisis of the 1970s. But it wasn't.

On July 16, 1982, those on the losing end of the scheme sued in the Los Angeles Superior Court, claiming fraud and misrepresentation. For a man who paid off other drivers to keep them from calling authorities in a mishap, the prospect of going to court terrified Herbert. He lived in fear that his conviction for murder would once again be brought up, that he'd be forced to return to prison, that his standing in the Hollywood community would crumble. Most knew him only as a computer analyst for Twentieth Century Fox, the man who lit their cigarettes and bought their drinks and was always smiling—no matter what—even as his blood pressure climbed with anxiety and his heart beat harder in his thickened arteries. His doctor told him to quit drinking and lose weight, but he ignored the advice.

As the day of the fraud trial approached, the invitations came as usual. There were parties, boozy fests in swank houses and hotels. Christmas came with lights strung through palm trees. Then came New Year's Eve, and 1983 slipped in with cheers, the blare of party horns, and "Auld Lang Syne." It would be his last new year. That year spring tiptoed in balmy and blue—as blue as his long-remembered marble. He was small again. The boy fit only for execution. A blight on society. The voices imprinted in his memory surfaced again, haunting him until he cried out in his sleep.

"He was afraid he'd go to prison again," Paul Niccolls said.

•

Over the years, Herbert had been interested in alternative religions. He found comfort in the idea of Krishna, the embodiment of divine joy and love who destroys all pain and sin, and in the Hindu scripture *Bhagavad Gita*.

On a warm April day, Herbert took Jonathan aside and gave him two tickets to see Yul Brynner's 4,000th performance of *The King and I* at the Pantages Theatre in Los Angeles, telling him to take Patricia if he himself couldn't go. Then father and son spent their usual Sunday together, this time driving down the Sunset Highway toward the coast. They stopped at an ashram. They sat on chairs with their eyes closed, listening to the song of the birds and the splash of fountains and feeling the breeze shifting lightly through the room.

Two days later at the family's Hollywood apartment, Herbert was sitting in his chair in the evening, watching Johnny Carson with Jonathan. Herbert pushed himself up from the chair slowly and headed toward his bedroom. Jonathan suddenly was moved to call to his father, "I love you, Dad."

"I love you, too, son," Herbert replied.

•

Shortly after four a.m. on April 24, 1983, Jonathan awoke to hear muffled cries. At first, he thought his father was having a nightmare so he rose and went to his father's bed. He found his father kneeling on the bed moaning in pain. Suddenly Herbert pitched forward as if he had been punched. Jonathan called 911 and tried to help his father as the precious minutes passed while they waited for an ambulance. Herbert was rushed to Hollywood Presbyterian Hospital. All the arteries of his heart were heavily clogged, preventing the passage of blood. By 5:26 a.m. he was dead. The cause of death was hypertensive, arteriosclerotic cardiovascular disease.

"We found out later that his nitroglycerine bottle was empty and the doctor said he hadn't refilled it in two months," Jonathan said. "He had just given up."

Two hundred people came to the funeral. Herbert was buried at the Hollywood Memorial Park in good company—with the Hollywood celebrities he admired.

Although his daily world was far from the conditions in which he grew up, he never forgot the day in Asotin that had changed his life—leaving a family without their beloved patriarch and a town without its most respected leader. More than anything, his brothers say, he wanted to erase the shame of his crime and be loved despite his past.

Epilogue

MANY YEARS AFTER Herbert Niccolls's death, his wife and son were still living in the same Hollywood apartment, where thorny red roses spilled over a cyclone fence. I pushed the button on the security gate and waited. At last I heard a crackling sound and the voice of an elderly woman. It was Patricia. Jonathan Niccolls, a young man with a husky build and dark hair, came to the gate and let me in.

The Niccolls's apartment was filled with worn furniture, a bookcase with paperbacks, and on a shelf, one blue marble, the color of sky and water that Jonathan had found and given to his mother. Patricia was ill (and later died in 2008) and retreated to another room shortly after I arrived. As Jonathan talked about Herbert, he described him as a good man and a kind-hearted father.

"He was a peach of a dad. Every Sunday we would make a day of it, going to movies or fishing on the Santa Monica pier," Jonathan said.

On most nights, "he'd come home after work, kiss Mom. We'd talk, he'd have his nightcap and fall asleep in his chair, listening to Johnny

Carson. "Dad would do anything for people," Jonathan said. "And people loved him."

Then I asked the question that would forever change his memories of his father: "Did he talk much about his life in Washington?"

Jonathan looked perplexed and insisted that his father had grown up in Idaho. "What made you think he lived in Washington?"

"There are news stories and records," I said.

"About my dad?" Jonathan asked. "What was my dad doing in the news?"

Almost as soon as I realized that he knew nothing about his father's past, Patricia walked into the room. Our eyes met. Jonathan begged for information.

I told him the story his father had kept secret. Jonathan was quiet for a long time. Finally, he told me how his father had tried to help so many street kids, taking them under his wing, and that often he retreated into brooding depression. Once, after listening to a news program about cuts in jail funding, Jonathan, without knowing why, had asked his father, "Have you ever been in jail?"

"I don't want to talk about it," was the reply.

"This explains so much," Jonathan said. "So very much."

Herbert had once told his brothers that going to prison saved his life. He knew little about the fight Father Flanagan had waged to bring him to Boys Town. He also likely never knew that when the newspapers had carried the story about his getting his high school diploma in prison, Flanagan had written to Mrs. Lamson expressing his regret that Herbert had not received his diploma from the Boys Town High School.

Herbert likely would have flourished at Boys Town. The arrangement at the prison allowed him to have food, shelter, and clothing, freedom from beatings, a structured environment, and an education. But a warden and prison guards are poor substitutes for family and friends. Prison would never have offered him the chance to heal from the violence he had experienced during his early years, let alone the humiliation and terror he endured during the trial and prison. The hobgoblin of "bad" heredity stalked him for the rest of his days, though the occurrences of crime and mental illness in Herbert Niccolls's ancestral family probably had more to do with the generational cycles of child abuse that were unbroken until the death of John Wormell.

•

In 2004, John Wormell was added to the list of the state's officers who had died in the line of duty and his name would be listed on the accompanying website. Many law enforcement officers, citizens of Asotin, and others around the country have added their comments. As one officer wrote on Wormell's page, "Sheriff, your service to your county has set a very high bar. To be elected for so many terms speaks to the respect you were given. To be handling calls at 1 a.m. speaks to your character as a law enforcement officer. Rest in Peace, your job on earth is done."

Another also weighed in with an opinion that had echoed from the past: "On . . . the 76th anniversary of your murder, I would like to say thank you for your service and sacrifice for the citizens of Asotin County. I think it was a travesty of justice that your murderer only served [nine] years in prison."

As Herbert told his brothers, he lived with the memory of what he had done. There is no greater punishment, he said, than living with a recurring nightmare—a secret he had never revealed even to a beloved son. And that, he said, "is a punishment far greater than any of man's laws."

Notes

•

Preface

p. x   *DuBuc had attended*: Washington State Penitentiary, No. 14201, 5 Mar. 1932.

Holds the record: Washington Department of Corrections, "Persons Executed Since 1904 in Washington State," www.doc.wa.gov/offenderinfo/capitalpunishment/executedlist.

Niccolls committed: "Executions in the United States, 1608-2000: The Espy File," Inter-University Consortium for Political and Social Research, Headland, Ala., 2004, www.icpsr.umich.edu.

p. xi   *In 1929*: Andrea Tortora, "Kentucky 6-year-old tried for murder," *Cincinnati Enquirer*, 5 Mar. 2000.

But unlike the Kentucky: Ibid.

p. xii *A 2003 case*: Jonathan Martin, "Supreme Court clears the way for trial of two boys," *Seattle Times*, 5 Feb. 2005.

From century to century: G. Pearson, quoted in "Executions in the United States, 1608-2000: The Espy File," Inter University Consortium for Political and Social Research, Headland, Ala., 2004, www.icpsr.umich.edu.

Chapter 1

p. 3   *This was not his*: "Many Want Star," *Lewiston Morning Tribune*, 9 Aug. 1931, 1.

p. 3   *He walked to the lumberyard*: Ibid.

p. 4   *He had made from the leather*: "Young Murderer Shows No Signs of Remorse; Sleeps after Tragedy," *Lewiston Morning Tribune*, 5 Aug. 1931, 1.

    He had taken the gun: "Boy Takes All," *Lewiston Morning Tribune*, 6 Aug. 1931, 1.

    Each time: Murphy Watkins, personal interview, 5 May 1996.

p. 5   *Into the bag*: "Slayer 12, Plays Harmonica, Waits Decision by Jury," *Seattle Times*, 23 Oct. 1931.

    He hadn't owned shoes: "Youth Pleads Insanity," *Walla Walla Daily Bulletin*, 27 Oct. 1931, 1.

p. 6   *He wondered why*: Wesley Niccolls, personal interview, 8 June 1996.

    Who dared: Ibid.

    No, not me: Ibid.

    Bert Niccolls raised the shotgun: Ibid.

p. 7   *As Junior was filling the bag*: "Sheriff of Asotin Slain by Boy Burglar in Store," *Seattle Times*, 5 Aug. 1931.

    Suddenly the store's: Ibid.

p. 8   *Then Bezona saw*: Judge E.V. Kuykendall, Elmer S. Halsey, Lillian M. Carse, superintendent, Children's Home, Boise, Idaho, Statement of Trial Judge and Prosecuting Attorney, Asotin County Superior Court, circa October 1931.

    Bezona had tried to tell: Jack Bezona, personal interview, 8 Aug. 1996.

    "Come out or I'll kill you!": Ibid.

    A boy less than five feet tall: Ibid.

p. 9   *"What did you do this for?"*: "Boy Burglar Kills Sheriff Wormell," *Asotin Sentinel*, 7 Aug. 1931, 1.

    That's what the Niccolls children: Wesley Niccolls, personal interview, 8 June 1996.

    She was a gentle soul: Ibid.

    What a blight . . . on the town: Judge Elgin V. Kuykendall, "Historic Glimpses of Asotin County, Washington," *East Washingtonian*, 1954, 56-57.

    Even in the pre-dawn: Ibid.

p. 10   *The ticking of the regulator*: Robert Weatherly, personal interview, 8 Aug. 1996.

    The boy was sprawled: "Young Murderer Shows No Signs of Remorse; Sleeps after Tragedy," *Lewiston Morning Tribune*, 5 Aug. 1931, 1, 3.

    Nothing could be done: "11-year-old Slays Sheriff John Wormell," *Lewiston Morning Tribune*, 5 Aug. 1931, 1.

p. 11   *"Old Bill Robison?"*: "Veteran Officer Murdered," *Asotin Sentinel*, Aug. 1931, 1.

    Young Murphy Watkins was jarred: Murphy Watkins, personal interview, 8 Aug. 1996.

p. 12   *"What? You want to arrest me?"*: Jean Seibel, personal interview, 8 Aug. 1996.

"Please don't take him!": Ibid.

Chapter 2

p. 13   *They gathered in amazement*: "Young Murderer Shows No Signs of Remorse; Sleeps after Tragedy," *Lewiston Morning Tribune*, 5 Aug. 1931, 1, 3.

"Is he the one?": "Young Murderer Shows No Signs of Remorse; Sleeps after Tragedy," *Lewiston Morning Tribune*, 5 Aug. 1931, 1, 3.

p. 14   *"For doing things"*: "Murder Blame, Bill Robinson Exonerated," *Asotin Sentinel*, 8 Aug. 1931, 1.

Anyone in those parts: George Day, *The Best of Jawbone Flat Gazette*, vol. 3 (Bob Weatherly Books, 1987), 153.

p. 15   *"If I didn't get him"*: "Barefoot Boy who Killed Asotin Sheriff on Trial," *Lewiston Morning Tribune*, 26 Oct. 1931, 1

"Life is a game": Author's observation from visiting the former jail, 8 Aug. 1996.

Outside the jail Junior: Judge Elgin V. Kuykendall, "Historic Glimpses of Asotin County, Washington," *East Washingtonian*, 1954, 56-57.

p. 16   *The town had a history*: "Musty Old Sheriff's Book Tells of Early Lynchings," source uncertain.

p. 17   *As thousands from nearby*: Judge Elgin V. Kuykendall, "Historic Glimpses of Asotin County, Washington," *East Washingtonian*, 1954, 56-57.

When the mob swarmed: Ibid.

"Hang them!": Ibid.

p. 18   *Wayne Bezona knew this*: Jack Bezona, personal interview, 8 Aug. 1996.

She was a blue blood: Linda Spencer, interview, 8 Aug. 1996.

p. 19   *Over the years*: Jack Bezona, interview, 9 Aug. 1996.

Chapter 3

p. 20   *Not that he would have been eligible*: Judge Elgin V. Kuykendall, "Historic Glimpses of Asotin County, Washington," *East Washingtonian*, 1954, 56-57.

p. 21   *In a time when the average age*: "New Leaflet for Visitors to Penitentiary Gives Data," *Walla Walla Daily Bulletin*, 23 May 1930, 3.

How excited he had been: Judge Elgin V. Kuykendall, Elmer S. Halsey, Lillian M. Carse, superintendent, Children's Home, Boise, Idaho, Statement of Trial Judge and Prosecuting Attorney, Asotin County Superior Court, circa Oct. 1931.

p. 22   *But on August 2, 1929, he tried to persuade*: Ibid.

Saying she was trying: Murphy Watkins, interview, 8 Aug. 1996.

p. 22   *Impressed by the boy's*: Garfield Davis, Washington State Penitentiary, "Statement of Facts: A Biographical History of the Niccolls Family," 17 Apr. 1933.

She told the judge: "Slayer, 12, Plays Harmonica, Waits Decision by Jury," *Seattle Times*, 23 Oct. 1931.

p. 23   *But moments later*: Washington State Penitentiary, "Statement of Facts: A Biographical History of the Niccolls Family," Garfield Davis, 17 Apr. 1933.

His grandmother came: Ibid.

Then after fifteen months: Ibid.

No one knew him, except his: "Tragic side to Case Is Bared," *Walla Walla Daily Bulletin*, 30 Oct. 1931.

p. 25   *"Shoot to kill," the boy replied*: "Veteran officer murdered," *Lewiston Morning Tribune*, 7 Aug. 1931, 1.

And then he heard someone: "Home Life of Boy Enters the Trial," *The Daily Northwestern*, Oshkosh, Wis., 28 Oct. 1931.

After the others had left: "Boy Slayer Sorry, Wants to Do Right; Hans Damm to Aid," *Seattle Times,* 31 Oct. 1931, 1.

For many hours: Lewiston Morning Tribune, 7 Aug. 1931, 1.

"I hid behind the vinegar": Ibid.

p. 26   *The boy began to invent*: "Veteran officer murdered," *Lewiston Morning Tribune*, 7 Aug. 1931, 1.

"I was just sore because": "Suspect Freed," *Seattle Times*, 6 Aug. 1931.

Gilliam came back to the boy's: "Young Slayer Now in Prison," *Reno Evening Gazette*, 30 Oct. 1931.

The boy recited the story: Ibid.

p. 27   *The body of John Wormell*: "Solemn Rites Held for John Wormell," *Lewiston Morning Tribune*, 7 Aug. 1931, 1

p. 28   *"He talks freely about it"*: "Board to Name Sheriff This Afternoon," *Lewiston Morning Tribune*, 7 Aug. 1931.

Chapter 4

p. 30   *"A meteor passed"*: "Fiery Star Struck in Blue Mountains," *Lewiston Morning Tribune*, 7 Aug. 1931.

The Tribune *reported that*: Ibid.

p. 31   *He was going to uphold*: Jack Bezona, interview, 9 Aug. 1996.

p. 32   *Patterson had needed to send*: Armene Lamson, letter to Gov. Clarence Martin, 25 May 1933.

p. 33   *A. G. Farley of Pomeroy*: Ibid.

p. 34   *It was as if he was detached*: "Tragic Side to Case of Young Killer Seen," *Walla Walla Daily Bulletin*, 30 Oct. 1931, 1.

           Doyle, as a father: "Hubert Nicolls (*sic*) Cries as Jurors Get Killing Case," *Walla Walla Daily Bulletin*, 28 Oct. 1931, 1.

Chapter 5

p. 36   *The trousers were long*: "Youth Pleads Insanity," *Walla Walla Daily Bulletin*, 27 Oct. 1931.

           His dark curling lashes: R. B. Bermann, "Child Delinquency Problem Is Presented," *Seattle Post-Intelligencer*, 25 Oct. 1931.

p. 37   *Enterprising members*: "Boy, 12, May Hear Fate in Slaying Trial Today," *Seattle Times*, 27 Oct. 1931.

           He smiled and waved: "Youth Pleads Insanity," *Walla Walla Union Bulletin*, 27 Oct. 1931, 1.

           She paused, clasped her hands: Ibid.

p. 38   *"May every possible bad"*: "Historic Glimpses of Asotin County, Washington," *East Washingtonian*, 1954.

           Crackpot, Kuykendall: Ibid.

p. 39   *Kuykendall suspected that Farley was merely* : Judge Elgin V. Kuykendall, Elmer S. Halsey, Lillian M. Carse, superintendent, Children's Home, Boise, Idaho, Statement of Trial Judge and Prosecuting Attorney, Asotin County Superior Court, circa Oct. 1931.

p. 40   *Although he would*: In the Superior Court of the State of Washington, No. 3281 Verdict, 28 Oct. 1931.

p. 41   *Of the witnesses*: Asotin County Superior Court Subpoenas 3281 and 3282, 16 Oct. 1931.

p. 42   *"I am an old man"*: "Boy Guilty of Murder," *Los Angeles Times*, 29 Oct. 1931, 1

           "Smokeless cartridges": John W. Schaefer, letter to King County Superior Court Judge William J. Wilkins, 24 Sept. 1940.

p. 43   *"Come on out"*: "Boy, 12, May Hear Fate in Slaying Trial Today," *Seattle Times*, 27 Oct. 1931.

           The newspapers carried Bezona's: "State Ends Case against Niccolls," *Walla Walla Daily Bulletin*, 27 Oct. 1931, 1.

           Several days before: Garfield Davis, Washington State Penitentiary, "Statement of Facts: A Biographical History of the Niccolls Family," 17 Apr. 1933.

           He then asked her to continue: Ibid.

p. 44   *"Hey Junior. Wanna shoot"*: Murphy Watkins, interview, 13 May 1996.

           With seven children: Jean Seibel, interview, 13 May 1996.

p. 44   *"But he can't go home"*: Ibid.

p. 45   *Junior leaped from*: Ibid.

Chapter 6

p. 46   *Hostetler was at first*: Joyce Hostetler, interview, 8 Aug. 1996.

p. 47   *A woman in the crowd*: "Hubert (sic) Niccolls, Murderer of Sheriff Wormell, Tried and Verdict is Guilty," *Asotin County Sentinel*, 30 Oct. 1931, 1

"He's a murdering little": Ibid.

After about an hour: Ibid.

p. 48   *"Too many pancakes"*: "Boy Murderer Termed Insane," *Los Angeles Times*, 28 Oct. 1931, 10.

"He has no conscience": "Slayer, 12, Plays Harmonica, Waits Decision by Jury," *Seattle Times*, 28 Oct. 1931.

Sheriff Patterson said: Ibid.

J. B. Tucker, who had bought the suit: Ibid.

"He's a congenital psychopath": "Hubert (sic) Niccolls, Murderer of Sheriff Wormell, Tried and Verdict is Guilty," *Asotin County Sentinel*, 30 Oct. 1931, 1.

"No wonder he's sick": *Asotin County Sentinel*, 30 Oct. 1931, 1

p. 49   *His mother, Hazel Niccolls*: Mrs. O. E. Lamson, "The Herbert Niccolls Case," Seattle, Wash., undated.

The children always went: Ibid.

"Who knows how they kept": Ibid.

She described Bert Niccolls: Ibid.

p. 50   *After Mrs. Frazier was murdered*: Ibid.

Mrs. Addington detailed: "Youth Pleads Insanity," *Walla Walla Daily Bulletin*, 27 Oct. 1931, 1.

On the day of the murder: "Boy Murderer Termed Insane," *Los Angeles Times*, 28 Oct. 1931, 10.

"He's possessed by a demon": "Slayer, 12, Plays Harmonica, Waits Decision by Jury," *Seattle Times*, 28 Oct. 1931.

p. 51   *"I'm better at math"*: "Hubert (sic) Niccolls, Murderer of Sheriff Wormell, Tried and Verdict is Guilty," *Asotin County Sentinel*, 30 Oct. 1931, 1

"I like books and magazines": "Slayer, 12, Plays Harmonica, Waits Decision by Jury," *Seattle Times*, 28 Oct. 1931.

"I saw some tobacco": Ibid.

"For holding a duck under water": Ibid.

p. 52   *As far as the attorneys were concerned*: E. J. Doyle, letter to Rev. E. J. Flanagan, 30 Oct. 1931.

p. 52   *He was haunted by them*: Wesley Niccolls, personal interview, 8 June 1996.

Papa was hitting Mama: Ibid.

In November, Mary Addington: Garfield Davis, Washington State Penitentiary, "Statement of Facts: A Biographical History of the Niccolls Family," 17 Apr. 1933.

p. 53   *Since their father had given up smoking*: Wesley Niccolls, personal interview, 8 June 1996.

Hazel Niccolls pleaded: Ibid.

"Forget about it," Mrs. Addington: Garfield Davis, Washington State Penitentiary, "Statement of Facts: A Biographical History of the Niccolls Family," 17 Apr. 1933.

When Bert Niccolls: Wesley Niccolls, personal interview, 8 June 1996.

p. 54   *"Prepare to meet your Jesus!"*: Ibid.

Chapter 7

p. 56   *The case became a symbol*: R. B. Bermann, "Child Delinquency Problem is Presented: Prosecutor Will Not Demand Death Penalty," *Seattle Post-Intelligencer*, 26 Oct. 1931.

p. 57   *"Junior turned his usual beam on the crowd"*: "Boy, 12, May Hear Fate in Slaying Trial Today," *Seattle Times*, 27 Oct. 1931.

"Junior simply has bad 'heredity'": "Slayer, 12, Plays Harmonica, Waits Decision by Jury," *Seattle Times*, 28 Oct. 1931.

He stole from them—jewelry and money: Garfield Davis, Washington State Penitentiary, "Statement of Facts: A Biographical History of the Niccolls Family," 17 Apr. 1933.

p. 58   *He burglarized the post office*: "Church Fire and Robbery Laid to Convicted Boy," *Seattle Times*, 21 Dec. 1931.

"He shot Mr. Wormell": "Boy Guilty of Murder," *Los Angeles Times*, 29 Oct. 1931, 1.

In his closing, Doyle played to the jury's: Ibid.

p. 59   *"Wayne told me not to."*: "Tragic Side to Case Is Bared," *Walla Walla Daily Bulletin*, Oct. 1931, 74.

"Better have some": Ibid.

p. 60   *"Nothing"*: "Jury Finds Hubert (*sic*) Niccolls Jr., Guilty of First Degree Murder," *Seattle Times* 29 Oct. 1931, 1

Chapter 8

p. 61   *Flanagan was at Mercy*: Charles P. Graves, *Father Flanagan Founder of Boys Town* (Garrard Publishing Company, 1972).

p. 61   *"To Mr. J. C. Applewhite and Mr. E. J. Doyle"*: Rev. E. J. Flanagan, telegram to John C. Applewhite and E. J. Doyle, 30 Oct. 1931.

p. 62   *John Wormell had been a wise and good leader*: Fran Connelly, personal interview, 7 July 1997.

       When the boy called to it: "Tragic Side to Case of Young Killer Seen," *Walla Walla Daily Bulletin*, 30 Oct. 1931, 1.

       "Stand up, Herbert": "Jury Finds Hubert (sic) Niccolls Jr., Guilty of First Degree Murder," *Seattle Times*, 29 Oct. 1931, 1

       It really mattered little: "Hubert (*sic*) Niccolls Cries as Jurors Get Killing Case," *Walla Walla Daily Bulletin*, 28 Oct. 1931, 1.

       "He's a boy who wanted": "Twelve Years Old and in Prison for Life," *Indiana Evening Gazette*, 5 Nov. 1931, 6.

p. 63   *"I'm glad they didn't"*: "Jury Finds Hubert (*sic*) Niccolls Jr., Guilty of First Degree Murder," *Seattle Times*, 29 Oct. 1931, 1

       "We wanted to say good-bye": Murphy Watkins, personal interview, 5 May 1996.

       Murphy muttered his reply: Ibid.

       In his hospital bed: Rev. E. J. Flanagan, radio address, 12 Nov. 1931.

       It was too late, the attorneys wrote: E. J. Doyle, letter to Rev. E. J. Flanagan, 30 Oct. 1931; John C. Applewhite, letter to Rev. E. J. Flanagan, 1 Nov. 1931.

p. 64   *"The boy had previously"*: "Mackintosh Regrets Failure to Hang," *Walla Walla Daily Bulletin*, 30 Oct. 1931, 1.

       Only three months earlier, the commission: "Junior Prisons Are Condemned," *Lewiston Morning Tribune*, 9 July 1931, 1.

p. 65   *Flanagan was so enraged*: Rev. E. J. Flanagan, telegraph statement to *Seattle Post-Intelligencer*, 1931.

       Katherine Lenroot, acting chief: "Bureau Assails Boy Sentences," *Los Angeles Times*, 4 Nov. 1931.

       When Sheriff Wayne Bezona called Long: Armene Lamson, letter to Gov. Roland Hartley, 23 June 1932.

       In the meantime, the boy: "Boy Slayer Kept Away From Men in State Prison," *Seattle Times*, 5 Dec. 1931, 1.

p. 66   *Junior stood outside the courthouse*: "Tragic Side to Case of Young Killer Seen," *Walla Walla Daily Bulletin*, 30 Oct. 1931, 1.

       But Halsey did tell one: "Boy Slayer Due Today to Start Life in Prison," *Walla Walla Daily Bulletin*, 29 Oct. 1931, 1.

       "Have you read it?": "Tragic Side to Case of Young Killer Seen," *Walla Walla Daily Bulletin*, 30 Oct. 1931, 1.

       The quotes on pages 66 through 70 are also from the *Walla Walla Daily Bulletin* of 30 Oct. 1931.

Chapter 9

p. 72   *That a man of Father Flanagan's*: Gov. Roland Hartley, letter to Rev. E. J. Flanagan, 19 Dec. 1931.

Hartley thought they were nothing: Gov. Roland Hartley, letter to H. S. Kocher, 25 Apr. 1931.

"The people are not asking": Gov. Roland Hartley, address to the state legislature, 14 Jan. 1925.

p. 73   *He also questioned the money*: Dave James, "Ex-Governor Hartley, Now 82, Still is Fiery," *Seattle Times*, 8 Dec. 1948.

"The American people today": Gov. Roland Hartley, address to the state legislature, 14 Jan. 1925.

Hartley believed that much: "Hartley Advises Silence as Best Depression Cure," *Walla Walla Daily Bulletin*, 31 Aug. 1931, 1.

p. 74   *They cried to one another*: "Tee, Governor's Pet Gull, His Best Friend: Others May Desert but Bird Always Comes Back; Hartley Tells You Why," *Seattle Star*, 7 Mar. 1929.

p. 75   *The way he "collected" celebrities*: "Henry Broderick: Builder of Seattle, is Dead at 94," *Seattle Post-Intelligencer*, 8 Oct. 1975.

Hartley acknowledged that Flanagan: Gov. Roland Hartley, telegram to Rev. E. J. Flanagan, 21 Nov. 1931.

p. 76   *The men slipped into the leather*: "Henry Broderick, Builder of Seattle, Is Dead at 94," *Seattle Times*, 8 Oct. 1975.

p. 77   *Since he took office*: Washington Department of Corrections,"Persons Executed Since 1904 in Washington State," ww.doc.wa.gov/offenderinfo/capitalpunishment/executedlist

Walter DuBuc's crime had been: Biographical Statement of Inmate No. 14201— Walter Dubuc, Washington State Penitentiary, 5 Mar. 1932.

"He was standing in": Ibid.

p. 78   *Hartley studied Flanagan's letter*: Rev. E. J. Flanagan, letter from to Gov. Roland Hartley, 4 Nov. 1931.

"Were it not that we have": Ibid.

Chapter 10

p. 81   *There was no such thing as a bad boy*: "Sketch 2842, Msgr. E.J. Flanagan Founder of Boys Town," The Associated Press Biographical Service, 13 July 1986.

p. 82   *On the snowy Christmas*: Charles P. Graves, *Father Flanagan Founder of Boys Town* (Garrard Publishing Company, 1972).

The man mumbled: Ibid.

p. 82   *He told his critics*: Barbara Lonnborg, editor, *Boys Town: A Photographic History*, (Boys Town Press, 1992), 14.

So it had seemed like a good: Ibid.

p. 83   *"The Boys' Home, for which"*: Ibid.

p. 84   *Patterson had written*: Sheriff James Patterson, letter to Rev. E. J. Flanagan, 29 Oct. 1931.

And according to Ed Doyle: E. J. Doyle, letter to Rev. E. J. Flanagan, 30 Oct. 1931.

p. 85   *An attorney named Farley*: A. G. Farley, letter to Rev. E. J. Flanagan, 31 Oct. 1931.

"The Divine Master forgives": Elva Timms, letter to Rev. E. J. Flanagan, 2 Nov. 1931.

p. 86   *A letter from a Mrs. O. F.*: Armene Lamson, letter to Rev. E. J. Flanagan, 30 Oct. 1931.

I've been approached: Armene Lamson, letter to Rev. E. J. Flanagan, 29 Dec. 1931.

He wrote back to her immediately: Rev. E. J. Flanagan, letter to Armene Lamson, 10 Nov. 1931.

In a second letter, Doyle: E.J. Doyle, letter to Rev. E. J. Flanagan, 31 Oct. 1931.

p. 87   *As Johnson wrote*: Ruth Johnson, letter to Rev. E. J. Flanagan, 30 Oct. 1931.

"I am ashamed of the way": Ibid.

p. 88   *"Within the gray walls"*: Rev. E. J. Flanagan, letter to seventy-three radio stations in the United States and Canada, 10 Nov. 1931.

"Dear Radio Friends": Rev. E. J. Flanagan, radio speech, 12 Nov. 1931.

As heinous as the deed was: Rev. E. J. Flanagan, interview following radio speech with KVOS-Bellingham, Wa., 12 Nov. 1931.

p. 89   *The boy's conscience*: Rev. E. J. Flanagan, radio speech 12 Nov. 1931.

There was no Clarence: Ibid.

Flanagan placed the blame on society: Ibid.

"This is indeed, an important": Ibid.

p. 90   *Hartley heard "Dear Radio Friends"*: Rev. E. J. Flanagan radio speech, 15 Nov. 1931.

p. 91   *"We must rest our case"*: Ibid.

p. 92   *Then Flanagan took on Mackintosh*: Ibid.

"I want to say right here": Ibid.

Chapter 11

p. 93   *On the boy's first day in*: "Boy Slayer Sorry, Wants to do Right; Hans Damm to Aid," *Seattle Times*, 31 Oct. 1931.

"Maybe you could play with me?": "Childish Murderer Would Reform: Father Fla-

nagan Anxious to Take Boy of 12," *The Helena (Mont.) Independent*, 31 Oct. 1931.

p. 94 *She wrote to him all about Jesus*: Garfield Davis, Washington State Penitentiary, "Statement of Facts: A Biographical History of the Niccolls Family," 17 Apr. 1933.

His mother had written: Ibid.

He never heard from his father: Ibid.

p. 95 *Someone had adopted him*: Hudson Shake, personal interview, 7 June 1996.

The prisoners had filed in: "Boy Slayer Applauds at Prison Play," *Seattle Times*, 9 Nov. 1931.

Flanagan had heard all about that life: "Sketch 2842, Msgr. E.J. Flanagan Founder of Boys Town," The Associated Press Biographical Service, 13 July 1986.

p. 96 *Oliver Morris, city editor*: Oliver Morris, city editor, *Seattle Post-Intelligencer*, telegram to Nathan Jacobs, Union Pacific Pullman, Shoshone, Idaho, 19 Nov. 1931.

Morris Jacobs had contacted: Morris Jacobs, letter to Henry Luce, editor, *Time* magazine, 20 Nov. 1931; Morris Jacobs, letter to Walter Winchell, *The Daily Mirror*, 21 Nov. 1931.

Morris had run news stories: "Father Flanagan Still Hopes to Set Boy Free: Persons Interested in Welfare of Hubert (sic) Niccolls Preparing to Receive Priest on Mercy Errand," *Seattle Times*, 20 Nov. 1931, 2.

At the agency's urging: Nathan Jacobs, telegram to Tracy Clark, California Council of Dads Clubs, 18 Nov. 1931.

p. 97 *Morris had sprinkled in quotes*: "Father Flannagan Still Hopes," *Seattle Times*, 20 Nov. 1931, 2.

Nebraska Governor Charles W. Bryan: Charles P. Graves, *Father Flanagan Founder of Boys Town* (Garrard Publishing Company, 1972), 236.

p. 98 *He stepped into a taxi*: Nathan Jacobs,"Will Rogers Joined with Father Flanagan to Obtain pardon for Niccolls," 21 Nov. 1931, press release sent to Tom Porter, Associated Press, Homer Gruenther, United Press.

The following day, after: Ibid.

Rogers took a notepad: Ibid.

p. 99 *To save the man, save the boy*: Rev. E. J. Flanagan, interview following radio speech with KVOS-Bellingham, WA, 12 Nov. 1931.

As the daughter of the head: "Who Is She?" *The Seattle Times*, 12 June 1938.

p. 101 *It was her favorite—cutaway velvet*: Robert Lamson, personal interview, 3 Mar. 1999.

The reception and dinner passed: "Father Flanagan to Visit Hartley Monday on Plea," *Seattle Times*, 21 Nov. 1931.

As he told the gathering: Ibid.

p. 102 *"Of the 3,000 boys we"*: Ibid.

p. 102　*His words were met by*: Ibid.

"If I am defeated": Rev. E. J. Flanagan, interview following radio speech with KVOS-Bellingham, WA, 12 Nov. 1931.

The Seattle Times, *to*: "Misplaced Sympathy," editorial, *Seattle Times*, 23 Nov. 1931.

p. 103　*"Will be at Washington Hotel"*: Gov. Roland Hartley, telegram to Rev. E. J. Flanagan, 21 Nov. 1931.

"Governor Hartley gave": "Parole board to act on priest's plea for slayer," *Seattle Times*, 23 Nov. 1931, 5.

p. 106　*"Yesterday, I sent you"*: Morris Jacobs, letter to Henry Luce, Editor, *Time* magazine, 20 Nov. 1931

"Here's a stunt you": Morris Jacobs, letter to Walter Winchell, *The Daily Mirror*, 21 Nov. 1931.

"I have a boy staying": Charles Holly, letter to Rev. E. J. Flanagan, 26 Dec. 1931.

All over the country children: "America's Wild Children," *Seattle Post-Intelligencer*, 28 Apr. 1932.

p. 107　*"The Governor is on his way"*: R. M. Kinnear, telegram to Rev. E. J. Flanagan, 30 Nov. 1931.

p. 108　*"Dear Father, I had a talk"*: F. G. Burns, letter to Rev. E. J. Flanagan, 23 Dec. 1931.

p. 109　*"I had intended writing"*: Rev. E. J. Flanagan, letter to Armene Lamson, 23 Dec. 1931.

Then he added the courtesies: Ibid.

"It is very fine and very beautiful": Rev. E. J. Flanagan, letter to Armene Lamson, 30 Dec. 1931.

p. 110　*"The writer speaks of"*: referring to a letter from F. G. Burns to Rev. E. J. Flanagan, 23 Dec. 1931.

"Thanking you dear Mrs.": Rev. E. J. Flanagan, letter to Armene Lamson, 15 Dec. 1931.

Hartley had been called: "Controlled Washington," *Time* magazine, 8 Aug. 1932.

p. 111　*The garage was so deluxe*: "A mansion-sized task," *Seattle Post-Intelligencer*, 27 Oct. 1984.

"Because of the youth": Gov. Roland Hartley, letter to Rev. E. J. Flanagan, 19 Dec. 1931.

Further quotes on pages 111 through 115 are also from Governor Hartley's letter to Father Flanagan, 19 Dec. 1931.

p. 115　*They also carried a story*: "Youth Described as Young Tiger," *Walla Walla Daily Bulletin*, 21 Dec. 1931.

p. 116　*In another story*: "Niccolls is 'Happy' in Jail," *Seattle Times*, 29 Dec. 1931, 1.

p. 116   *In every single Hearst*: "Father Flanagan's rebuke of Governor Hartley," *Seattle Post-Intelligencer*, 24 Dec. 1931.

"In upholding the sentence": Ibid.

p. 118   *"Father Flanagan's interest"*: "Savior of Wayward Youth is Defended by Mrs. Lamson," *Seattle Post-Intelligencer*, 22 Dec. 1931, 1

Oliver Morris had written to congratulate: Oliver Morris, city editor, *Seattle Post-Intelligencer*, letter to Rev. E. J. Flanagan, 25 Dec. 1931.

"On the whole, your": Ibid.

p. 119   *Flanagan couldn't agree more*: Charles O. Holly, letter to Rev. E. J. Flanagan, 29 Dec. 1931.

p. 120   *Did the world not understand*: Rev. E. J. Flanagan, interview following radio speech with KVOS-Bellingham, WA, 12 Nov. 1931.

The fight to save Herbert: "Flanagan's Fight for Niccolls Wins Big Farm for Home," *Seattle Times*, 30 Dec. 1931.

Mr. and Mrs. Elias Smithier: Ibid.

Chapter 12

p. 121   *Then he added*: "Father Flanagan Accused of Misquoting," *Seattle Times*, 23 Dec. 1931.

p. 122   *"This boy has winning ways"*: Gov. Roland Hartley, "State of Washington v. Herbert Franklin Niccolls," 11 Jan. 1932.

During the trial, the boy: Ibid.

"With an insane father": "Who is the Real Murderer?" editorial, *Seattle Times*, Dec. 1931, originally published in *New Haven (Conn.) Journal-Courier*.

p. 123   *Hartley had only a few years*: Gov. Roland Hartley, letter to Dr. E. E. Straw, 15 June 1926.

He hated the Times: Gov. Roland Hartley, letter to H. S. Kocher, 25 Apr. 1932.

Blethen had topped: "Application for Timber Was Signed By Governor," *Seattle Times*, 10 Sept. 1926.

He didn't dare even leave: "Hartley Brands Gellatly as One of 'Pirate Crew,'" *Seattle Times*, 4 Feb. 1932.

That's why he made it plain: Ibid.

p. 124   *Now Gellatly*: Ibid.

"Anybody can see": Ibid.

DuBuc would be the youngest: Washington Department of Corrections, "Persons Executed Since 1904 in Washington State."

p. 125   *Mrs. Lamson wrote to tell Flanagan*: Armene Lamson, letter to Rev. E. J. Flanagan, 16 Aug. 1932.

p. 125 *As head of the Boys' Home, Flanagan had written*: Lillian Carse, superintendent, The Children's Home Finding and Aid Society of Idaho, letter to Rev. E. J. Flanagan, 31 Dec. 1931.

She added that Mrs. Niccolls was: Ibid.

p. 126 *What he found disturbing*: Armene Lamson, letter to Rev. E. J. Flanagan, 31 Jan. 1933.

p. 127 *The governor with the heart of stone*: F. G. Burns, letter to Rev. E. J. Flanagan, 23 Dec. 1931.

Flanagan had written: Rev. E. J. Flanagan, letter to Armene Lamson, 23 Dec. 1931.

"Father Flanagan [is] asking": Gov. Roland Hartley, letter to Rev. E. J. Flanagan, 19 Dec. 1931.

The governor then turned: Gov. Roland Hartley, "State of Washington v. Herbert Franklin Niccolls," 11 Jan. 1932.

p. 128 *"Herbert's father seemingly"*: Ibid.

There was a nine-year-old: "Priest Answers Hartley on Parole of Boy Slayer," *Los Angeles Examiner*, 23 Dec. 1931, 6.

There was a boy who had shot: "Father Flanagan to Visit Boy Patricide," *Seattle Times*, 7 Apr. 1937.

Chapter 13

p. 130 *It was ten minutes before noon*: Henry Broderick, "Little Break," *Commandment Breakers of Walla Walla*, 1934, 50.

Further quotes on pages 130 through 132 are also from the *Commandment Breakers of Walla Walla*, 1934.

p. 133 *More than anything, he wanted*: "Niccolls Boy Pleads for One More Chance," *Seattle Post-Intelligencer*, 20 July 1932.

p. 134 *The execution of DuBuc and*: Henry Broderick, *Commandment Breakers of Walla Walla*, 1934, 46-48.

When the trap springs open: Ibid.

p. 135 *Then they scrawled across an ink-blotched page*: Superior Court of the State of Washington for Thurston County Return of Death Warrant, Walter DuBuc, statement of prisoner, 16 Apr. 1932.

"Even the hardest ones blubber": Henry Broderick, *Commandment Breakers of Walla Walla*, 1934, 46-48.

p. 136 *"You try to follow everything"*: Ibid.

Damm is" a good old soul": Ibid.

Chapter 14

p. 137   *Hartley was smugly:* Gov. Roland Hartley, letter to H. S. Kocher, 25 Apr. 1932.

      He had filed a lawsuit: "Hartley Grilled in Trial Seeking Access to Books," *Seattle Times,* 16 June 1932.

p. 138   *The* Walla Walla Daily Bulletin: "Hartley, 'Secrecy Foe,' Fighting Investigation," *Walla Walla Daily Bulletin,* 29 Jan. 1932.

      Nevertheless, he again: Ibid.

      In the meantime, some of: "'Long-Geared (sic) Son-of-a-Gun of a Lieutenant-Governor Likely to Raise Hob' on the Job, Says Governor," *Seattle Times,* 29 Apr. 1932.

      As far as he was concerned: Ibid.

      "If I go away they can": Ibid.

p. 139   *Leo Bozell, of Bozell:* Armene Lamson, letter to Rev. E. J. Flanagan, 6 Apr. 1933

      The fight seemed to: Ibid.

      "The governor [is] . . . spreading": Ibid.

      There were supportive letters: B. J. Gibson, letter to William Wilkins, 13 Apr. 1939, 8 May 1939.

      Lamson believed that no mother: Armene Lamson, letter to Rev. E. J. Flanagan, 15 Apr. 1933.

p. 140   *When Mrs. Lamson wrote:* Ibid.

p. 141   *The meeting took two hours:* Armene Lamson, letter to Rev. E. J. Flanagan, 21 June 1932.

      During the last few months: Ibid.

      The prison library: Ibid.

p. 142   *He sat at a desk beneath:* C. F. Rose, letter to J. M. McCauley, 17 Jan. 1934.

      "Herbert was not always": Ibid.

      Herbert had an amazing appetite: Ibid.

p. 143   *The first was twenty-three-year-old:* "Herbert Niccolls Will Lose Tutor if Mother Succeeds in Obtaining her Son," *Lewiston Morning Tribune,* 1 Dec. 1932, 1931.

      Rose noted that the boy: Ibid.

      His booking information: Ibid.

p. 144   *On his intake form:* Washington State Register Description of Convict, No. 7343, 9 May 1913.

      He had started a fund: Henry Drum, superintendent, Washington State Penitentiary, letter to Gov. Louis Hart, 20 March 1921.

      He had certainly argued: Ibid.

p. 144   *That's what Rose told*: "Mrs. Lamson Describes Life Herbert Niccolls is Leading in Washington Penitentiary," *Father Flanagan's Boys Home Journal*, Sept. 1932, 3.

In the beginning, Rose: C. F. Rose, letter to J. M. McCauley, 17 Jan. 1934.

p. 145   *The boy doesn't have*: J. M. McCauley, superintendent, Washington State Penitentiary, letter to Gov. Clarence Martin, 10 July 1933.

"Then he is not being prepared": Armene Lamson, letter to Rev. E. J. Flanagan, 22 June 1932.

Teaching him about good: Ibid.

The only thing that concerned: Armene Lamson, letter to Gov. Roland Hartley, 22 June 1932, 2.

It is simply not humanly: Armene Lamson, letter to Rev. E. J. Flanagan, 22 June 1932.

p. 146   *In addition to the women*: Ibid.

Mrs. Lamson commented: Ibid.

p. 147   *She sat across from him*: Ibid.

Then she told him: "Niccolls Boy Pleads for One More Chance," *Seattle Post-Intelligencer*, 20 July 1932.

Further quotes on pages 147 through 148 are also from *Seattle Post-Intelligencer*, 20 July 1932.

p. 149   *In fact, even the warden*: Armene Lamson, letter to Gov. Roland Hartley, 23 June 1932.

And to think that only: Armene Lamson, "An Answer to Governor Hartley's Letter Regarding the Herbert Niccoll's (sic) Case," Published by the Homeless Boys of Father Flanagan's Boys Home, Omaha, Neb., Feb. 1933.

A soft-spoken turnkey went: Richard Morgan, Washington State Penitentiary Superintendent, personal interview, 6 Aug. 1996.

p. 150   *With the first blow*: Ibid.

Daily the guards would: "Herbert Niccolls, Boy Killer, Facing Life's Crisis," *Seattle Star*, 29 Aug. 1938.

While early spring rains: *Walla Walla Daily Bulletin* digest, 1932,Whitman College Archives.

p. 151   *Ellis Woodward and W. D. Moxley were gone*: Ibid.

Sixteen days later, another: Ibid.

p. 152   *She had, of course*: Armene Lamson, "An Answer to Governor Hartley's Letter Regarding the Herbert Niccoll's (sic) Case," published by the Homeless Boys of Father Flanagan's Boys Home, Omaha, NE, Feb. 1933.

"It does not matter how": Ibid.

About the same time, Time: "Controlled Washington," *Time* magazine, 8 Aug. 1932.

p. 152 *The Hartley machine, as*: Armene Lamson, telegram to Rev. E. J. Flanagan, 14 Sept. 1932.

p. 153 *When Flanagan received the telegram*: Ibid.

p. 154 *The bands played*: Bob Weatherly, "The History of the Round Log Dance Hall," in *The Best of Jawbone Flat Gazette* (The Valley American, 1984), 22.

Mary Addington had paid: Gov. Roland Hartley, "State of Washington v. Herbert Franklin Niccolls," 11 Jan. 1932.

Chapter 15

p. 156 *As Broderick would describe*: Henry Broderick, "Peter Miller Pioneer Public Enemy," *Commandment Breakers of Walla Walla*, 1934, 9.

p. 157 *As anti-German sentiment*: John Edwin Ayer, letter to Gov. Louis Hart, 27 Dec. 1922.

Miller was placed in a dark cell: Dudley Wooten, letter to Gov. Louis Hart, 12 Apr. 1921.

He confessed to the brutal conditions: *Washington v. Peter Miller*, No. 9442 (Washington 1912).

p. 158 *The youth was entirely alone*: Ibid.

That winter the prison: "Blizzard in Umatilla County Kills Thousands of Sheep," *Walla Walla Daily Bulletin*.

On February 9, when the inmates: Ibid.

Even the Plymouth-Umatilla: Ibid.

p. 159 *Eleven days later, McCauley*: "Our New Superintendent," *The Agenda*, Mar. 1933.

McCauley, however, brought: "State Starts $107,000 New Building Program at the Pen," *Walla Walla Daily Bulletin*, digest 1933, Whitman College Archives.

p. 160 *"There is a public curiosity"*: "Repeaters Given Too Much Stress," *The Agenda*, Aug./Sept. 1937, 12.

p. 161 *With Flanagan's encouragement*: Armene Lamson, personal letter to Gov. Clarence Martin, 2 Feb. 1933.

"My heart is filled with gratitude": Rev. E. J. Flanagan, letter to Gov. Clarence Martin, 6 Feb. 1933.

Unless Martin acts soon: Rev. E. J. Flanagan, letter to Armene Lamson, 28 Feb.1933.

p. 162 *In the shadowed corners*: Garfield Davis, Washington State Penitentiary, "Statement of Facts: A Biographical History of the Niccolls Family," 17 Apr. 1933.

In Star, Idaho, Davis found: Ibid.

p. 163 *By that April, Martin*: Gov. Clarence Martin, personal letter to Armene Lamson, 30 Mar. 1933.

p. 163   *According to Davis*: Garfield Davis, Washington State Penitentiary, "Statement of Facts: A Biographical History of the Niccolls Family," 17 Apr. 1933.

"While she has tried to convey": Ibid.

p. 164   *Mrs. Addington is what is known*: Ibid.

Bert Niccolls's maternal: Ibid., 3.

It's the modern theory: King County Superior Court Judge Everett Smith, letter to Gov. Clarence Martin, 3 Apr. 1933.

p. 165   *Mrs. Addington, Davis said*: Ibid., 2.

Even the guards were talking: Wanda Jacobson, personal interview, 12 Dec. 1997.

p. 166   *When summer arrived*: Ibid.

p. 167   *During June, July and August*: *Walla Walla Daily Bulletin* digest, Whitman College Archives, 1933.

The 1,500 prisoners: Ibid.

On July 28, Ollie Lee: "Ollie Lee Stratton Hanged for Murder," *Walla Walla Daily Bulletin* digest, 1933, Whitman College Archives.

Shortly before the meeting: State Penitentiary Superintendent Henry Drum, letter to Gov. Louis Hart, 20 Mar. 1921.

p. 168   *He, of course, wanted to return*: Dudley G. Wooten, letter to Gov. Louis F. Hart, 12 Apr. 1921.

"It was evident that": Henry Broderick, "Peter Miller Pioneer Public Enemy," *Commandment Breakers of Walla Walla*, 1934, 9.

When Miller asked the board: Henry Broderick, "Peter Miller Pioneer Public Enemy," *Commandment Breakers of Walla Walla*, 1934, 9.

p. 169   *They hated the youth*: Armene Lamson, letter to Gov. Clarence Martin, 25 May 1933.

Chapter 16

p. 170   *It was one p.m.*: "February 12, 1934, Riot," *The American Detective*, date unknown.

He saw a flicker of motion: Ibid.

p. 171   *She had left again and*: Wanda Jacobson, personal interview, 12 Dec. 1997.

They were lifers with no: "February 12, 1934, Riot," *The American Detective*, date unknown.

When the last of them was: Ibid.

Officer Burnett was watching: Ibid.

p. 172   *Turnkey George Binder ran*: Ibid.

Guard Jackson was talking: Ibid.

Jackson grabbed a: Ibid.

p. 173 *Suddenly an inmate stepped*: Floyd Jackson, Western Union telegram to Gov. Mon Wallgren, 27 Dec. 1948.

He kicked out the glass, took: "February 12, 1934, Riot," *The American Detective*, publication date unknown.

The No. 1 Tower guard: Ibid.

There were numerous reports: Armene Lamson, letter to Rev. E. J. Flanagan, 19 Nov. 1933.

p. 174 *"What do you think you're doing"*: "February 12, 1934, Riot," *The American Detective*, publication date unknown.

"Well, in that case, let's": Ibid.

p. 175 *In order to stall the mob*: Henry Broderick, "The Big Break," *Commandment Breakers of Walla Walla* (1934), 53.

"Open up the gate, or we'll": "February 12, 1934, Riot," *The American Detective*, date unknown.

p. 176 *Another inmate popped his head*: "One Inmate Slain; Another Wounded in Prison Break," *Walla Walla Daily Bulletin*, 28 Dec. 1934, 1.

One man in solitary: Henry Broderick, "The Big Break," *Commandment Breakers of Walla Walla*, 1934, 53.

Chapter 17

p. 178 *One by one the chained men*: "Striped Suits and Clipped Hair," *The Agenda*, Apr./May 1936, 19.

He was a small-boned: Washington State Penitentiary Commitment Record, 15 June 1934.

p. 179 *He was educated at Oxford*: Louis Bunge, Board of Prison Terms and Parole, letter to Gov. Clarence Martin, 14 Oct. 1937.

Then the detective struck him: Albert Rosellini, personal interview, June 10, 1994.

He was born in Holyoke: Washington State Register Description of Convict, No. 15589.

He bought her an automobile: "Pretty wife of accused literary agent says husband told her he had to 'keep up' with the crowd," *Seattle Times*, 23 Apr. 1934.

p. 180 *Once when Mrs. Shannon*: "Mrs. Shannon tells jury Ashe was treated with 'utmost severity,'" *Seattle Times*, 24 Apr. 1934.

It wasn't to his benefit: "Women well-wishers back Ashe as he faces second trial," *Seattle Times*, 15 Mar. 1934.

p. 181 *He had done unspeakable*: Albert Rosellini, personal interview, 10 June 1994.

But the judge instead: "Ashe, 'Smart Guy,' Starts for Prison," *Seattle Times*, 16 June 1934.

p. 181 *The warden himself suggested*: "Ashe in Prison, Tutors Boy Who Killed Sheriff," *Seattle Times*, 1 Aug. 1934.

p. 182 *Financial matters put*: "Pretty wife of accused literary agent says husband told her he had to 'keep up' with the crowd," *Seattle Times*, 23 Apr. 1934.

p. 183 *They wrote of sleighs*: "Christmas Eve at Grandma's," *The Agenda*, Dec./Jan. 1938, 18.

p. 185 *Workers spent days stringing*: "The Radio," *The Agenda*, Feb. 1935.

Chapter 18

p. 186 *As for Herbert Niccolls*: Armene Lamson, letter to Rev. E. J. Flanagan, 16 Aug. 1932.

He still wanted to see: Rev. E. J. Flanagan, letter to Armene Lamson, 14 Sept. 1932

"He likes to play politics": Ibid.

High winds swept through: *Walla Walla Daily Bulletin* digest, Whitman College Archives, 1935.

p. 187 *McCauley remained to console*: Wanda Jacobson, personal interview, 12 Dec. 1997.

p. 189 *Eight had escaped from*: "Eight Convicts Dig Way Out of Cell Block, Main Walls," *Walla Walla Daily Bulletin*, 9 Dec. 1935.

The escapees had removed: Ibid.

p. 190 *It opened December 11 to*: "Third Annual revue," *The Agenda*, Dec./Jan. 1935, 10-13.

Chapter 19

p. 192 *Father Flanagan was sitting*: Barbara Lonnborg, editor, *Boys Town: A Photographic History*, (Boys Town Press, 1992).

p. 194 *But on July 8, nine*: "Nine Convicts Dig Tunnel But Fail," *Seattle Times*, 8 July 1936, 5.

p. 196 *He heard his wife's cry*: Wanda Jacobson personal interview, 12 Dec. 1997.

p. 198 *"Freeze! Don't move or I'll shoot"*: Ibid.

p. 199 *The killing of the young suitors*: Ibid.

p. 200 *Most prisoners become better*: "Repeaters Given Too Much Stress," *The Agenda*, Aug./Sept. 1937, 12.

Chapter 20

p. 201 *At nine p.m. the bedtime whistle*: "New Year's Eve in Prison," *The Agenda*, Dec./Jan. 1936, 5-7.

p. 202 *Then the Rocky Mountain*: Ibid.

p. 203 *Roosevelt visited the Grand Coulee Dam*: Dorothy Brant Brazier, "Another Voice

Says 'Save the Mansion!'" *Seattle Times*, 30 June 1965.

p. 203 *In the meantime brief*: "Governor's Wife, Hurt in Fall, Recovering," *Seattle Times*, 11 Jan. 1937.

In July 1940 she would: "Wife of Governor Has Broken Wrist," *Seattle Times*, 10 July 1940.

Martin remarried: "Ex-Governor Martin Weds in California," *Seattle Times*, 17 Apr. 1944.

McCauley was proud: "Move State Pen Asked in Report," *Spokesman Review*, 2 Feb. 1927.

p. 204 *With the exception of the new cellblock*: "Attack on State's Prison Refuted," *Walla Walla Daily Bulletin*, 1937.

"Examination of the records": "Paroles Fewer: Prison Warden Defends Actions of Governor," *Tacoma News Tribune*, 22 Apr. 1935.

"When we are satisfied that he will do well": "Prison Walls to Dim Youth's 18th Birthday," *Seattle Times*, 29 June 1937.

"Of course, freedom means more": Ibid.

p. 205 *James Ashe's eyes were infected*: Louis Bunge, Board of Prison Terms and Paroles, letter to Gov. Clarence Martin, 14 Oct. 1937.

George R. Perry of the J. G. White Co: George Perry, letter to Board of Prison Terms and Paroles, 26 June 1937.

"He has lost the sight of one eye": Louis Bunge, Board of Prison Terms and Paroles, letter to Gov. Clarence Martin, 14 Oct. 1937.

King County Prosecuting Attorney: B. Gray Warner, King County prosecuting attorney, letter to Louis Bunge, Board of Prison Terms and Paroles, 11 Oct. 1937.

p. 206 *Perry, his future employer*: Office of the Governor, Conditional Pardon, Inmate No. 15589, James Ashe, 14 Oct. 1937.

By June 1938 Herbert had completed: "Young Niccolls Given a Diploma," *Seattle Times*, 5 June 1938.

p. 207 *"It occurred to me it would be a very fine"*: Armene Lamson, personal letter to Rev. E. J. Flanagan, 2 June 1938.

"This week's newspaper carried": Armene Lamson, personal letter to Gov. Clarence Martin, 4 June 1938.

p. 208 *In August, Seattle Star reporter*: Stuart Whitehouse, "Boy Convict Will Go to College," *Seattle Star*, 27 Feb.1938.

"Vows of eternal allegiance between": "Post Office Box 520," *The Agenda*, Dec./Jan. 1938-39, 1.

p. 209 *Herbert was now used to movies*: Armene Lamson, letter to Rev. E. J. Flanagan, 22 June 1932.

That fall, Herbert: "Boy Convict Will Go to College," *Seattle Times*, 27 Feb. 1938.

p. 209 *It was common for trustees*: Richard Morgan, Washington State Penitentiary Superintendent, personal interview, 6 Aug. 1996.

p. 210 *In April 1936, McCauley*: Wanda Jacobson, personal interview, 12 Dec. 1997.

Prisoners there often: Richard Morgan, Washington State Penitentiary Superintendent, personal interview, 6 Aug. 1996.

During the first seven: Washington Department of Corrections, "Persons Executed Since 1904 in Washington State."

Chapter 21

p. 211 *It was an idea favored by Kern*: W. M. Kern, letter to Gov. Clarence Martin, 16 May 1939.

Martin asked an associate to contact Boeing: G. V. Alexander, letter to Gov. Clarence D. Martin, 4 Nov. 1939.

"The years since Herbert arrived": W. M. Kern, letter to Gov. Clarence Martin, 2 May 1939.

p. 212 *He still clung to his idea of placing*: Chairman of the Board of Prison Terms and Paroles, King County Superior Court Judge William J. Wilkins, letter to W. M. Kern.

"Mr. Wilkins wrote to me some": W. M. Kern, letter to Gov. Clarence Martin, 6 May 1939.

p. 213 *"I hesitate to subscribe to the idea"*: Gov. Clarence Martin, letter to W. M. Kern, 19 May 1940.

Kern also suggested: W. M. Kern, letter to Gov. Clarence Martin, 16 May 1939.

"Even though Niccolls has been away": John W. Schaefer. letter to Chairman of the Board of Prison Terms and Paroles, King County Superior Court Judge William J. Wilkins, 24 Sept. 1940.

p. 214 *Tracy had inscribed it*: "Boys Town priest gets Tracy's Oscar," *Seattle Times*, 1 Mar. 1939, 14.

Days later, four boys: "Youths steal auto for trip to Boys Town," *Seattle Times*, 14 Mar. 1939, 9.

That month, Flanagan's board: "Boys Town will help 200 more," *Seattle Times*, 19 Mar. 1939.

He learned to bind books: "Boy Binds Book for Broderick," *Seattle Times*, 25 Feb. 1939.

p. 215 *There is a vast difference*: Herbert Niccolls, "Bookbinding," *The Agenda*, Apr./May 1939, 6-9.

p. 216 *Herbert wrote back, updating*: Herbert Niccolls, letter to Gov. Clarence Martin, 7 July 1939.

p. 217 *"Is there any way that"*: Gov. Clarence Martin, letter to W. M. Kern, 8 May 1939.

p. 217　*"This young man is"*:Gov. Clarence Martin, letter to Eastern State Hospital Superintendent Dr. M. E. Conway, 28 June 1939.

p. 218　*Landis was only sixteen when*: Washington State Register Description of Convict, No. 13015.

　　　　"I know that you will agree": Pat McCarran, Western Union telegram to Gov. Mon Wallgren, 27 Dec. 1948.

p. 219　*Photographers captured Martin helping*: "Lifer at 12, Life Begins for Him at 21," 20 July 1940, 1.

　　　　"Boy lifer gets first air": "Boy lifer gets first air ride leaving prison," *Walla Walla Daily Bulletin*, 6 Nov. 1939, 1.

　　　　The flight was "the greatest day of": "Niccolls, Young Slayer, Awaits Freedom Test," *Seattle Times*, 6 Nov. 1939.

p. 220　*Martin—who told reporters*: "Niccolls, Young Slayer, Awaits Freedom Test," *Seattle Times*, 6 Nov. 1939.

　　　　The town council passed: Asotin Mayor Joe A. Forgey, letter to Gov. Clarence Martin, 10 Nov. 1939.

　　　　"We have gone to very great extremes": B. H. German, Special Agent in Charge, National Automobile Theft Bureau, personal letter to Gov. Clarence Martin, 18 July 1933.

p. 221　*"We surely enjoyed the attention"*: Clarkston Mayor A. Ray Johnson, letter to Gov. Clarence Martin, 4 Sept. 1940.

　　　　"A person shouldn't say": Mrs. R. L. Berlinghoff, Lewiston, Idaho, letter to Gov. Clarence Martin, 15 Nov. 1939.

　　　　In all, four from Clarkston: "Herbert Niccolls," *Clarkston Herald*, 10 Jan. 1941, 2.

p. 222　*Seven hundred came to the funeral*: "Officials Here for Warden's Rites Sunday," *The (Dayton) Chronicle-Dispatch*, 11 Jan. 1940.

　　　　Yet, midway through Herbert's: "Lifer at 12, Life Begins for Him at 21," 20 July 1940, 1.

p. 223　*Herbert "seems happy"*: Ibid.

　　　　News photographers: "Martin Paroles Herbert Niccolls," *Seattle Post-Intelligencer*, 7 Jan. 1941, 1.

　　　　"It is needless to say": Ibid.

　　　　"He has been an excellent": Ibid.

Chapter 22

p. 225　*Martin had arranged*: "Martin Paroles Herbert Niccolls," *Seattle Post-Intelligencer*, 7 Jan. 1941, A1.

　　　　Headlines announced: Ibid.

p. 225 *"You must remember I've"*: Ibid.

p. 226 *"Do you know who I am?"*: W. H. Stillman, assistant parole officer, Board of Prison Terms and Paroles, report, 19 Mar. 1942.

p. 227 *"He loafed on the job and"*: Ibid.

Not only did he instruct: Ibid.

*Then one day he was reconnect*ed: Wesley Niccolls, personal interview, 10 Oct. 1996.

"What was it like?" Wesley: Ibid.

p. 228 *Herbert moved to Tacoma*: George Fahey, report to Fred Emard, Board of Prison Terms and Paroles, 3 Feb. 1944.

Herbert made a good salary: Ibid.

Shortly before Christmas: Ibid.

"We have heard informally": Chairman A. M. Murfin, Board of Prison Terms and Paroles, memorandum to Ross L. Cunningham, secretary, 14 Dec. 1943.

p. 229 *Martin protested and*: Ibid.

Fahey noted that Herbert: George Fahey, report to Fred Emard, Board of Prison Terms and Paroles, 3 Feb. 1944.

Although Fahey found nothing: Ibid.

One month later, Herbert: Herbert Niccolls, letter to Gov. Arthur Langley, 8 Mar. 1944.

p. 230 *Langlie replied that*: Gov. Arthur Langlie, letter to Herbert Niccolls, 8 Mar. 1944.

p. 231 *In April 1945, the*: Board of Prison Terms and Paroles Memorandum to Herbert Niccolls, 20 Feb. 1945.

On September 19, 1945, Herbert: Vincent O'Leary, chief parole and probation officer, letter to the Board of Prison Terms and Paroles, 7 Nov. 1956.

Chapter 23

p. 232 *He saw the footprints*: Paul Niccolls, personal interview, 10 June 1997.

p. 233 *On his first day*: "The Tabulating Department," *Action*, June 1950, 6-9.

Slowly the studio: Patricia Niccolls, personal interview, 3 June 2002.

p. 234 *L. Ron Hubbard seemed to have the answer*: Paul Niccolls, personal interview, 15 Nov. 2001.

The harder he tried: Ibid.

p. 235 *Even the studio*: "How You Can Fight the Bomb," *Action*, Apr. 1951, 14.

His brother Paul: Wesley Niccolls, personal interview, 12 Nov. 2001.

Long after Herbert left prison: Rev. E. J. Flanagan, letter to B. J. Gibson, 8 Oct. 1941.

p. 236 *"It costs so little to teach"*: Boys Town web site, http://www.boystown.org/about/
father-edward-j-flanagan/father-flanagan-quotes

A sixteen-year-old sentenced: "Young Slayer is Offered Place in Boys' Town," *Seattle Times*, 24 May 1941; "Fr. Flanagan Pleads for Sailor Slayers," *Seattle Times*, 28 Dec. 1944.

Until the day of his death: "$25,000 Bail Paid for Boy Slayer," *Seattle Times*, 7 May 1944.

He continued to preach that: "Sketch 2842, Msgr. E.J. Flanagan Founder of Boys Town," The Associated Press Biographical Service, 13 July 1986.

In the meantime, the studio's: *Action*, 20th Century Fox Studio Club, Los Angeles, Calif., Feb. 1949.

The studio's bowlers: Ibid.

p. 237 *Then one day, Herbert*: Katherine Wills, Board of Prison Terms and Paroles, letter to John Lamb, 6 Nov. 1946.

And although he had "audited": Jonathan Niccolls, personal interview, 12 Nov. 2011.

Meanwhile, back in the: Judge Elgin V. Kuykendall, "Historic Glimpses of Asotin County, Washington," *East Washingtonian*, 1954, 56-57.

They had often used him: Jonathan Niccolls, personal interview, 12 Nov. 2011.

p. 238 *One night a friend invited*: Patricia Niccolls, personal interview, 9 June 2010.

p. 239 *A partial hysterectomy*: Ibid.

"You'd think you invented": Ibid.

"They want me to": Ibid.

Over the years: Jonathan Niccolls, personal interview, 14 Nov. 2011.

p. 240 *"He wasn't happy but he tried"*: Wesley Niccolls, personal interview, 12 Nov. 2001.

Herbert tried to bring: Ibid.

p. 241 *Pat Boone endorsed the product*: Advertisement, Trend Marketing insulation and distributorships.

p. 242 *"He was afraid he'd go to"*: Paul Niccolls, personal interview, 10 June 1997.

He found comfort in: Jonathan Niccolls, personal interview, 14 Nov. 2011.

On a warm April day, Herbert: Ibid.

Then father and son: Ibid.

Herbert pushed himself: Ibid.

p. 243 *"I love you, Dad"; "I love you, too, son"*: Ibid.

The cause of death: Los Angeles County death certificate

"We found out later": Ibid.

Two hundred people came: Wesley Niccolls, personal interview, 14 Nov. 2001.

p. 243 *Although his daily world*: Ibid.

More than anything: Paul Niccolls, personal interview, 8 June 1996.

Epilogue

p. 244 *"He was a peach of a dad"*: Jonathan Niccolls, personal interview, 10 Aug. 2002.

On most nights: Ibid.

p. 245 *"Dad would do anything"*: Ibid.

"What made you think": Ibid.

"About my dad?": Ibid.

Once, after listening: Ibid.

"I don't want to": Ibid.

"This explains so much": Ibid.

p. 246 *In 2004, John Wormell*: Officer Down Memorial Page, http://www.odmp.org/officer/14513-sheriff-john-l-wormell

As one officer wrote: Ibid.

Another also weighed in: Ibid.

And that, he said: Wesley Niccolls, personal interview, 12 Nov. 2001.

Note on Sources

HISTORY IS MORE than bare facts and figures. The real story, the human story beneath the surface, is often missing from the basic accounts as first recorded. To bring this slice of history to life, I visited the places familiar to Herbert Niccolls—the prison; Star, Idaho; Hollywood; and rural Asotin. While these settings have changed in varying degrees over the years, I hoped that by putting myself in the actual places, it would help me re-create them with accuracy. Asotin was the richest place to find historical details, since some of the old structures still remain. The mortuary is now a museum and the jail where Herbert was first held is now a garage. The barred windows remain, as well as a ring used for shackling prisoners and the inscriptions on the walls. The park where Sheriff John Wormell's funeral was held is still there and the old bridge over Asotin Creek remains at the edge of town.

I've interviewed many people with firsthand recollections, though most have now passed on. I was fortunate to connect with two of Herbert Niccolls's playmates, his brothers, and his wife and son. Others I interviewed told me about life in the town of Asotin in the 1930s, detailed stories about relatives, the people who were involved in the case, and those that could provide me with bits of information to help weave a portrait of the time, the place, and the boy known as the "barefoot-boy murderer."

I am indebted to the late Murphy Watkins, Herbert Niccolls's childhood friend, who gave me detailed information about Herbert's early life with his grandmother and about what transpired on the day of the murder, including how he had presented Herbert with a blue marble. I'm also grateful to Watkins's sister, Jean Seibel, another playmate, who detailed how Herbert's grandmother abused him.

The late Paul Niccolls, Herbert's brother, was especially helpful in giving me details about Herbert's life in Hollywood, as was his brother, Wesley Niccolls, and his son, Jonathan Niccolls. The late Wanda Jacobson, Warden James McCauley's step-daughter who lived at the mansion, gave me wonderful information about little-known aspects of the warden's life. And I'm fortunate that the late Seattle real estate developer Henry Broderick wrote annual Christmas letters in self-published booklets he sent to friends. The booklets were about activities in which he was involved, and they now are unique historical documents. I've drawn heavily on his *Commandment Breakers of Walla Walla* to portray the parole board and prison life in the 1930s. Boys Town's Tom Lynch provided me with hundreds of letters pertaining to the case; this book would not have been possible without them. Wayne Bezona's daughter, Fran Connelly, and his grandson, Jack Bezona, gave me information about the deputy sheriff and his friendship with Sheriff John Wormell. And Linda Spencer and Doug Wormell gave me information about their grandparents, John and Annie Wormell.

In creating this work of literary nonfiction, I've used primary and secondary documents and interviews conducted with those who have firsthand knowledge of the relevant people and events. All direct quotes come either from newspaper stories, private correspondence, other documents or interviews.

I have attempted to create literary characters based on the best, most factual information available. Characters' points of view and reflections are drawn from these sources. I've attempted to be as accurate as possible. If I have failed in any way, I take full responsibility.

Finally, I am indebted to the late Ruth Harris, Asotin Museum curator, who was extremely helpful and gave me newspaper clippings and access to the museum's files, and to the late Asotin historian Bob Weatherly. I am also grateful to the Academy of Motion Picture Arts and Sciences Margaret Herrick Library for research help, to Chuck and Karen Hindman for their hospitality on my many research trips, and to my son, James McDonald, for his help in many ways. In the Notes section, I have attempted to list sources for the parts of this work that need attribution; I have not listed sources for information that is well known.

Index